The World of Classic Stamps

To my Wahine

James A. Mackay

THE WORLD OF
CLASSIC STAMPS
1840-1870

G. P. Putnam's Sons · New York

Photos by Bill Grout

73-12708

G. P. Putnam's Sons
200 Madison Avenue
New York, N.Y. 10016

Published in the United States of America
in 1972

© 1972 by Office du Livre, Fribourg
(Switzerland)

Library of Congress Catalog Card
Number : 72-75945

Published simultaneously in Canada by
Longmans Canada Limited, Toronto.

Printed in Switzerland

CONTENTS

PREFACE

Philately, the science of stamp-collecting, is the hobby and serious pursuit of millions in every part of the world. The humble postage stamp, originally designed to indicate the prepayment of postage, has long been collected and studied for its aesthetic qualities and—in the case of the stamps considered in this book—for its antiquarian interest. This volume is devoted to the stamps of the world issued during the classic period (1840–70). Contrary to popular belief not all the stamps of this era are priced beyond the reach of the average collector. While the classics include the 'blue chips' of philately, such as the 'Post Office Mauritius', the Hawaiian 'Missionaries' and the British Guiana 'Cottonreels', there are also many stamps which can still be purchased for a very small sum. Condition is an important factor in assessing the value of the classic stamps. Many stamps are quite plentiful in poor or fair condition but excessively rare in really fine condition. Thus this is an area of philately which can still be tailored to suit the pocket of the individual collector.

I am indebted to my friends in the philatelic trade for their advice in compiling this book. Many of the stamps illustrated in this work are reproduced by courtesy of the Trustees of the British Museum and I am grateful to Bill Grout for taking the photographs. I should also like to record my thanks to Arthur Blair, the Editor of *The Stamp Magazine* for assistance with illustrations and much helpful advice at every stage of this book, and to Mrs Joyce O'Halloran who typed the manuscript.

J. M.

CHAPTER I
THE CLASSIC STAMPS

In 1870, for the first time, all the postage stamps known to philatelists as 'the classics' (those produced in the period from 1840 to 1870) also qualified for that much-abused appellation 'antique'. Thus interest in the first thirty years of the postage stamp is doubly justifed, and the incunabula of philately will now certainly show a greater increase in value commensurate with the larger amount of attention being focused on them.

At the present time there are some two hundred and thirty stamp-issuing countries. A century ago there were approximately half as many, whose combined output of new issues was about a twentieth of that produced today. Curiously enough, there were more than thirty other countries which had issued stamps since 1840 but which had ceased to exist by 1870—the Canadian provinces, the Swiss cantons and the old states of Italy and Germany—and it is from some of these countries that the great rarities of nineteenth-century philately came.

In philately, as in so much else in the mid-nineteenth century, British influence was prodigious. Of the 108 countries issuing stamps in 1870, no fewer than forty-seven were in the British Empire. By contrast, at that time only two French colonies —Réunion and New Caledonia—had the distinction of having had their own stamps. Indeed, with the exception of the famous Hawaiian 'Missionaries', the most valuable stamps of the classic period all emanated from the British territories, particularly from the more remote and exotic places, such as Guiana, Mauritius and Bermuda.

There have been stamps of comparable rarity from other countries, but none has captured the imagination like the unique One Cent of British Guiana, 1856—often referred to as the world's most valuable stamp. Frederick Small paid $ 40,000 for it when he purchased it in 1940; in March 1970 he sold it in New York for $ 280,000 —a handsome return on his original outlay.

Barely a dozen each of the Penny and Twopence 'Post Office' Mauritius stamps exist today, and these now have a price tag of $44,880 (£22,000) each, in the 1971 edition of the Gibbons' catalogue (a lift of 10 per cent over the 1970 quotation). The so-called 'Postmasters' issues of Bermuda, produced at Hamilton and St George's between 1848 and 1861, are now in the $12,250–14,280 (£6–7,000) range, while the 'Cottonreels' of British Guiana vary from a mere $620 (£300) up to $20,400 (£10,000).

The fact that astronomic sums of money are paid for pieces of paper measured in millimetres indicates that the rarest of the classic stamps far outrank the greatest of the Old Masters, and constitute the most valuable class of man-made object in the world, on a proportionate basis. Sensational reports of the prices paid for these stamps, however, give a false impression. An analysis of the 5,400 different stamps issued between 1840 and 1870 shows that more than 50 per cent are still obtainable in reasonable condition for $10.20 (£5) or less. No other form of antique is available so cheaply.

Age alone, in this context, is not a factor determining the value of a postage stamp, and although the world market is vast, with the number of collectors currently estimated at thirty-five to fifty million, certain stamps were issued in such astronomic quantities that there is no shortage of them even now. The British Penny Red, for example, was released in February 1841, and was in use for thirteen years before perforation was introduced. Perforated Penny Reds with stars in their upper corners were current from 1854 till 1864 when the stamps appeared with letters in all four corners and remained in use till 1880. Countless millions of Penny Reds were used during a period of almost forty years and though certain rarities such as the Penny Red of 1864 from plate 77 are priced in hundreds or thousands of pounds, the majority of these stamps must still be reckoned in pence.

The latest edition of the Gibbons' catalogue has raised the price of the cheapest Penny Black from $12.20 (£6) to $16.30 (£8), indicating the inexorable rise in value of this relatively common, though eminently desirable, stamp. I would guess that a fair proportion of the seventy-two million of the world's first stamp is still in existence— 5 per cent would be a conservative estimate —but such is the demand for this stamp that its value is bound to go on rising steadily.

It should be remembered that a recent market research survey revealed a figure of over two million collectors in the United Kingdom alone, and it is reasonable to suppose that it is the aim of every British collector to possess at least one example of a Penny Black. The French equivalent, the 20 centimes Black of 1849, is even cheaper, being rated at $4–6 (£2–3) today in fine used condition, and one can even cite examples of countries—Honduras (1866) and Nicaragua (1862), for example—whose first stamps may still be purchased for a few cents or pence only.

The postal services in the United States a century ago were less sophisticated than their European counterparts and, of course, the population of the country was only a fraction of what it is today. Since the number of stamp collectors in America today outnumbers the total population of the United States in 1850, it is almost inevitable that early American stamps should be relatively scarce and correspondingly more expensive than the early British or French stamps.

The first 5 cent (Washington) and 10 cent (Franklin) stamps of the United States were issued in 1847, and are catalogued today at $42.84 (£21) and $142.80 (£70) respectively in fine used condition. Many of the 'Postmasters' stamps of the 1840s which preceded the general issue of 1847 are major rarities, such as the Buchanan 5 c (1845) and the St Louis 'Bears' (1845–7), or the New Haven 5 c (1845). Even the lower denominations of the 1869 pictorial series are priced in pounds or dollars rather than in pence or cents.

Somewhere between the extremes of British and American stamps of the very early period come the issues of the majority of European countries. Lower standards of living in the populations of these countries and lower standards of literacy generally militated against such a widespread use of the postal services as in Britain.

In addition, Europe in the 1840s and 1850s was in a state of political transition, out of which emerged such powerful nation-states as Italy and Germany. Consequently the stamps of the numerous kingdoms, principalities and grand duchies, which disappeared at the unification of these countries, had a relatively brief usage, and many of them are scarce and expensive nowadays, particularly in fine used condition.

The unification of Germany, a decade after Italy, was crucial to the philately of that country. Indeed, the stamps of the German Empire, which made their debut in January 1872, do not come within the category of the classics. When the first of the German states, Schleswig-Holstein and Hanover, were swallowed by Prussia as a result of the Seven Weeks' War of 1866, the philatelic press of the period was sufficiently well organized to be able to warn its readers of the impending disappearance of these countries from the stamp album, while enterprising dealers in Hamburg and elsewhere capitalized on the situation and acquired vast stocks of the obsolete stamps. The international market in the intervening years has absorbed these stocks, although, to this day, nicely used copies generally have the edge over mint specimens.

This is true of the other German states, which ceased to have separate issues in 1868 when the North German Confederation, under Prussian hegemony, came into being. Apart from the comparative plenitude of mint stamps, there are also the reprints with which Continental stamp dealers flooded the market in the late nineteenth century and even now many collectors shy away from the stamps of the German states on account of the numerous pitfalls which trap the unwary.

In recent years, however, there has been a tremendous upsurge of interest in the stamps of the Italian and German states. The law of supply and demand has had a marked effect on the value of stamps which, not so long ago, were not very highly rated. Although there are more collectors in the United States than in any other country, both Italy and Germany have a high density of stamp collectors in relation to the population in general, and these philatelists have stimulated the market in the early stamps of their respective countries.

Postage stamps had, by 1870, penetrated to all the civilized countries, and a good number of the more backward ones as well, but communications on a global scale were severely limited. By and large the classic issues of non-European countries are likely to be fairly expensive today—provided they are in good condition. There are exceptions to this rule, of course, mainly among the emergent nations of Latin America which often, optimistically, provided themselves with stamps before their postal services were ready to cope.

Thus the 2 reales stamps of Honduras, issued in 1866, are not known in postally used condition, the first actual postal service for which stamps were required being introduced eleven years later. Vast quantities of these Honduran stamps were around at one time, and every Victorian schoolboy collection contained some examples, but nowadays they are increasingly elusive, especially in blocks and larger multiples.

Fashions in philately have also changed over the past century. Whereas the early collectors preferred their classics in all their pristine glory, the modern collector is showing an increasing awareness of postmarks and has a predilection for stamps on cover. Many stamps which are very cheap as used singles become major rarities when found on their original envelope. Unusually early or late dates of usage are factors which may add considerably to the value of otherwise common stamps.

But it is probably on aesthetic grounds that the classics of philately deserve their enduring popularity. This was a period dominated by the beautiful line-engraved stamps of Perkins Bacon, a London firm which in its heyday produced the stamps of Britain, most of the colonies, and many other countries all over the world. In New York, Messrs Rawdon, Wright, Hatch & Edson, later known as the American Bank Note Company, recess-printed the early issues not only of the United States but also of Canada and subsequently of Mexico and other Latin American countries. The high standards of design and printing produced by these companies have contributed largely to the eternal appeal of the classic stamps, and though there are many other categories of stamps which have appeared since then, these are still the 'blue chips' of philately.

CHAPTER II
THE GENESIS OF POSTAGE STAMPS

Neither the prepayment of letters by stamps nor the use of adhesive labels to prepay taxes were novel in the 1830s; the prepayment of letters by means of adhesive labels was. Since the time of Dockwra in 1680 *hand-struck* postage stamps existed in Great Britain and many other postal services used hand-struck stamps to indicate prepayment also. Since 1802 adhesive labels had been used by the Board of Customs and Excise in Great Britain (forerunner of the present-day Board of Inland Revenue) to prepay taxes on patent medicines and other dutiable articles. Stamped wrappers or letter sheets, on which the device indicating prepayment was printed or impressed *before* the letter was written, also existed before 1840. If we discount the Sardinian letter sheets of 1819-20, with their printed or embossed stamps in denominations of 15, 25 or 50 centesimi, as paying a tax rather than a postal charge (and this supposition can be argued back and forth interminably), we cannot overlook the embossed wrappers and letter sheets used for prepaid correspondence in Sydney, New South Wales, from 1838 onwards. In 1834 Charles Whiting suggested stamped wrappers for newspapers transmitted by post but nothing came of it.

In *The Romance of the Postage Stamp* Gustav Schenk produces an astonishing statement which I quote in full: 'In 1811, a Scottish shipping line used adhesive stamps for its private postal service, though unfortunately little is known about these.' Tantalizingly, no more explicit details are given; it would be fascinating to know the name of this company and intriguing circumstances of this forerunner of the Penny Black.

From Scotland also comes the closest rival to Sir Rowland Hill's fame. Time was when the *Encyclopaedia Britannica* used to claim for James Chalmers, the Dundee bookseller, the title of the inventor of the adhesive postage stamp, but for several editions now this premier reference work has deleted all mention of Chalmers. The facts of the Chalmers-Hill controversy may briefly be stated.

Chalmers undoubtedly took a keen interest in problems of posts and communications; in 1825 he successfully proposed a scheme which led to a great acceleration in the coach service between Dundee and London. It is highly probable that he studied the problem of postal reform following the agitation in Parliament of Mr Robert Wallace, M. P. for Greenock (who, significantly, was Rowland Hill's inspiration as well). When the Treasury Competition of 1839 was announced, Chalmers submitted some essays which were subsequently turned down as unsuitable. He thereupon wrote to Rowland Hill on October 1st 1839: 'If slips (i.e. stamps) are to be used I flatter myself that I have a claim to priority in the suggestion, it being nearly two years since I first made it public and submitted it in a communication to Mr Wallace, M. P.' This would therefore place the first publication of Chalmers' scheme at no earlier than the end of 1837. This is confirmed in other correspondence where Chalmers gives the date at which he *first* published his plan as November 1837. The italics are his.

In his pamphlet advocating Post Office reform, published on February 22nd 1837, Rowland Hill wrote: 'Perhaps this difficulty (of using stamped envelopes in certain cases) might be obviated by using a bit of paper just large enough to bear the stamp, and covered at the back with a glutinous wash, which the bringer might, by the application of a little moisture, attach to the back of the letter, so as to avoid the necessity of re-directing it.'

Thus Sir Rowland Hill had published his plan and outlined the concept of the adhesive stamp nine months before Chalmers. The latter undoubtedly arrived at the same conclusion independently of Hill; his letter of October 1839 shows that he was until then unaware of Sir Rowland's earlier publication. When he realized this he wrote again to Hill candidly withdrawing his own claim. In a letter to his 'rival', dated May 18th 1840, he wrote : 'My reason for not replying sooner proceeded from a wish to see the stamps in operation, which, although not general, they now are. I therefore conceive it only an act of justice to myself to state to you what induced me to become a competitor; for in that capacity I never would have appeared if I had known that anyone, particularly you, had suggested anything like the same scheme... I have only to regret that, through my ignorance, I was led to put others and myself to trouble in the matter, besides some unavoidable expense, while the *only* satisfaction I have had in this, as well as in former suggestions (all original to me), is that these have been adopted, and are likely to prove beneficial to the public.'

James Chalmers, in his own lifetime, acknowledged that Sir Rowland Hill had prior claim. Not till 1879, in which year Sir Rowland Hill died, did Chalmers' son, Patrick, dare to challenge Hill's claims. In the *Dundee Advertiser* he challenged Sir Rowland's reputation and charged him with having deliberately concealed his father's plan. The pamphlet vendetta which was waged between Patrick Chalmers and Rowland's son, Pearson, lasted almost twenty years. Patrick published no less than thirty-five pamphlets blasting and counterblasting the Hills, and Pearson Hill, who was a real chip off the old block, gave as good as he got. Between 1884 and 1889 Judge Tiffany took it upon himself to investigate the relative merits of the arguments in the Chalmers-Hill controversy. He corresponded during this period with both Patrick Chalmers and Pearson Hill in an attempt to evaluate their respective claims. Tiffany's collected correspondence, together with copies of the numerous pamphlets which the protagonists were publishing even at that late date, are bound together in one volume in the Crawford Library at the British Museum and make interesting reading, casting valuable light on the characters of the two men concerned.

This unseemly squabble was carried into the third generation with Chalmers' granddaughter, Leah, and Colonel Hill taking up the verbal cudgels as late as 1940. Patrick went so far as to obtain sworn testimonies from several old Dundonians who had been in his father's employment in the 1830s and allegedly remembered James Chalmers printing stamp essays in 1834. One of these men, unfortunately, overstated the case, thereby destroying it. In the *American Philatelic Journal* of September 1887 a Mr Whitelaw stated that he was employed by Chalmers in 1834 and remembered his 'setting to work to draw up a plan of adhesive stamps when it had been settled that the Penny Postage system was to be adopted.' In 1834 the Penny Postage system had not even been heard of, let alone settled, so the evidence put forward by Mr Whitelaw, relying on his memory of events in his teens fifty years earlier, was highly suspect.

The year 1834 also figures in the only claim made against Sir Rowland Hill in his own lifetime. Dr John Gray of the British Museum was impelled to challenge him in the correspondence columns of *The Times,* after he had been knighted and had many honours heaped upon him. Gray claimed to have pioneered postal reforms, including the introduction of prepayment by means of adhesive stamps, as early as 1834. Dr Gray's bibliography lists almost 1,200 articles and pamphlets published by him between 1819 and 1874 on all manner of subjects, from snakes and butterflies to artisans' education and municipal drainage. He also wrote copiously about decimal coinage and is best remembered by philatelists for his early stamp catalogues—but nowhere in this mass of writings is there any published account on postal reform. It must be conceded that Hill's claim stands unsullied, since he beat all his rivals and competitors into print.

Patrick Chalmers ingeniously explained his father's stamps of 1834—three years before Sir Rowland Hill's plan was published—by linking it with the claims of another man, Samuel Roberts of Llanbrynmair. Roberts, a Welsh nonconformist with a deep interest in social problems of all sorts,

claimed to have been engaged in postal reform since 1827 but, like James Chalmers, had published nothing to prove his contentions. In 1889 the Marquis of Carmarthen petitioned the House of Commons on behalf of Mr Francis Worrell Stevens 'the real Inventor of the Penny Postage System'. Stevens claimed to have submitted plans for prepayment of postage by means of adhesive stamps to the Chancellor of the Exchequer in 1833. By an interesting coincidence a fellow master at his school, Albion House, Loughton, Essex, at the time was none other than Rowland Hill. He discussed his ideas with Hill, who borrowed his papers. Shortly afterwards Stevens left Loughton and emigrated to New Zealand where he forgot all about the matter, until 1876 when he learned of Sir Rowland Hill's fame and promptly wrote to him accusing him of breach of copyright. Sir Rowland never replied to this. Stevens' petition eventually reached the G.P.O. but there the matter rested and no action was taken.

The Austrian Empire has produced two claimants to have invented the adhesive stamp. In 1938 a letter was unearthed in a family Bible in the town of Millstattin, Carinthia, which fourteen years later created a philatelic sensation. Dated February 20th 1839, from Spittal to Klagenfurt, it bore a one kreuzer stamp printed on a light-brown burele background with the letters 'O.P.' in dark brown. A party of responsible Austrian philatelists examined the letter and pronounced the stamp genuine and the family which owned it were even offered three million Austrian schillings for it. The stamp had been invented by Ferdinand Egarter, postmaster of Spittal and father of the lady who had written the letter. At that time it was customary for postmen to receive a one kreuzer tip for handling letters and Herr Egarter apparently hit upon this method of gathering his dues. Thus, the 'stamp' was nothing more than a Collecting Fee label and has no real status as a postage stamp. The letters 'O.P.', once thought to mean Österreichische Post, are now supposed to stand for Orts Post (local post) and it has even been suggested that the stamp is merely a twentieth-century hoax. Until another specimen turns up it will be impossible to make a more definite pronouncement.

In 1936 Yugoslavia issued a set of four stamps in memory of Laurence Kosir, 'ideological creator of the first postage stamp'. Kosir, or Koschier, became a civil servant in the Austrian Empire and served in various capacities in Laibach and Venice, becoming registrar to the Illyrian court post book-keeping office in 1836. On May 11th of that year he put forward a scheme to the Austrian Government outlining a series of postal reforms. The Austrian authorities took no action in this matter. Kosir, however, is alleged to have communicated his proposals to an English trade agent named Galloway and he, in turn, passed on this information to Rowland Hill. Kosir continued to rise steadily in the Austrian civil service, eventually becoming Vice-State Auditor for Croatia-Slavonia in 1857. He died in Zagreb in 1868.

Another contender for the title of inventor of the prepaid postage stamp is Lieutenant Curry Treffenberg (1791-1875), who devised a scheme for stamped stationery in 1823. His proposal was laid before the Swedish parliament but was never implemented. He proposed 'various kinds of stamped paper bearing different values, which could be sold like *Carta Sigillata*, but for the purpose of containing letters which could be handed over to a post office without further payment being required.'

The *Carta Sigillata* referred to were the forms used in legal transactions and were stamped with the duty levied on such transactions. Stamped paper of this nature had been in use in Sweden since 1660.

Treffenberg's scheme envisaged letter sheets bearing a circular device with the three crowns of Sweden and values expressed in skillings. It seems likely that Treffenberg modelled his proposal on the *Cavallini* of Sardinia. Although his idea was not adopted for letters, it undoubtedly served as the basis of the scheme, introduced in 1824, of newspaper stamps. As in many other countries at this time, these stamps primarily represented a tax on newspapers, but, as a concession, permitted their transmission by post without further charge. Significantly the earliest of these *tidningsstämplarna* incorporated the three crowns emblem in designs closely resembling the Treffenberg essays. These newspaper stamps, in various forms, survived until 1872. They were struck directly onto the newspaper and were not produced as adhesive stamps.

So much for the fathers of the postage stamp; but one other claim deserves mention. In the 1840s M. Piron, *Sous-Directeur des Postes aux Lettres* in Paris, discovered in the archives of the French Post Office some documents showing that M. de Velayer had, between 1653 and 1665, established in Paris a private post under royal approbation and had placed posting-boxes at the corners of the streets for the reception of letters wrapped up in envelopes which were bought at offices established for that purpose. De Velayer also devised printed forms, or *Billets port payé*, for prepaying postage but as none of them has survived we have no means of knowing what form they took. Legend (for that is all it is) has it that de Velayer's scheme owed its inspiration to the Duchesse de Longueville who suggested that strips of paper, impressed with the royal arms and a value of two sous (ten centimes), could be affixed to letters by isinglass wafers. This would enable people to post their letters in street posting-boxes unobserved, instead of having to declare the contents of their correspondence to officials of the secret police who examined all the mail at the post office. So, perhaps, it is not a case of who fathered the postage stamp—but who was its mother, after all!

In 1831 a type-set label inscribed in Greek 'tesserakonta lepta' (40 lepta) was produced in connection with a charity-raising fund for the relief of refugees following the Cretan insurrection of that year. Recent evidence, in the form of letters passing through Athens and Piraeus in the 1830s, seems to suggest that these labels may have performed postal duty. If this is the case, Greece may well usurp Britain's claim as inventor of the adhesive postage stamp. On the evidence so far presented, however, it seems more probable that the labels were intended merely to embellish letters—in much the same way as Christmas and other charity seals are used today. The use of the 'tesserakonta lepta' labels in correspondence was a relatively isolated occurrence and it was not until 1861 that Greece adopted adhesive stamps.

CHAPTER III
GREAT BRITAIN 1840-1870

On January 10th 1839 the fourpenny rate was reduced and Uniform Penny Postage introduced in Great Britain. Rowland Hill had also envisaged the prepayment of letters (not considered polite up till then) and proposed the use of stamped envelopes or wrappers and adhesive labels 'just large enough to bear the stamp and smeared on the back with a glutinous wash'. James Chalmers, Henry Cole and others had produced essays for such stamps as early as 1838 and in the following year the Treasury sponsored a competition to find suitable designs for such stamps. Many weird and wonderful designs were submitted, none of which was subsequently used, and in the end it was the simple design, showing the queen's head in profile, which Rowland Hill himself had suggested, that formed the basis of the world's first adhesive postage stamps.

The earliest adhesive stamps of the United Kingdom were recess-printed from line-engraved plates. This process required an engraver to cut lines into a polished soft steel die, in the reverse of the intended design. The die, when completed, was then hardened by a chemical process and a roller of soft steel passed over it under great pressure. The design of the stamp would then be transferred to the roller and one roller could take up several impressions from the die. The design now appeared in

positive form. The transfer roller was then hardened and rolled carefully, under pressure, over a steel plate, in such a way that the impressions were transferred to the latter in twenty rows of twelve. The plate was then hardened and ready for printing. Strictly speaking the stamps were recess-printed while the plates were line-engraved, but it is customary to refer to the stamps produced in this way as 'the line-engraveds'.

They were printed by the firm of Perkins, Bacon & Petch, who had perfected a press about twenty years earlier for printing banknotes. This was combined with another Perkins device, the Rose engine, which produced spiral patterns of high geometrical precision and intricacy, thus defeating the forger. These engine-turned patterns were used as a background to the banknotes and this device was incorporated in the postage stamps.

The portrait chosen for the stamps was based on the profile of Queen Victoria at the age of fifteen, when she was still princess, but first appeared in relief form on the obverse of the medal engraved by William Wyon in 1837 to commemorate the young queen's visit to the Guildhall, following her Coronation. Henry Corbould, F.S.A., made a number of sketches from this profile, from which the engravers Charles and Frederick Heath produced the master die for the stamps.

Recess-printing involves the inking of the *recesses* of the plate instead of the *surface* of it as in the letterpress process. Once the plate has been inked and the colour worked thoroughly into all the grooves the plate is wiped clean and polished. This, of course, does not remove the ink which lies in the grooves. The paper usually had to be dampened in order to make it more absorbent, and it was then laid on top of the plate and forced down under great pressure, so that the plate bit into the paper. The paper squeezed into the grooves picked up the ink; and this gives stamps and banknotes printed in this fashion their characteristic ridged surface. Recess-printing was used for all the stamps up to and including the 2 d value, from 1840 till 1880, and for all the definitive high values (2 s 6 d to £ 1) since 1913.

The first adhesives were put on sale on May 1st 1840, although they were not valid for use until May 6th. Nevertheless a few copies exist with authentic dates from May 2nd onwards. The Penny Black was printed from eleven different plates, some of which can be found in several states, while the Twopence Blue was printed from only two plates. All the penny stamps up till 1880 bore the plate number in the corners of the sheet and the interesting marginal inscription 'PRICE 1 d Per Label. 1 s PER ROW of 12. £ 1 0 s 0 d Per Sheet. Place the Labels ABOVE the address and towards the RIGHT-HAND SIDE of the Letter. In Wetting the Back be careful not to remove the Cement.' Similar inscriptions appeared on the other line-engraved stamps.

An unusual feature of the first British stamps, continued in the later issues down till 1887, was the inclusion of small letters in the corners, as a further check on the activities of the would-be forger. Down till 1864 the letters only appeared in the bottom

1 *Great Britain, Penny Black, 1840*

2 *Great Britain, Penny Red, 1841*

3 *Great Britain, Twopence Blue, 'white lines', 1841*

4 *Great Britain, Penny Red with perforations, 1858*

5 *Great Britain, ¹|₂ d, 1870*

6 *Great Britain, 1¹|₂ d, 1870*

7 *Great Britain, 6 d, embossed, 1854*

8 *Great Britain, 4 d, surface-printed by De La Rue, 1855*

2

3

5

6

8

corners, but, as it was feared that people might use the unobliterated portions of two used stamps joined together to make one apparently unused stamp, the letters, in reverse order, were added to the upper corners as well, in place of the little star ornaments. The lettering ran across the top row thus : AA, AB, AC to AL, on the second row BA, BB, BC to BL, and so on down the sheet to the bottom row which was lettered from TA to TL. The letters were added to the plates by means of punches. One style of lettering was used for the Penny Blacks and Twopence Blues, but in the Penny Reds, which were introduced in 1841 and continued in use for almost forty years, three styles of punches were employed, known to specialists as Alphabets I, II and III. A fourth style of lettering, Alphabet IV, was hand-engraved not punched, on plates 50 and 51 of the Penny Reds in 1861.

The first major change in the British stamps was made at the end of 1840, when it was decided to alter the colour of the 1 d from black to red, so that the postmark could then be more readily distinguished. The first Penny Reds were used on January 17th 1841 and up till 1843 were printed 2 from plates 1, 2, 5, 8, 9, 10 and 11 of the Penny Black. It is thus possible to collect the black and red stamps in 'matched pairs', from identical positions on the same plates. At the same time the design of the Two- 3 pence Blue was altered by the inclusion of horizontal white lines above and below the portrait. These stamps were printed from two plates, numbered 3 and 4 and fairly easy to differentiate on account of their distinctive corner letters.

Altogether 204 plates, plus fourteen reserve plates (R1–R14), were used to print the original design of the penny stamps up till 1855. In that year the portrait was re-

engraved by William Humphrys, the chief differences being that the eye was more deeply shaded and the chin given a firmer appearance. The Humphrys' engraving is known as die II to distinguish it from the Heaths' master die. Using die II, 1 d stamps in plates numbered from 1 to 225 and R15 to R20 were printed up till the end of 1879. With die I, 2 d stamps in plates from 1 to 6 were used up till 1858 and, using die II, from 7 to 15 till the line-engraveds were withdrawn in 1880.

The paper used in the earlier issues has a pronounced bluish tinge caused by the presence of prussiate of potash, either in the paper itself or in the printing ink. After 1856 the paper used for the line-engraveds was no longer blued, though some instances occurred in later stamps. A further check against forgery was the use of a small water-mark repeated throughout the sheet so that one occurred on each stamp. A small crown watermark was used on the stamps from 1840 till 1855, when it was superseded by a large crown.

Perforation was introduced in 1854, the 4 first gauge being 16. Experiments by Henry Archer and David Napier preceded the general adoption of perforation, and such stamps are extremely elusive and highly prized by collectors. In the Penny Red series, from die II, the stamps with letters in all four corners were also inscribed in the vertical side panels with minute figures signifying the number of the plate. The first plate with letters in all corners was plate 69. Both plates 69 and 70 (and also 75, 126 and 128) were manufactured, but rejected on account of defects before print-ing took place. Consequently no stamps bearing these numbers can exist and the lowest number which may be found is 71. Plate 77 was likewise rejected, but in this case a few stamps were printed and put into circulation. No more than ten are known to exist, however, and these are extremely rare. Most of the other plate numbers are easy to obtain for only a few cents or pence, but several, including 225 which was the last one to be used, are scarce and command a premium.

In 1870 a change of postal rates and the introduction of a printed paper rate necessitated the issue of ½ d and 1½ d stamps. The ½ d was produced in a very small horizontal format, about half the size of the 1 d stamp. It bore a script watermark—'halfpenny'—extending over three stamps, and was perforated 14 in sheets of 480. Plate numbers were engraved in the spandrels at the side of the portrait and stamps from plates 1, 3-6, 8-15, 19 and 20 were issued between October 1870 and October 1880. The 1½ d stamp had been produced as early as 1860, in anticipation of a change in postal rates which did not in fact materialize. Consequently, the original printing, in rosy-mauve, was scrapped, and when the stamp was eventually released it appeared in shades of red, similar to the ½ d and 1 d stamps. It went on sale at the same time as the ½ d. Only two plates were used in the decade in which this stamp was current. Plate 1 bore no figures, but plate 3 had tiny figures engraved in the spandrels on the lower left and right-hand sides of the design. A few specimens of the rosy-mauve variety have survived in unused condition.

The line-engraveds are a happy hunting ground for the specialist. The fact that the stamps in each sheet bore different corner letters made their plating (especially in the numbered series after 1858) a popular pastime. The reconstruction of the eleven plates of the Penny Black has long since been achieved, but much research remains to be done, and many problems solved, in the imperforate Penny Reds and the later

issues up to 1858, so that there is still opportunity for the student who wishes to accept the challenge of a fascinating series. The stamps also abound with flaws and re-entries (the latter as a result of the transfer roller being reworked over a defective or worn part of the plate), and every collector remains eternally optimistic about turning up a plate 77 Penny Red, a Treasury roulette, or a 1½ d lettered OP-PC (in error for CP-PC).

Embossing, a process seldom used in the production of adhesive stamps, is still in use for postal stationery (envelopes and registered envelopes) and is in fact the most enduring process used, having been employed for this purpose continually since 1841. Prior to that it was in use since the reign of William and Mary for the impressing of the tax label on legal documents, a practice which continues at the Stamping Department of the Board of Inland Revenue till this day. It is not surprising therefore that this process was suggested in many of the essays submitted in the Treasury Competition of 1839 and some of them, notably those entered by Charles Whiting and Robert Sievier, were extremely elegant in appearance. The individual method of production, however, made embossing too tedious a process to be used in the manufacture of adhesive stamps and consequently its use was confined to three denominations current between 1847 and 1856.

In embossing, the original die is engraved rather like a cameo, the details being achieved by variations in the depths of the sculpture. Intermediate dies (known as 'punches') are struck from the master die and then working dies struck from the punches. The ink is spread on the flat portions of the die and the paper pressed on to the die with great force, either using a 'male' matrix in steel, or a pad of leather, to squeeze the paper into the recesses of the die. Simultaneously the paper takes up the ink from the unrecessed portions of the die. Thus the design is shown in colourless relief against a flat, coloured background. So far as the author is aware, no method of impressing two dies at once has been used in the manufacture of embossed British stamps. Each impression was struck individually and, as a result, the spacing of stamps on the sheet was often irregular, sometimes overlapping.

William Wyon engraved the dies for the postal stationery, beginning with the 1 d pink envelope stamp used from 1841 till 1902, using as his model the obverse of the 1837 Guildhall Medal. This portrait was retained by Wyon for the adhesive 1 s green stamp which was embossed at Somerset House and released on September 11th 1847. This stamp, like the 10 d brown stamp which appeared the following year, was embossed on special paper manufactured by John Dickinson and shows two vertical silk threads impregnated in each stamp. This is an easy way of differentiating these stamps from undated postal stationery cut-outs of the 1890s which are often confused with the adhesives.

7 A 6 d lilac stamp was produced in March 1854 and bore a watermark 'VR' in single-lined letters, which may be found upright, inverted or reversed. The 6 d is also unique in that later printings had the gum tinted green to aid the printer in distinguishing the gummed side of the paper.

At first, when the adhesive stamps were only valid for postage in the United Kingdom, denominations of 1 d and 2 d were held to be sufficient, but by 1847 Britain had negotiated postal treaties with other countries, notably the United States and France, and stamps in higher denominations were thus required.

Die numbers were indicated on these stamps by minute figures engraved on the base of the bust, together with the letters W. W. (Wyon's initials). Two dies of the 1 s were used (1-2), four for the 10 d (1-4) and one only for the 6 d. Some stamps from die I of the 10 d exist without the die number showing, while, generally speaking, the die numbers tend to be rather indistinct. The stamps were issued imperforate and good, four-square copies are worth a premium. It seems to have been an unfortunate practice by Victorian collectors to trim these stamps to fit the octagonal space allotted them in the early printed stamp albums.

In 1855 a radical change was made in British stamp production when the firm of Thomas De La Rue & Co. Ltd was given the contract to print a 4 d stamp by the letterpress or typographic process. Dissatisfaction with this laborious embossed process was a contributory factor in this change. At this time, also, perforation was coming into use for the line-engraved low values and a great deal of trouble in perforating the sheets was being experienced. Because the paper had to be dampened prior to printing, uneven shrinkage of the dried sheets made it extremely difficult to get any uniformity in perforation. The fact that in the typographic process it was not necessary to dampen the sheets was a point in De La Rue's favour. The authorities were nevertheless worried about fraud, but De La Rue convinced them of the efficacy of their special fugitive inks which prevented the cleaning and re-use of stamps.

Their first order was to print the Draft and Receipt stamps for the Board of Inland Revenue in 1853, and the competent manner in which this was carried out led to the award to De La Rue of a contract two years later to print the 4 d postage stamp. Hence- 8 forward De La Rue printed an increasing number of postage as well as fiscal stamps and eventually, in 1880, wrested from Perkins Bacon the contract to print the low values from ½ d to 2 d. De La Rue excelled their rivals in their scientific approach to the subject of security printing and the efficiency with which they achieved results. From then until the end of the reign of King Edward VII, De La Rue had a monopoly of the printing of postage and fiscal stamps in Great Britain, as well as printing the vast majority of Colonial and Indian stamps.

Between 1855 and 1880, however, De La Rue had to be content with printing the higher values only, ranging from 3 d to £ 1. During that period many different designs were produced, often varying in comparatively minor details, so that the beginner tends to be bewildered by their profusion. To complicate matters further, the stamps were not issued in sets, as is so often the case nowadays, but in ones and twos as the occasion demanded. All the De La Rue typographed issues bore the Corbould version of the Wyon medallion portrait, engraved by one of the greatest exponents of the *en épargne* process, Jean Ferdinand Joubert de la Ferté.

The first 4 d stamp was printed in shades of carmine and considerable variation occurred, not only in the quality of paper used (ranging from highly glazed and deeply blued to ordinary white), but in the watermark (small, medium or large garter emblem). The 4 d was followed in late 1856 by stamps in denominations of 6 d lilac and 1 s green. The 4 d had been introduced to prepay the minimum letter rate to France, while the 6 d and 1 s denominations superseded the embossed stamps. The two latter were printed on paper of varying thickness and coloration bearing a watermark showing the floral emblems of the United Kingdom.

9 *Great Britain, 6 d, 1856*

10 *Great Britain, 3 d, wing-margin, 1862*

11 *Great Britain, 4 d, 1862*

12 *Great Britain, 9 d, 1862*

10

13

14

15

16

17

These three stamps were devoid of any corner letters or plate numbers, but in 1862 it was decided to incorporate letters in all four corners, a practice extended to the 1 d and 2 d stamps two years later. Small white letters on a coloured background were used at first, making their debut with a new 4 d 11 stamp issued on January 15th 1862. On the same day a 9 d stamp, printed in bistre, 12 was issued, to be followed by a 3 d stamp 10 in May and 6 d and 1 s values on December 1st. Plate numbering was not indicated on the stamps in the straightforward manner of Perkins Bacon. The earliest 3 d was, for example, printed from plate 2, plate 1 having been rejected before printing commenced. No indication was given on the stamp at all, but stamps from the ephemeral plate 3 may be distinguished by the appearance of white dots in the frame opposite the queen's chin and chignon. Similarly the first of the 9 d and 1 s stamps were printed from plate 2—though in the case of the latter the stamps actually bear the figures '1' in the spandrels!

The 4 d plates were even more complicated. Stamps from plate 3 have a Roman numeral I next to the bottom corner letters, while those from plate 4 have a Roman II and small hair-lines cut across the corners. The 9 d 'with hair-lines' (plate 3) and the 3 d 'with white dots' are what are termed 'abnormals'. It was customary to print at Somerset House, or an approved factory under the control of the Board of Inland Revenue, six sheets of stamps from every plate approved for printing. One sheet was retained in imperforate condition as the approved 'registration' or 'imprimatur' sheet, but some of the others were perforated and subsequently issued in the usual way, whether the plate was brought into regular employment or not. There are a number of other 'abnormals', of which the 6 d

13 *Great Britain, 3 d, 1865*

14 *Great Britain, 6 d, 1865*

15 *Great Britain, 10 d, 1867*

16 *Great Britain, 1 s, 1865*

17 *Great Britain, 2 s, 1867*

plate 10 (1869), the 10 d plate 1 (1867) and the 2 s plate 3 (1868) are well-known examples.

In 1865 the corner letters of the typographed stamps were increased in size to make them more distinct. Between March 1st and December 1st, the 3 d, 4 d, 6 d, 9 d, and 1 s were issued with redrawn corner letters. The 4 d bore the large Garter watermark, while the others showed the Floral Emblem watermark. This, incidentally, consisted of two roses, a thistle and a shamrock. A few 3 d stamps have been recorded with the error of watermark showing three roses and a shamrock. From the middle of 1866 onwards, the Garter emblem on the 4 d watermark was invariably inverted.

A new watermark, showing a spray of rose, was introduced in 1867 and gradually replaced the Emblem design. Between July 1867 and February 1880 the 3 d, 6 d, 9 d, 10 d and 1 s were reprinted on this watermark. By error, at least one sheet of the 10 d was printed on the obsolete Emblem watermark: less than a dozen have since turned up, most of them bearing the postmark of the British Post Office in Constantinople. Two types of 6 d appeared in this period, both with and without a hyphen between SIX and PENCE.

Britain's only 2 s denomination was issued on July 1st 1867 and remained in use until the early 1880s, being originally printed in blue and latterly in brown. A 5 s stamp was designed in November 1866 and put on sale the following July. It was decided to produce the stamp in a larger format, similar to that used for the contemporary Revenue stamps. They were sold in panes of twenty for £ 5 but printed in four panes to the sheet.

CHAPTER IV
THE 1840s: THE POSTAGE STAMP SPREADS ABROAD

Although Rowland Hill seems to have originally pinned his faith on the Mulready envelopes and wrappers, the general public took more readily to the adhesive stamps, the Penny Black and Twopence Blue, and by the end of 1840 the use of these labels was well established and the prepayment of letters had become the custom rather than the exception, though it was not until 1853 that prepayment became compulsory.

The fact that some seventy-two million Penny Blacks were issued in the period from May 1840 to January 1841, when they were superseded by the Penny Red, gives some indication of the popularity of adhesive stamps in Britain at a comparatively early stage. Yet it is surprising that other countries were so slow to adopt this innovation, and even more surprising was the order in which they did so.

Although the French postal administration was closely watching developments in Britain from 1840 onwards, nine years elapsed before they introduced adhesive stamps. Conversely it was in the New World, rather than Europe, that the first adhesive stamps outside Britain were released. The honour of having produced the world's second stamps must be given to the United States which, although delaying the government use of postage stamps till 1845, witnessed the issue of stamps by various private despatch companies and semi-official carriers much earlier.

UNITED STATES

The first of these appeared in 1842, some nineteen months after the issue of the Penny Black, and owed its origin to an English gentleman, Henry Thomas Windsor, who lived in Hoboken, New Jersey, from May 1841 till the autumn of 1842. He had been impressed by the working of the new postal system in England and thought that the same could be applied on a smaller scale in the United States. Accordingly he formed a partnership with an American businessman, Alexander M. Greig. The service which they initiated was colloquially known as 'Greig's Post' and commenced operations in New York City on February 1st 1842. Charles Windsor, son of the founder, recalled in later years that his father 'strained every nerve to get the post in full working order before St Valentine's Day, which he expected would be a heavy day, and so it turned out, for the Post was so inundated with letters that, owing to the arrangements not being thoroughly completed, so many complaints of irregularity were made, that he greatly feared it would be the deathblow of the Post.'

His fears, however, proved to be groundless and the service, known officially as the City Despatch Post, flourished until the Government postal authorities decided that it infringed their monopoly—and suppressed it. The service was heralded by a circular which, in view of its being the earliest reference to the use of adhesive stamps in the Western hemisphere, is worth quoting at some length:

New York City Despatch Post
Principal Office, 46 William Street

'The necessity of a medium of communication by letter from one part of the city to another being universally admitted, and the Penny Post lately existing having been relinquished, the opportunity has been embraced to reorganize it under an entirely new proprietary and management, and upon a much more comprehensive basis, by which Despatch, Punctuality and Security—those essential elements of success—may at once be attained, and the inconvenience now experienced be entirely removed.

'Branch Offices—Letter-boxes are placed throughout every part of the city in conspicuous places; and all letters deposited therein not exceeding two ounces in weight, will be punctually delivered three times a day ... at three cents each.

'Post Paid Letters—Letters which the writers desire to send free, must have a free stamp affixed to them. An ornamental stamp has been prepared for this purpose ... 36 cnts per dozen or 2 dolls. 50 c. per hundred.

'No money must be put in boxes. All letters intended to be sent forward to the General Post Office for the inland mails must have a free stamp affixed to them.

'Unpaid Letters—Letters not having a free stamp will be charged three cents, payable by the party to whom they are addressed, on delivery.

'Registry and Despatch—A Registry will be kept for letters which it may be wished to place under special charge. Free stamps must be affixed for such letters for the ordinary postage, and three cents additional be paid (or an additional free stamp affixed), for the Registration.'

United States

18 *3 c, United States City Despatch Post (cover), 1842–5*

19 *Philadelphia Despatch Post (cover), 1842*

20 *3 c, City Despatch Post, 1842*

21 *25 c, Adam & Co's Express, 1853*

22 *'20 for a dollar', American Letter Mail Co., 1844*

23 *The American Letter Mail Co., 1844*

24 *Barr's Penny Dispatch, 1858*

25 *Bentley's Despatch, 1857*

26 *Blood's Penny Post, 1843*

27 *D.O. Blood & Cos City Despatch, 1847*

28 *Blood's Penny-Post: Kochersperger & Co., 1848*

29 *2 c, Boyce's City Express Post, 1852*

30 *'20 for one dollar', Brainard & Co., 1843*

31 *2 c, Boyd's City Express, 1844*

32 *1 c, Brady & Co., 1858*

33 *Broad-way Post-Office, 1848*

34 *1 c, Brady & Cos Chicago Penny Post, 1857*

35 *Bank & Insurance Delivery Office, 1862*

36 *2 c, Browne & Cos. City Post, 1852*

37 *2 c, Browne's Easton Despatch, 1856*

38 *5 c, City Delivery, G. & H San Francisco*

39 *10 c, California City Letter Express, 1862*

40 *Floyd's Penny Post, 1860*

41 *1 c, Glen Haven Daily Mail, 1854*

42 *1 c, Grafflins One Cent Despatch, 1856*

43 *Frazer & Co. City Despatch Post, 1847*

44 *2 c, Gordon's City Express, 1848*

45 *'20 for 1 dollar', Hale & Co., 1843*

46 *1 c, Hourly Express Post, 1859*

47 *2 c, California Penny Post Co., 1855*

48 *5 c, Carnes San Francisco Letter Express, 1864*

49 *2 c, Cheever & Towle, 1850*

50 *Chicago Penny Post, 1862*

51 *City Dispatch, 1860*

18

19

20

21

22

23

24

25

26

27

28

29

30

31

32

33

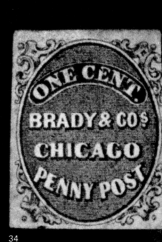

34

NOTICE
DELIVERY OFFICE
BANK & INSURANCE
82, BROADWAY.

35

BROWNE & Cos.
CITY POST.
2
CENTS

36

BROWNES
Easton Despatch
TWO CENTS

37

5 5
CITY DELIVERY
G. & H
P. SAN FRANCISCO 5

38

10 cents
Wedding cards, Notices
and Letters delivered,
by the California
City Letter Express
Co. Office at Hoogs
& Madison's, Real
Estate, House Bro-
kers & Rent Collectors,
418 Montgomery St.
10 cents
10 cents

39

FLOYDS
PENNY POST

40

41

42

43

44

45

46

47

48

49

50

51

52

53

54

55

56

57

58

59

60

61

62

63

65

66

67

68

69

70

71

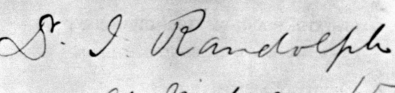

73

74

75

76

77

78

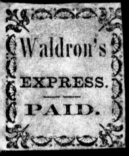

79

80

79

81

82

Lydia Hazard

Washington Hollow

Dutchess County

New York

86

87

88

89

90

Messrs Corcoran & Riggs

Washington City

D.C.

91

United States

52 *1 c, City Express Post, 1850*
53 *Cornwell Post Office, 1850*
54 *City Letter Express, 1860*
55 *2 c, Cumming's City Post, 1846*
56 *Dupuy & Schenck Penny Post, 1846*
57 *Eagle City Post, 1847*
58 *East River P.O., 1850*
59 *2 c, Essex Letter Express, 1856*
60 *25 c, Humboldt Express*
61 *Hussey's Post, 1854*
62 *2 c, Hussey's Bank & Insurance, 1862*
63 *2 c and 1c, M. W. Mearis City Despatch (used pair), 1846*
64 *Messenkope's Union Square Post Office (on cover, in combination with the US 3 c of 1851)*
65 *2 c, McIntires City Express Post, 1860*
66 *2 c, Menant & C⁰ Express Post, 1863*
67 *One Cent Despatch, 1844*
68 *Priest's Paid Despatch, 1854*
69 *5 c, Penny Express Company, 1866*
70 *J. H. Prince Letter Dispatch, 1861*
71 *2 c, Price's City Express, 1857*
72 *2 c, Price's City Express on local cover, 1857*
73 *Russell Post Office, 1853*
74 *2 c, Smith's City Express Post, 1857*
75 *1 c, Snow's Express*
76 *1 c, Squier & Co's City Letter Dispatch, 1847*
77 *3 c, Staten Island Express Post, 1851*
78 *Swarts City Dispatch Post, 1846*
79 *Waldron's Express*
80 *Teese & Co Penny Post, 1852*
81 *25 c, Wells Fargo Pony Express, 1861*
82 *2 c, Walton & Co's City Express, 1846*
83 *Wells Fargo & Co. newspaper stamp, 1861*
84 *2 c, Union Square P.O., 1850*
85 *Westervelt's Post, 1863*
86 *West Town (on cover with US 3 c of 1851), 1859*
87 *Carriers' stamp, U.S.P.O. Despatch, 1849*
88 *Carriers' stamp, One Cent Despatch, 1852*
89 *Carriers' stamp, Honour's City Post, 1851*
90 *Carriers' stamp, Government City Dispatch, 1860*
91 *Carriers' stamp, 2 Cents, Honour's City Post (on cover with a pair of the 5 c US government issue of 1847), 1850*

The 'free stamps' referred to in the above circular consisted of a 3 c recess-printed in black on greyish paper. A portrait of George Washington appeared in an upright oval, with the inscription 'CITY DESPATCH POST' around the top and the words 'THREE CENTS' at the bottom. The stamps were printed in sheets of forty-two by the New York firm of Rawdon, Wright and Hatch (later to become the American Bank Note Company) and cancellation was effected by means of a red marking inscribed 'FREE' in a double-lined frame.

According to Charles Windsor the post was suspended for a time, on the orders of the Government postal authorities, but the protests of the citizens of New York led to a resumption of the service some time later. In the meantime his father had been called to London on business and did not return to the United States. This statement is only partially true. Local delivery of letters had been authorized by an Act of Congress as early as July 1836 and reinforced by an Act of 1851, by which the Federal Government undertook the collection and delivery of letters within certain city areas for a fee of one or two cents (the 'penny post' referred to in the circular). Alongside the official carrier services, which derived their authority from the US Postmaster General, were many private services which, acting unofficially, frequently performed the same services.

Greig's Post came in the latter category and whether it was actually suppressed in the manner suggested by Charles Windsor cannot be vouchsafed. However, on August 1st 1842 the Postmaster General established a carrier service in New York known as the United States City Despatch Post. Greig's Post was sold to the United States Post Office on August 15th 1842 and recommenced the following day as the United States City Despatch Post, under the superintendence of Alexander Greig, who was appointed a US letter-carrier for that purpose. The City Despatch Post stamps were accepted for the service of the United States City Despatch Post and cancellation was usually effected by a small octagonal mark inscribed US, but sometimes a circular date-stamp was also used. This stamp, which began its career as a private issue, thus deserves to be regarded as the first official issue of the United States Post Office.

Subsequently the stamp was re-issued, between the end of 1842 and 1845, in black on unsurfaced paper of various colours—blue, rose or green—or on glazed paper coloured green or blue on the surface only. The three cents postage was made up of one cent for the fee on 'drop letters' (i.e. those sent to the addressee at the post office) and the carrier's fee of two cents. When the drop letter postage was abolished in June 1845 the stamps were revalued at 2 c, by surcharging the new value in red. The Government postal service ceased operation late in November 1846, but the following year the City Despatch Post was revived under private enterprise again, the proprietor of this service being Abraham Mead. The same design was used for the stamps as before, but the value was inscribed 'TWO CENTS'. Between 1847 and 1850 these stamps additionally bore the letters CC beside Washington's portrait, the initials of Charles Cole, who took over the service from Mead.

Some idea of the proliferation of local postal services in the United States may be gained from the fact that there were more than fifty companies operating in the decade up to 1850 and issuing adhesive stamps for the prepayment of postage. In addition a number of the carriers appointed by the US Postmaster General also issued stamps which can be regarded as semi-official in nature. In addition to the United States City Despatch Post already referred to, carriers' stamps were produced in Boston, Charleston, Philadelphia and St Louis in 1849, and though the Federal Government issued carriers' stamps of its own in 1851, a number of distinctive issues continued to appear until well into the 1850s. Many of these issues bore the names of the carriers and were similar in appearance to the local stamps of the private companies, hence the confusion which exists in the minds of many collectors regarding their function and status. Others bore such inscriptions as 'Government Despatch', 'Post Office Despatch' or 'US Penny Post' which gave some indication of their semi-official status.

By an Act of Congress of March 3rd 1845, which came into effect on July 1st of that year, the postal rates within the United States were regulated. Single letters (i.e. those consisting of a single sheet of paper) conveyed a distance of three hundred miles or less were charged five cents; those conveyed any distance over three hundred miles were charged ten cents. Double letters (and this theoretically included letters enclosed in a wrapper or envelope) were charged at twice these rates, while treble letters were also charged accordingly. However, it was found more expedient to regard any letter or packet weighing less than half an ounce as a single letter, and multiples of that weight were treated as double, treble or quadruple letters as the case might be. All drop letters, or letters placed in a post office for local delivery only, were charged at the lower rate of two cents each. Various rates were applied to circulars, newspapers and pamphlets.

Curiously enough there was a considerable time lag between the passage of this

18

19
20-86

87-91

Act and the Act of March 3rd 1847 which permitted the Postmaster General to issue adhesive stamps. In the intervening period of two years it was left to the postmasters of various towns and cities to remedy this omission by producing their own provisional stamps. The first of the 'Postmasters' issues appeared, as one might 93 expect, in New York barely a fortnight after the Act came into effect. Again George Washington formed the subject of this 'first' and the task of recess-printing the stamps was entrusted to Messrs Rawdon, Wright & Hatch. The 5 c stamps were printed in black on bluish paper, the portrait being from the die used in the production of the banknotes then current. The stamps were usually initialled in red 'A.C.M.' (Alonzo Castle Monson), a postal clerk, but rarely they may be found with the initials 'R.H.M.' (the Postmaster, Robert H. Morris) or 'M.M. Jr.' (Marcena Monson). Mr Morris is also believed to have prepared stamped envelopes, but although these were advertized in a circular of July 7th 1845, none has so far come to light.

101 James Madison Buchanan, Postmaster of Baltimore, Maryland, issued 5 and 10 c stamps in 1845, consisting of his signature above the denomination, enclosed in a thin rectangular frame. The make-up of the printing plate is unknown, though eleven varieties of the 5 c and three of the 10 c have been recorded. The stamps were printed in black on white or bluish paper. Buchanan also produced postal stationery, consisting of envelopes bearing his signature above the word 'PAID' and the value in a circle.

John M. Wimer, Postmaster of St Louis, Missouri, also released stamps late in 1845; these stamps are known to collectors as the 98 'St Louis Bears', from the fact that they featured the coat of arms of Missouri, whose supporters were American grizzly bears.

The stamps were engraved in a plate of six subjects (three 5 c and three 10 c) by J. M. Kershaw and each stamp differed slightly from its neighbours. The need for 20 c stamps led to a further re-engraving of the plate. The values on two of the 5 c stamps were obliterated by placing the plate face downward on a hard surface and hammering on the reverse at the required point. The new value was then engraved by hand. Subsequently the need for 20 c stamps diminished and the plate was again reworked, to convert the 20 c subjects back to 5 c once more. The redrawn 5 c stamps differed slightly from the originals. In addition there were considerable retouching and repairs to the impressions, thus giving rise to distinct varieties. The stamps were printed in black on paper of different colours (greenish or grey-lilac) and textures (wove or pelure).

The St Louis Bears were in use for little more than fifteen months and the numerous variations which they underwent in that period have resulted in a relative scarcity of individual items.

During 1846 'Postmasters' stamps also appeared in Alexandria (Virginia), Annapolis (Maryland), Boscawen (New Hampshire), Brattleboro (Vermont), Lockport 100 (New York), Millbury (Massachusetts), New Haven (Connecticut) and Providence 99 (Rhode Island). They range aesthetically from the crudely hand-struck 5 c produced by Hezekiah Scovell at Lockport, to the woodcut portrait of George Washington issued by Asa Waters at Millbury. The circular, type-set design of the Alexandria 5 c issued by Daniel Bryan was subsequently plagiarized by the Russian *zemstvo* (local) post of Aleksandria (Kherson district), which issued a 10 kopek stamp in a strikingly similar design in 1870. The mystery deepens when it is realized that the American stamp was not in fact discovered by philatelists till 1872.

Although the Postmaster General of the United States was so tardy in introducing a general issue of postage stamps, it is interesting to note that the New York Postmaster's 5 c stamp was sold not only in New York but also in the post offices of Albany, Boston, Washington and Philadelphia. It has been stated that the United States Postmaster General, Cave Johnson, authorized the sale of the New York stamps in these other cities, but only for use on mail addressed to New York. This was done for a short time only during 1846, apparently to test the practicability of the use of adhesive postage stamps on a nationwide scale. In general, however, the Postmasters issues were not recognized beyond the areas served by the individual postmasters.

The first general issues appeared on 5th August 1847. Section II of the Act of March 3rd 1847 stated that the Postmaster General was authorized to prepare postage stamps '... which, when attached to any letter or packet, shall be evidence of the payment of the postage chargeable on such letter'.

This Act also made it illegal for the postmasters '... to prepare, use, or dispose of any postage stamps not authorized by and received from the Postmaster General'.

The stamps, in denominations of 5 and 92 10 c, were recess-printed by Messrs Rawdon, Wright, Hatch & Edson and portrayed 94 Benjamin Franklin (the first Postmaster General of the United States) and George Washington (the first President) respectively.

Although the stamps should have been released on July 1st, over a month elapsed before the printers had the first consignment ready. The *Hartford Times* of August 5th

92 *United States Government issue, 5 c, Franklin, 1847*

93 *United States Postmaster's stamp, 5 c, New York, 1845*

94 *United States Government issue, 10 c, Washington, 1847*

95 *United States Government issue, 15 c, inverted centre, 1869*

96 *United States Government issue, 24 c, inverted centre, 1869*

97 *United States Government issue, 30 c, inverted centre, 1869*

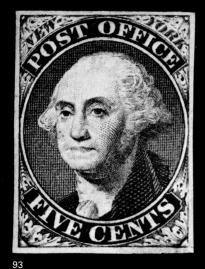

93

92

94

95

96

1885 contained an interesting account concerning the issue of the first stamps. Henry Shaw, a prominent citizen of New York, happened to be in the Postmaster General's office on the morning of August 5th 1847 when Cave Johnson entered with one of the printers and examined sheets of the new stamps. Johnson showed the stamps to Shaw, who thereupon drew 15 cents from his purse and purchased one of each denomination. The 5 c he kept as a curiosity while the 10 c he subsequently presented to Governor Briggs '... as an appropriate gift'.

A total of 4,400,000 of the 5 c and 1,050,000 of the 10 c were printed, some $ 8,229 worth being redeemed or exchanged when the series was superseded in July 1851. The quantity of stamps sold in that four-year period seems small in comparison with the 409,320,000 Penny Blacks and Penny Reds printed in the comparable period of 1840-3 in the United Kingdom, but it should be remembered that the public were less inclined to prepay postage in the United States than in Britain, despite repeated exhortations by the US Post Office to encourage prepayment. In a memorandum to postmasters, the Postmaster General pointed out the advantages : '... it saves time and trouble to all offices both in the mailing and delivery of letters; and if you supply your neighbourhood in the manner stated, an increased proportion of letters will come to you prepaid to be mailed, and your commissions will be correspondingly augmented.'

102 Lower denominations of 1 and 3 c, also portraying Franklin and Washington, were
103 introduced in 1851, then new 10 c and 12 c (Washington) and 5 c (Jefferson) were issued between 1851 and 1856. Several
104-106 distinct types were produced of each value, distinguished by minor details. In 1860,

24 and 90 c (Washington) and 30 c (Franklin) stamps were added to the series. 107-109 Having appeared piecemeal over the previous decade, the definitive series was reissued in 1861 in amended designs, a further mark of distinction being the addition of perforation for the first time. The 110-117 introduction of local delivery in 1862 resulted in the 2 c of that year portraying 118 Andrew Jackson, known to collectors as the 'Black Jack' or 'Big Head' (on account of the disproportionate area taken up by the portrait). A black 15 c appeared in June 1866 portraying the recently murdered 119 President Lincoln. This stamp has been hailed as the first mourning stamp to be issued.

In order to prevent dishonest people from washing off the postmark, a device consisting of an embossed grill was introduced in 1867. The grill was supposed to break up the fibres of the paper thus enabling the obliterating ink to penetrate deeply into the paper. Grills appeared on the 1867 and the two succeeding definitive issues, but were abandoned as impracticable in 1871.

The series of 1869, recess-printed by the National Bank Note Co., portrayed Franklin, Washington and Lincoln on the 1, 6 120-129 and 90 c denominations, but adopted pictorial motifs for the remaining values. Communications were represented by the Pony Express rider (2 c), locomotive (3 c) and steamship *Adriatic* (12 c). The 15 and 24 c stamps struck a historical note, with tableaux of the landing of Columbus and the signing of the Declaration of Independence respectively. The eagle and heraldic emblems of the United States were shown on the 10 and 30 c stamps. The four top values were printed in two colour combinations, and examples of the 15, 24 and 30 c have been recorded with the centres inverted. 95-97

The pictorial experiment was short-lived, the United States reverting to a policy of portraying prominent statesmen on the definitive series of 1870. This, with very few isolated exceptions, has remained the rule down to the present day.

130-140

The introduction of the local delivery service sounded the death-knell of the private local mail companies which had proliferated in the 1850s, each with its own distinctive stamps. Among the last to survive was the Wells Fargo Pony Express which closed in 1864, but not before it had the distinction of issuing $ 4 stamps—at that time a world record for high face value.

BRAZIL

Although the United States was the first country other than Britain to issue adhesive postage stamps of any kind, it is to another country in the New World that credit should be given for first considering the adoption of stamps. A Brazilian consular official, J. D. Sturz, was serving in Europe in the early 1840s and was able to examine at close quarters the working of this new system in Britain. He was convinced of its efficacy, so that early in 1842, on his return to Brazil, he began agitating for the introduction of adhesive stamps in that country. Eventually a decree was signed on November 29th 1842 by the Minister of Posts, C. J. Aranjo Vianna (later Vicomte de Sapucahy), authorizing the issue of stamps. Article 5 of this decree stated : 'The postage of letters in the Imperial Post will be defrayed in advance by stamped paper or stamps of the value of 30, 60 and 90 reis.'

Whereas the British stamps had borne the profile of Queen Victoria, and the City Des-

98 *United States Postmaster's stamp, 10 c, 'St Louis Bear', 1845*

99 *United States Postmaster's stamp, Providence, Rhode Island, 1846*

100 *United States Postmaster's stamp, Brattleboro P.O., Vermont, 1846*

101 *United States Postmaster's stamp, Baltimore 5 c on cover, December 1845*

102 *United States Government issue, 1 c, Franklin, 1851*

103 *United States Government issue, 3 c, Washington, 1851*

104 *United States Government issue, 5 c, Jefferson, 1856*

105 *United States Government issue, 10 c, Washington, 1855*

106 *United States Government issue, 12 c, Washington, 1856*

107 *United States Government issue, 24 c, Washington, 1860*

108 *United States Government issue, 30 c, Franklin, 1860*

109 *United States Government issue, 90 c, Washington, 1860*

110 *United States Government issue, 1 c, Franklin, 1861*

111 *United States Government issue, 3 c, Washington, 1861*

112 *United States Government issue, 5 c, Washington, 1861*

113 *United States Government issue, 10 c, Washington, 1861*

114 *United States Government issue, 12 c, Washington, 1861*

115 *United States Government issue, 24 c, Washington, 1862*

116 *United States Government issue, 30 c, Franklin, 1861*

117 *United States Government issue, 90 c, Washington, 1861*

98

99

100

102

103

104

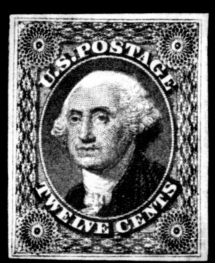

105

106

107

108

109

110

111

112

113

114

115

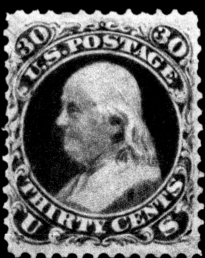

116

117

118

119

120

121

122

123

124

125

126

127

128

129

130

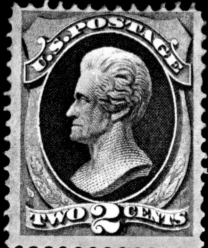

131

132

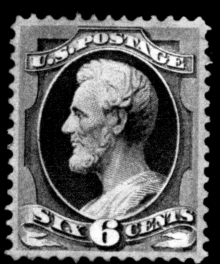

133

134

135

136

137

138

139

140

118 *United States Government issue, 2 c,*
Jackson, 'Black Jack', 1863

119 *United States Government issue, 15 c, Lincoln*
(the world's first mourning stamp), 1866

120 *United States Government issue, 1 c,*
Franklin, 1869

121 *United States Government issue, 2 c,*
Pony Express Rider, 1869

122 *United States Government issue, 3 c,*
Locomotive, 1869

123 *United States Government issue, 6 c,*
Washington, 1869

124 *United States Government issue, 10 c,*
Shield and Eagle, 1869

125 *United States Government issue, 12 c,*
Steamship Adriatic, 1869

126 *United States Government issue, 15 c,*
Landing of Columbus, 1869

127 *United States Government issue, 24 c,*
Declaration of Independence, 1869

128 *United States Government issue, 30 c,*
Shield, Eagle and Flags, 1869

129 *United States Government issue, 90 c,*
Lincoln, 1869

130 *United States Government issue, 1 c,*
Franklin, 1870

131 *United States Government issue, 2 c,*
Jackson, 1870

132 *United States Government issue, 3 c,*
Washington, 1870

133 *United States Government issue, 6 c,*
Lincoln, 1870

134 *United States Government issue, 7 c,*
Stanton, 1871

135 *United States Government issue, 10 c,*
Jefferson, 1870

136 *United States Government issue, 12 c,*
Clay, 1870

137 *United States Government issue, 15 c,*
Webster, 1870

138 *United States Government issue, 24 c,*
Winfield Scott, 1870

139 *United States Government issue, 30 c,*
Hamilton, 1870

140 *United States Government issue, 90 c,*
Commodore Perry, 1870

patch Post of New York had portrayed George Washington, the first stamps of Brazil departed from precedent by featuring the numerals of value against an engine-turned background. At that time the young Dom Pedro II had been emperor of Brazil for little more than two years, and was to have an illustrious reign lasting half a century, so at first sight it seems odd that his portrait did not grace the stamps of Brazil. It was, in fact, out of respect for the emperor that his portrait was not used. The idea was at first mooted, but the Director of the Rio de Janeiro Mint, regarding the obliteration of the royal effigy by means of a postmark as virtual lese-majesty, wrote to the Minister of Posts on February 13th 1843 raising objections to the original proposal and these were duly admitted.

The early stamps of Brazil were produced in a workshop attached to the National Treasury in Rio. The dies were engraved by Carlos Custodio de Azevedo and Guintino José de Faria, and the stamps recess-printed on a machine press by Clementino Geraldo de Gonvea and Florentino Rodrigues Prado. The use of an engine-turned background, in imitation of the device adopted by Perkins Bacon when they printed the first British stamps, made the stamps difficult to forge. The designs were extremely utilitarian nonetheless, with the figures of value on an oval background bereft of any inscription. Their curious appearance led to their nickname the 'Bull's- 142 Eyes'. The stamps were printed in black on papers of various qualities, ranging from thin yellowish paper to thicker greyish paper. The yellowish paper was, in fact, originally white but had become toned with age. The stamps were printed together in nine horizontal rows of six stamps, three rows of each value. The block of eighteen of each denomination was surrounded by a thin outer line and there was an additional line across the plate between the 30 and 60 and between the 60 and 90 reis stamps. The panes were theoretically cut apart before being issued, but mint vertical pairs of 30 and 60 r stamps *se-tenant* (two different stamps side by side in the same sheet) have been recorded, while a strip of three used stamps consisting of two 30 r and one 60 r was formerly in the collection of Charles Lathrop Pack and fetched the sum of $23,460 (£11,500) when it was sold at a Stanley Gibbons auction in February 1969.

Large sheets consisting of the 60 r alone were also produced and the late E. W. Mann, an authority on the early stamps of Brazil, proved by plate reconstructions that two plates of the 60 r, probably consisting of sixty subjects, were used, in addition to the pane of eighteen. The plates of the 'Bull's-Eyes' stamps rapidly deteriorated and later impressions of the stamps present a blurred, worn appearance. The stamps remained in use for less than a year. They were first put on sale on August 1st 1843 and withdrawn on June 30th 1844, notice of this having been given in a postal decree of February 13th that year. Although they were withdrawn from sale they remained valid for postage and examples are known with cancellations dated as late as 1845.

On July 1st 1844 a new series of three stamps, in the same denominations, was substituted. These stamps also had the numerals of value on an engine-turned background, but were smaller and neater in design and from the sloping character of the numerals were dubbed the '*Inclinados*'. Curiously enough, the postal decree authorizing these stamps was not signed till the following December. This decree also reserved the right to issue stamps of other denominations. The earliest printings of the 30, 60

141

141 *Brazil, 60 r, 'Inclinado', 1844*
142 *Brazil, 90 r, 'Bull's Eye', 1843*

141

142

and 90 r Inclinados were made on thick yellowish paper. Later printings of these values, released in May 1845, were on thin yellowish paper or thin blue-grey paper. At the same time 180, 300 and 600 r values in similar designs were introduced, while a 10 r denomination was released in September 1846. The various additional values may be found on either yellowish or grey-blue paper, both papers being of comparable degrees of rarity. The 10, 30, 60 and 90 r values are known in sharp (early) impressions or worn, rather blurred (late) impressions. The Inclinados were superseded by another numeral series on New 143 Year's Day, 1850. Sixteen years elapsed before the numerals were replaced by a series by the American Bank Note Co. por-144-150 traying Dom Pedro in various designs.

SWISS CANTONS: ZURICH, GENEVA, BASLE

The first country on the continent of Europe to issue adhesive stamps was, surprisingly enough, Switzerland. In the early 1840s Switzerland consisted of a remote mountain fastness which could not be regarded as a single political entity by any stretch of the imagination. Prior to 1847 Switzerland was a loosely knit Confederation of twenty-five cantons and half-cantons, differing widely in political and religious complexion, in economic structure and importance, in language, population and geography. There were, at this time, few effective Federal organs. Significantly the army was one, but the postal services were disunited. This explains why certain parts of the country were quick to adopt adhesive stamps while other parts did not introduce stamps until they were thrust upon them by Federal decree in 1850.

One of the largest of the liberal cantons was Zurich and it was here that innovations in postal matters were first and most readily embraced. Like many other postal administrators the Directors of the Zurich Cantonal postal service had paid close attention to the workings of postal reform in Britain. The decision to reform the postal system in Zurich was taken at the end of 1842 and a decree of the Postal Department, authorized by the Zurich Council, was published on February 25th 1843, intimating that '... in March 1843 the distance-tariff for the expedition of home letters will expire, and will be replaced by a fixed tax of 6 rappen for the whole canton, for single letters, that is, weighing less than ½ ounce.' Further clauses established a local post with a local tax of 4 rappen for each letter weighing less than half an ounce, and regulations concerning the registration of letters. Clause 4 announced: 'The Postal Administrations are requested to issue postage-stamps of 4 rappen for the Local post and 6 rappen for the Cantonal post.'

The stamps were lithographed in sheets of one hundred subjects by Orell, Fuessli & Co. of Zurich and placed on sale early in March, the earliest recorded date of use being March 12th. The stamps were print- 151 ed in black and were strictly functional, with large white numerals on a background of diagonally crossed lines. The name 'ZURICH' appeared at the top, while the respective denominations were inscribed 'Local-Taxe' or 'Cantonal-Taxe' at the foot. The stamps were produced in large quantities and the sheets kept locked in a safe along with the printing plates. When they were required a consignment would be taken out and an overall pattern of red lines overprinted as a form of control device. The lines come horizontally or vertically.

Reprints were made in October 1862 on thinner paper without the red lines. Five varieties exist of each denomination, repeated twenty times throughout the sheet. Complete strips, which are of the greatest rarity, are exhibited in the Tapling Collection at the British Museum. One example of a 4 rappen stamp bisected in conjunction with another 4 rappen stamp to make up the cantonal rate has been recorded. Local letters circulating in the city of Zurich were postmarked in red, while those in the country districts were cancelled in black. A few stamps are known with blue cancellations; these denote late usage after January 1849 when Federal cancellations in this colour were introduced.

The use of adhesives had been in operation in Zurich for barely ten weeks when M. Candolle proposed, in the Grand Council of Geneva, that similar labels should be introduced in that canton. The proposal was referred to the cantonal finance department for further consideration and on June 19th it was decided to introduce stamps and stamped envelopes. M. Candolle is believed to have been in England in 1839 shortly before the introduction of Uniform Penny Postage, and subsequently to have been impressed by the beneficial effects of a cheap postal system.

The Finance Department published a statement on September 13th to the effect that they had prepared postage stamps which would be placed on sale in the post offices of Geneva and Carouge. Two rates of postage were laid down, 10 centimes for letters under an ounce from one part of the canton to another, and 5 c for letters destined for addresses within the same postal delivery area (*Aufgabe-Ort*). Only one stamp was released, in a design whose ingenuity has never been surpassed. The stamp came to be known to collectors as 152 the 'Double Geneva' from the fact that it

143 *Brazil, 30 r, 1850*

144 *Brazil, 10 r, Dom Pedro II, 1866–8*

145 *Brazil, 20 r, Dom Pedro II, 1866–8*

146 *Brazil, 50 r, Dom Pedro II, 1866–8*

147 *Brazil, 80 r, Dom Pedro II, 1866–8*

143

144

145

146

147

148

149

150

151

consisted of two designs featuring the cantonal coat of arms. Each half was inscribed 5 c and 'Poste Genève-Port local', while across the top of each pair was the inscription '10 Port Cantonal Cent'. The bill from the printer, Schmidt of Geneva, was preserved in the archives of the Finance Department and from this it was deduced that a total of six hundred sheets was printed. The stamps were lithographed in black on green paper. Half-stamps are roughly four times commoner than the complete Double Genevas, while pairs cut the wrong way are twice as scarce again. These terms are relative, since any genuine examples of this stamp in good condition are major rarities.

A curious feature introduced with these stamps was the 50 per cent discount allowed on bulk postings of twenty letters or more. It is interesting to speculate to what extent this concession was used.

M. Candolle's suggestion that the stamps should be sold for 8 c instead of the nominal 10 c expressed on them was adopted by the Cantonal Grand Council in March 1844 and this concession is thought to have led to a marked increase in the number of prepaid letters handled after that date.

In 1845 a new tariff was introduced, involving a surtax of 5 c on letters coming into the canton from other parts of Switzerland. In connection with this, a new 5 c 153 stamp was lithographed by Schmidt in a single design featuring the cantonal coat of arms. This stamp is known to collectors as the Small Geneva Eagle. At the same time envelopes with this stamp impressed were prepared and sold for 5 c each. The adhesive stamps, on the other hand, were sold for 4 c in order to encourage the public to use them. There have been very few examples of 'cut-price' stamps (the Turkish 'Behie' stamps and the Belgian postwar 'Van Ackers' being outstanding exceptions)

148 *Brazil, 100 r, Dom Pedro II, 1866–8*

149 *Brazil, 200 r, Dom Pedro II, 1866–8*

150 *Brazil, 500 r, Dom Pedro II, 1866–8*

151 *Zurich, 4 rappen (the unique strip of five varieties), 1843*

and none has been as curious as the Geneva stamps of 1843–5.

Some 120,000 of the Small Eagle stamps were printed before a new design, known for obvious reasons as the Large Eagle design, was introduced in 1847. Like its predecessors this stamp was printed in black on coloured paper.

The last of the cantons to produce its own stamps in the Helvetian period was Basle which, not to be outdone by its allies Zurich and Geneva, embarked on a similar system in July 1845. The decision to introduce adhesive stamps was taken in June of that year and the Town Postal Service for the city of Basle was announced in the *Allgemeinen Intelligenzblatt der Stadt Basel* on June 30th. Publicizing the introduction of *Francozettelchen* (small franking labels) the announcement stated: 'For the greater convenience of the public, letters can now be accepted prepaid, for delivery within the town of Basle, so that the receiver gets them free of charge.' The stamps were to be available at '20 pieces for 5 batzen' and one was to be affixed to each letter weighing up to one *loth* for delivery within the city. Letters of heavier weight, or for delivery in the outer suburbs, '... have to bear two of these papers when they are prepaid'. Copious instructions were also given on how to affix the 'papers' to the letters.

157   The so-called '*Baslertäubchen*' or Little Basle Dove is an interesting stamp for several reasons. It was the first stamp to be printed in a country other than that which issued it, having been printed by a Herr Krebs of Frankfurt-am-Main in Germany. It was the world's first stamp to be produced in combined processes, involving embossing and typography. True to the precedents of Zurich and Geneva, which both produced stamps in more than one colour, Basle followed a similar policy but had to

152 *Geneva, 5 + 5 c, 'Double Geneva', 1843*

153 *Geneva, 5 c, 'Small Eagle', 1845*

154 *Geneva, 5 c, cut-out envelope stamp, 1849*

155 *Zurich, 2 1/2 r, 1850*

156 *Geneva, 4 c, 1849*

157 *Basle, 2 1/2 r, 'Little Basle Dove', 1845*

158 *Geneva, 5 c, 1850*

152

53

154

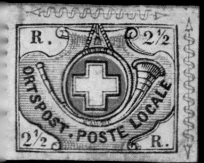

55

156

go a step farther and use three colours—black, carmine and blue. Examples of this stamp in black, vermilion and green are colour proofs.

Friction between the Catholic conservative cantons and the Protestant liberal cantons came to a head in 1847, when seven of the former established an alliance known as the Sonderbund. The Federal Diet ordered the dissolution of the Sonderbund, which was tantamount to secession from the Federation. The Federal Army, led by the Genevan General G. H. Dufour, marched against the seceding cantons and defeated them at the end of a short campaign in November 1847. The collapse of the Sonderbund led to the strengthening of the Federation at the expense of the individual cantons. A new constitution was promulgated in 1848, based on the American model. The new Federal authorities, in which the most moderate elements of the liberal party had a majority, set to work immediately. From the beginning of January 1849 the postal and telegraphic systems, the customs, the currency and weights and measures were unified and centralized.

The Federal Diet announced that '... the existing lawful and customary installations in the Cantonal Postal Administrations shall remain until the definite regulations of the Postal Department come into force.' This meant that the three cantons which had introduced stamps were permitted to retain them pending the release of Federal stamps. The Basle Dove inscribed 2½ rappen (the Federal currency) remained in use till May 1850, but new stamps had to be introduced in the other two cantons following the reorganization of the Federal postal system in June 1849.

In March 1850 Zurich released a 2½ rappen stamp featuring the Swiss cross in a

155

posthorn. This stamp was inscribed in German and French 'ORTSPOST POSTE LOCALE' and was officially designated as for use in Swiss Postal District VIII. Old stamp catalogues at one time attributed this stamp incorrectly to the town of Winterthur. Between the beginning of 1849 and the introduction of this stamp, the people of Zurich had to do without stamps and reverted to the old system of letters endorsed FRANCO with the amount of the postage written in red ink alongside.

The postal system of Geneva was taken over by the Federal authorities on June 4th 1849. To this period belongs the so-called Large Eagle in green on white paper. It was a transitional issue, made in the absence of other stamps pending the introduction of a Federal issue, and was produced from remnants of stamped envelopes for which there had been little demand. **154**

Geneva continued to use French currency until 1852, hence the continuance of stamps in centimes. A certain amount of confusion and mystery surrounded the stamps released in October 1849. They were inscribed 'POSTE LOCALE' and featured the Swiss cross in a posthorn. At first stamps were **156** issued in 4 c denominations, but when the rate was increased in January 1850 the numeral was altered by hand on each stamp of the plate. There are thus one hundred different varieties of the 5 c stamps which can be plated by means of this idiosyncrasy. These stamps, for some strange reason, were formerly attributed to the canton of Vaud.

In August 1850 a new 5 c stamp, featuring the Swiss cross on a upright format, was **158** released. This stamp, also inscribed 'POSTE LOCALE', was once erroneously attributed to the canton of Neuchâtel.

With the introduction of Federal stamps in May 1850 the issues of the cantons were gradually phased out.

FRANCE

The movement for postal reform which had taken place in Britain in the 1830s was closely followed by reformers on the other side of the Channel. Indeed, the first proposals for postal reform were made in France in 1832, some five years before agitation began in earnest in the United Kingdom. In that year the eminent Parisian journalist, Emile de Girardin, wrote an article advocating the introduction of a uniform postal tariff of 10 centimes for a simple letter (i.e. one comprising a single sheet). This idea fell on stony ground and it was not until the British reforms were going through Parliament in 1839 that the French reformers raised the matter again. Between 1839 and 1848 the question of postal reform was debated year in year out in the Chambre des Députés, but although the members had ample evidence of the operation and the success of uniform postage in Britain they were slow to realize the benefits of the system.

Eventually, in the early part of 1848, Etienne Arago, the Director General of Posts, sent to Garnier Pages, the Minister of Finance, a report outlining proposals for postal reform. This formed the basis for the government's resolution of May 8th 1848 (passed on the 26th) announcing the introduction of uniform postal rates and the prepayment of postage by means of adhesive stamps. After further debate and numerous amendments the decree became law on August 30th 1848 and contained the following announcements: Article 1 intimated that stamps would be introduced on January 1st 1849 and that letters weighing up to 7½ grammes could be sent from any post office in France, Corsica and Algeria for 20 centimes. Articles 2 and 3 laid down rates for letters from 7½ to 15 grammes

(40 c) and up to 100 grammes (1 franc). Article 5 authorized the postal administration to issue stamps of these denominations for the prepayment of postage.

The uniform design of the stamps featured the profile of Ceres, goddess of agriculture, in a classical border with the inscription 'REPUB. FRANC.' (French Republic) at the top and the figures of value and the word 'POSTES' at the foot. The dies for the stamps were engraved by Jean-Jacques Barre, the celebrated medallist and coin-engraver, while the production of the stamps was entrusted to the eccentric Anatole Hulot who, for reasons best known to himself, inserted one or more clichés upside down in relation to the others when constructing the printing plates. This idiosyncrasy gave rise to the very rare *tête-bêche* pairs which occur only on the 10 c and 1 franc stamps of 1849. This curious arrangement was also adopted for the 10, 15 and 25 c denominations which were added to the series the following year.

The stamps were typographed on unwatermarked paper, the 20 c in black, like Britain's first penny stamp, but oddly enough both the 40 c and 1 f stamps were printed in orange. Despite Article 5 of the decree, no 40 c stamps were issued during the first year of the scheme and double-weight letters had to be prepaid by pairs of 20 c stamps. When the 40 c stamps were being prepared it was decided to change the colour of the 1 f stamps to deep carmine to avoid any confusion between the denominations. An ungummed sheet of the 1 f in orange was discovered among Hulot's papers many years later and was subsequently disposed of by a Parisian dealer named Vervelle. Because these stamps were ungummed the 'Vervelle francs' are in a distinctly lighter shade and, though still expensive, are worth only about a quarter of the issued stamps in this colour. The Ceres stamps of the Second Republic remained in use until 1852, when they were gradually superseded by the series portraying Louis Napoleon, later the Emperor Napoleon III. As a mark of his success in the Italian campaigns of 1859–60, Napoleon appeared on the stamps of 1862–70 with victor's laurels on his temples. After the downfall of the Second Empire in 1870 the republican Ceres designs were re-introduced.

160, 161
165-169

BAVARIA

Three hundred years ago the Count of Thurn and Taxis established a branch of his postal system in the then duchy of Bavaria. By 1808, however, Bavaria had grown in size and status and the authorities within that state took over the operation of their own postal affairs. After the Napoleonic Wars, Bavaria was elevated to the status of a kingdom and in the mid-nineteenth century was one of the more liberal and forward-looking of the German states. The first railway in Bavaria was opened in 1835, mail-boxes were erected in the towns and cities of the kingdom as long ago as 1841 and an express delivery service established two years later. The public made increasing use of the postal services and, at the same time, demanded a simplification of the postal tariffs.

The decision to introduce adhesive stamps, in emulation of the Swiss cantons and France was taken by the Minister of Posts, Baron von der Pfordten, in February 1849. Peter Raseney, an engraver of the Mortgage and Exchange Bank of Bavaria, acted as consultant and negotiated the contract with Johann Georg Weiss, printer to the University of Munich, who typo-

graphed the first stamps of Bavaria. Franz Max Josef Seitz designed and engraved the dies for the first series of stamps and the plates were manufactured by Gustav Lorenz of Munich. An edict promulgated on October 23rd 1849 announced the impending release of 1, 3 and 6 kreuzer stamps for use on letters within the kingdom of Bavaria. Letters destined for addresses beyond the Bavarian frontier had to be prepaid in cash as before.

The first printing of the famous 'Schwarzer 162 Einser' (the black one), as the 1 kreuzer is affectionately known, was produced from a copper plate which proved to be too soft and liable to rapid deterioration. Subsequent printings of this stamp were therefore made from new plates made of brass. The stamps in the deep-black shade belong to the first printing, while the grey-black version belongs to the subsequent printings. A few of the first printing are known on experimental paper with a silk thread running through it, but it is not known whether these stamps were actually released to the public.

The design of the first stamp was simple and functional, with the numeral one in a rectangular frame surrounded by the inscription 'BAYERN FRANCO EIN KREUZER'. Shortly afterwards the 3 and 6 k stamps were released. These stamps were similar in design, but with the numerals set in circles of solid colour. The following year the series was re-issued in a uniform design showing the numerals on coloured circles similar to the design of 1849 but with the circles intact, whereas the design of 1849 had the top, bottom and sides of the frame cutting into the circle. In this modified design the stamps were issued in denominations of 1, 6, 9, 12 and 170 18 k, the higher denominations being introduced in 1854–8. This design lasted until the first of the embossed arms stamps appeared in 1867, having nevertheless in the meantime undergone changes of colour in 171, 172 1862–3. Perforation was adopted in 1870.

BELGIUM

The necessary postal reforms, which preceded the introduction of adhesive stamps, were carried out in Belgium in 1847—more than a year before similar reforms came into effect in France—and yet Belgium lagged behind her neighbour in the matter of issuing adhesive postage stamps.

The chief architect of postal reform in Belgium was Jacques Wiener and it was largely through his exertions that a uniform system of postal rates, envisaging the prepayment of postage, came into operation in 1847. Ultimately a law was passed authorizing the release of postage stamps on July 1st 1849 and in the early months of that year Jacques Wiener supervised the production of the first stamps.

A full-face portrait of Leopold I, king of the Belgians, in military uniform, designed by C. Baugniet, was engraved by J. H. Robinson on an engine-turned background and the stamps recess-printed at the Atelier du Timbre in Brussels. The stamps were instantly nicknamed 'Epaulettes' on account of the military appanages of the king's 163 uniform. Denominations of 10 and 20 centimes were printed on hand-made paper of varying thicknesses with a double L monogram watermark. The shade of these stamps varied a lot and in addition there were numerous minor varieties, re-entries and retouches. Two plates were used for the 20 c value, the frame-lines in the first plate being heavier, while the general impression of stamps from the second plate was coarser. The stamps were printed in

159 *France, 10 c, tête-bêche pair, 1850*

160 *France, 25 c, Napoleon III, 1853*

161 *France, 20 c, Napoleon III, laureated profile, 1867*

162 *Bavaria, 1 kreuzer, 'Schwarzer Einser', 1849*

163 *Belgium, 10 c, 'Epaulettes', 1849*

159

160

161

162

163

sheets of two hundred subjects. Three printings of these stamps were made between May 1849 and May 1850 and a total of 4,800,000 of both denominations was produced.

On April 27th 1849 a postal convention was concluded between France and Belgium to come into force on October 1st of that year, by which the rate of postage on letters from Belgium to France was reduced to 40 c. The release of a stamp of this denomination was announced on October 9th and the stamps were put on sale eight days later. The 40 c denomination differed from the preceding issues by framing the king's portrait in a circular device which sheared off the epaulettes. This stamp was the first of the series known from their layout as the 'Medallions'. In August 1850, new 10 and 20 c stamps in the same design were issued. The official circular published at that time explained the change '... establishing a perfect identity between the stamps, as they are all prepared from one original die, and there can only be added [the value] to the reproduced dies for each kind of stamp.'

The Medallions were designed by Baugniet and engraved by Robinson as before. This design had a comparatively long life of fifteen years, undergoing changes in watermark and eventually appearing on unwatermarked paper, appearing imperforate until 1863 and then using a variety of perforations from 11½ to 14½ in various combinations. De La Rue typographed a series, from 10 c to 1 franc, bearing a profile of King Leopold I, issued in 1865–6. Lower values, 1, 2 and 5 c, featuring the Belgian lion, were typographed at Brussels in 1866–7. A new series, with a couchant lion on the low values and a profile of Leopold II, was released gradually between the years 1869 and 1880.

TRINIDAD

The world's first postage stamps chose portraiture, heraldry or a more functional motif for their design; but already, in the first decade, the first pictorial stamp made its appearance, laying the foundations for the branch of philately known as thematic or topical collecting. To the West Indian island of Trinidad falls the honour of having been the first part of the British Commonwealth outside the mother country to issue adhesive postage stamps, albeit stamps which had only private and local validity.

There is, preserved in the archives of the Post Office in London, a file of correspondence which passed between the Postmaster General and the Governor of Trinidad in the early 1840s, in which the latter agitated unsuccessfully for the establishment of a proper postal service. By an irony of history the Governor in question was Sir Henry McLeod, whose wife was subsequently to lend her name to one of the most romantic stamps of the classic period.

Communications between the two major towns of the island in the mid-nineteenth century were usually made by sea. In 1845 Turnbull, Stewart and Company purchased a sixty-ton steamship, built by Napier of Glasgow, and installed her on the route between San Fernando and Port of Spain on November 3rd of that year. The ship was named *Lady McLeod* in honour of the Governor's wife. At the end of the month the proprietors announced, in the *Port of Spain Gazette*, that 'Letters, money and small parcels will be carried from this date for subscribers only, at one dollar per month from each Subscriber or Estate, payable quarterly in advance; letters of non-Subscribers will be charged ten cents each'.

Twelve months later Turnbull, Stewart sold the *Lady McLeod* to another Scottish businessman, David Bryce, who re-examined the system then adopted for the carriage of mail. The subscriber system was found to be unsatisfactory, the majority of letters being paid for individually in cash. Bryce felt that this was inconvenient not only to his customers but to himself and it was to overcome this problem that he decided to introduce stamps. The *Port of Spain Gazette* of April 16th 1847 contained the following notice: 'The Subscriber experiencing inconvenience in Collecting the Money for Letters of Non-Subscribers, has procured Labels, which may be had of him or the Agents for the Steamer, at five cents each, or Four Dollars per Hundred.

'No other Letters but those of subscribers who have paid *in advance*, or such as have these labels attached, will be carried, from and after the 24th instant.'

From this it may be deduced that the stamps were introduced on or about April 16th 1847, though Bryce appears to have relented somewhat and permitted unstamped letters to be carried by the ship. Examples of the Lady McLeod stamp were cancelled with a small cross in manuscript, others were left without obliteration, while yet another method of cancellation consisted of the novel expedient of lifting a corner of the stamp and tearing off a small portion. This accounts for the relatively high proportion of damaged Lady McLeod stamps now in existence. An example of this stamp appeared at auction in 1969 with more than 50 per cent of the design missing; the damaged portion of this stamp had been painted in by hand, but this excessive repair did nothing to enhance the value of the stamp! At any rate no examples are known with any form of dated postmark, so it is difficult to estimate how long the stamps remained in use. Too few are recorded on dated entire letters for their period of

currency to be accurately assessed. The ship remained in service until January 1852. David Bryce sold the ship in December 1849 to a syndicate of four businessmen in San Fernando, but whether they continued to use the stamps is a matter of conjecture. The repeal of the Navigation Acts in 1849 (which had restricted British commerce to British ships) heralded the era of free trade. Henceforward the *Lady McLeod* had to fight stiff competition from Dutch and American shipping and inevitably this led to a decline in the amount of freight, including mail, which she carried after that date.

The stamps were lithographed by an unknown (presumably Trinidadian) printer in sheets of one hundred, and sold for 5 cents each or $4 a sheet—another early example of stamps at a discount. The design was simple and pleasing, with a colourless silhouette of the steamship against a blue background. Below appeared the monogram 'LMcL'—the sole indication of the stamp's identity.

Twenty years elapsed after its issue before the Lady McLeod stamp apparently came to the notice of philatelists and at first its authenticity was discounted. L. N. and M. Williams in *Famous Stamps* record that the stamp was slow to achieve popularity with collectors and as late as 1915 a specimen was sold for only 13 guineas. At the time of publication (1940) the Williams brothers noted that the average auction realization was about $102 (£50), though today the Lady McLeod stamps fetch over $2,040 (£1,000) unused and up to $1,734 (£850) in used condition. The stamp is listed in the Gibbons catalogue but ignored by most other standard catalogues on the grounds that it was a private local issue without official validity.

Other steamship stamps of comparable status, such as the Gauthier Frères, La

Guaira, St Lucia and Danube Steam Navigation issues, are ignored by general catalogues and it is only now that the rarities among them are beginning to fetch sums commensurate with their true scarcity and in line with the market value enjoyed by the Lady McLeod. Despite the example set by David Bryce, more than four years were to elapse before the postal authorities in Trinidad introduced adhesive stamps of their own.

MAURITIUS

At the time of the introduction of adhesive stamps in Britain, the Indian Ocean island of Mauritius had been a British colony for barely thirty years, having passed from the French by conquest during the Napoleonic Wars. A British-style postal administration was established in 1811, largely to serve the needs of the extensive military garrison which was maintained there throughout the nineteenth century.

The colony made steady economic progress under British rule, but the postal system failed to keep pace with commercial growth. The reorganization of the postal service was sanctioned by an Ordinance dated December 1846, although a copy of this document 'providing for the conveyance and postage of letters in the Colony' was not despatched to the Colonial Secretary, Earl Grey, until February 9th 1847. In a covering letter to Earl Grey, the Governor of Mauritius, Sir William Gomm, wrote: 'The regulations hitherto in force are very scanty and found wholly insufficient for the increasing needs of the Colony in this respect; and it is hoped that by the more ample detail now introduced with the organization of the Post Office Department, the public convenience will be adequately provided for in this essential Branch of Administration.'

The Ordinance itself was printed in English and French in parallel columns, although, shortly before stamps were introduced, it was finally decided to adopt English as the island's official language. Had this decision not been made, we might have had examples of bilingual stamps, long before Canada and South Africa adopted this expedient. The Ordinance fixed the rate of island postage at 2 d per ½ oz for country letters and 1 d per ½ oz for letters posted and delivered within the Port Louis boundaries. These rates came into force on January 1st 1847. Article 5 of the Ordinance stated that 'the postage on inland letters if not prepaid by stamp may be paid for on delivery'. Although no adhesive stamps were actually available at this time, their issue was anticipated in Article 9 of the Ordinance: 'Every letter, newspaper, or packet of any kind liable to postage under this Ordinance, if posted within the colony and its dependencies, and having a stamp or stamps affixed thereto and appearing on the outside—such stamps being provided by the Government—and being of the value or amount required in each case according to the preceding tariff, and not having been used before, shall pass by the post free of postage.'

Bearing in mind that the new postal system was in force for nine months before stamps were introduced, it is interesting to note that a month before the Ordinance was signed a local craftsman, J. Barnard, was approached regarding the production of the stamps. Barnard, usually described in works of reference as half-blind, had a watch-making and jewellery *atelier* on the Chaussée in Port Louis. Major E. B. Evans, the noted philatelist who was stationed on Mauritius and carried out research into the early stamps of that island, found references to a certain Mr Nash, an engraver who was noted for his skilled work. Neither Evans nor any subsequent student could offer any explanation why Nash was not called upon to engrave the first, or any other, Mauritian stamps.

Barnard's estimate for the work is now preserved in the British Museum. The charge for engraving the plate was £ 10 and that for printing the 1 d and 2 d stamps was 10 s per thousand. Since Barnard only printed five hundred of each he was presumably paid £10 10s, although the face value of the stamps amounted to only £6 5s. Thus the so-called 'POST OFFICE' stamps of Mauritius are not only among the world's crudest in execution and appearance, but must surely be the most expensive ever produced!

Work on the stamps did not begin till mid-1847. Barnard engraved the designs, primitive parodies of the British Penny Red and Twopence Blue, on the reverse of a copper plate which had previously been used in the production of a lady's visiting card. Only one of each design was engraved and Barnard then printed the stamps laboriously one by one. Pairs or multiples are therefore impossible, though the late Arthur Hind once boasted to King George V that he had a pair of the 'Post Office' 2 d stamps. Considering the circumstances in which the stamps were produced they present a not entirely discreditable appearance and were certainly more aesthetically appealing than many of the island's subsequent issues.

There has been controversy in the philatelic press over the years on the question of whether the inscription 'POST OFFICE' was an error for 'POST PAID'. It has been stated that Barnard received his brief verbally and had been instructed to engrave the latter inscription, but that he promptly forgot it—until reminded by the legend on

187

188

164

165

166

167

168

169

170

171

172

173

174

175

176

177

178

179

180

181

182

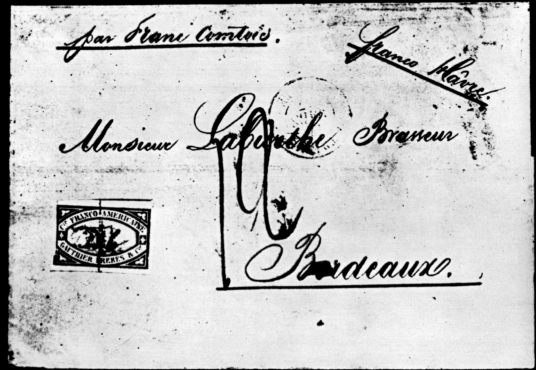

183

184

185

186

187

the facade of the Post Office. On the other hand 'Post Office Mauritius' was the customary inscription in the hand-struck postal markings which preceded the adhesive stamps. Failing the discovery of concrete evidence to the contrary, it must be accepted that the story of the 'error' is quite apocryphal.

Barnard was given a deadline to complete the production of the stamps, since Lady Gomm wished to use them on invitations sent out to a Ball at Government House held on September 30th 1847. Both the British Museum and Royal Collections contain examples of the 1 d stamp still adhering to the original envelope, while the latter collection even includes the actual invitation card. The stamps were placed on sale to the general public on September 21st and were apparently so popular that they sold out within a few days. The issue was not reprinted and, pending the production of the rather more ambitious POST PAID stamps the following year, the people of Mauritius had to revert to the former system of prepayment in cash.

Philately being hardly in an embryonic stage in the 1840s, it is not surprising that the existence of the POST OFFICE stamps should have been entirely overlooked by collectors until 1864, when Madame Borchard of Bordeaux discovered two 2 d and one 1 d stamps on correspondence addressed to her husband. One of the 2 d stamps was uncancelled and thus ranks today as one of the three unused specimens—the other two being in the Tapling and the Royal Collections. For the record this third example fetched $2,754 (£1,350) at Harmer's in 1938—and exactly ten times that sum in 1965 when it was purchased by Mr. Hiroyuki Kanai of Tokyo. A cover bearing one of each value was purchased for $10,200 (£5,000) in 1934 and fetched

178 *Steamship Company Stamp, Wanajavesi, 25 penni, 1866*

179 *Steamship Company Stamp, Danube Steam Navigation Company, 17 k*

180 *Steamship Company Stamp, St Thomas and La Guaira, ¹/₂ centavo, 1864*

181 *Steamship Company Stamp, Asia Minor Steamship Co, 2 piastres, 1868*

182 *Steamship Company Stamp, Turkish Admiralty Stamp, 1859*

183 *Steamship Company Stamp, Gauthier Frères, stamp on cover, 1856*

184 *Bermuda, 1 d, 'Perot', 1848*

185 *Hungary, Essay by Mor Than, 1848*

186 *Mauritius, 4 d, Britannia, 1854*

187 *Mauritius, 1 d, Post Office, stamp on cover, 1847*

$57,120 ($\pounds$28,000) in the Burrus sale of 1960. Another cover, bearing two copies of the 1 d stamp, was purchased in an Indian bazaar in 1897 for $102 ($\pounds$50) and sold for $322,300 ($\pounds$158,000) in 1969, when the Dale-Lichtenstein Collection was broken up—a world record price for a cover.

189 Towards the end of 1847 Barnard was engaged in the production of new stamps in the same denominations and similar designs, but with the amended inscription 'POST PAID'. These stamps were produced in plates of twelve subjects, each being engraved one at a time and thus differing in some detail from its neighbours. The seventh stamp in the sheet of 2 d stamps had the error of spelling (or rather the slip of the engraver's burin) 'PENOE' instead of 'PENCE'. The stamps were engraved on the backs of copper plates which had previously been used for the advertisements of the Grand Hotel d'Europe.

These plates proved to be too soft for repeated use and they rapidly wore out. Philatelists distinguish at least five states of the plates—earliest (clear, sharp lines), early (sharp and clear, but with some lines weakened), intermediate (white patches in the background where wear was beginning to show), worn (high points of the design worn away, but some diagonal lines still distinct) and latest (virtually none of the design showing, save the queen's head and the frame).

Although a public announcement concerning the release of these stamps did not appear till August 3rd 1848, various notices had already appeared in Mauritian newspapers and it is now known that they were put on sale some time in May. The POST PAID stamps remained in use for eleven years and it was not until March 1859 that new 2 d stamps superseded Barnard's. The 193 2 d stamps were the work of M. Lapirot

188 *Mauritius, 2 d, 'Post Office', 1847*

189 *Mauritius, 1 d, 'Post Paid', 1848*

190 *Mauritius, 1 d, 1859*

191 *Mauritius, 4 d, 1860*

192 *Mauritius, 6 d, 1861*

193 *Mauritius, 2 d, 'Tête de Singe', 1859*

188

189

190

191

192

193

and well deserved the epithet *Tête de Singe* (monkey's head). The Lapirot stamps were in use for only a few months but showed extensive signs of wear in even that short period and were scrapped in favour of 2 d stamps printed from the original Barnard plate, which had been re-engraved by a Mr Sherwin.

190   The last of the primitive issues of Mauritius consisted of 1 d and 2 d stamps lithographed by M. Dardenne and released in December 1859. In February 1859 Pearson Hill (son of Sir Rowland Hill) visited Mauritius to reorganize the island's postal administration. As a result of his recommendations Mauritius eventually super-seded its locally produced stamps by the attractive Britannia design engraved by
186, 192 Perkins Bacon of London. A series with the profile of the queen, surface-printed by
191 De La Rue, was introduced in 1860–72.

BERMUDA

Unlike the British island colonies of the Bahamas and the Caribbean, Bermuda was very tardy in introducing adhesive postage stamps, the first government series not being released till 1865. Prior to that date the prepayment of postage had been indicated by hand-struck markings. Unlike the majority of the Caribbean islands, Bermuda did not make use of British adhesives, and the fact that this island had employed adhesive stamps at all, in the period prior to 1865, was unknown till almost the end of the century. Then in July 1897 *Alfred Smith's Monthly Circular* described a curious circular stamp struck in carmine, with the signature 'W. B. Perot' and the value 'One penny' in manuscript. The *Circular* appeal-
184 ed for information, but none was forth-coming and interest in the discovery waned.

Then in May 1898 Mr B. W. Warhurst acquired a second copy of this stamp, from a correspondent in Bermuda. This specimen was struck in black and bore the date 1849 in the centre. An enquiry of the Postmaster of Bermuda elicited the somewhat vague information that 'it was the practice of the Postmaster at that time to issue stamps ... to persons who desired to post local notes—that is for places within the Colony. The impression of the stamp and the signature, etc., were made on a sheet of paper and cut off as required by the purchaser, and affixed to the note to be posted. These were not invariably used for postage, but only in cases where it was convenient to the sender. When a note was sent to the Post Office with a penny to pay the postage, the note was simply stamped with the date-stamp.'

The late Sir Edward Bacon investigated the status of this stamp and discovered that it had been produced by William Perot, the Postmaster at Hamilton from 1818 to 1862. Perot owned Par-la-Ville Park in Hamilton and operated the post office from his house at the entrance to the park. He was a keen gardener and his official duties being light, would often absent himself to attend to his garden. People would leave their notes in a post-box, together with the pennies for the postage. However, Perot soon found that certain dishonest persons were not leaving the money. It was in order to circumvent this problem that he struck off on sheets of paper twelve copies of his office stamp, omitting the day and month plugs and substituting his signature and the amount. He would then gum the sheets and sell them 'in shilling parcels', receiving them back on notes in payment of the local postage. The idea of adhesive stamps was suggested to Perot by his neighbour Mr J. B. Heyl, who ran a general store adjoining the post office. The colour of the post office ink-pad was changed in 1849 from black to red, hence the stamps dated 1848 and 1849 are known in black, whereas those of later dates are found in red. White paper was used for these stamps but from 1854 onwards blue paper was employed. Very few of these makeshifts have so far come to light; only those dated 1848, 1849, 1853, 1854 and 1856 have been recorded. In 1860–1 both Perot, and his counterpart at St George's, J. H. Thies, used their crowned Paid handstamps on gummed paper as a form of 'Postmasters' issues. Incidentally the date-stamp used by Perot to produce his adhesives in the late 1840s survived in use well into the 1860s and has been found as a cancellation on the first 'government' series of 1865.

HUNGARY

Although Hungary is only now celebrating the centenary of its first adhesive postage stamps, this event might have occurred some twenty years earlier but for the fortunes of war. In 1848 much of Europe was in a state of revolution and the Magyar people of Hungary seized the opportunity provided by the general unrest to press the Imperial Austrian government into recognizing their national aspirations. The Magyars, however, overplayed their hand by insisting that Magyar language, laws and traditions should be paramount in Hungary, at the expense of other nationalities, such as the Croats, Slovaks and Rumans. In July 1848 the Imperial government sent an army to invade Hungary under the command of Count Jelacic, Governor of Croatia. We are not here concerned with the unhappy train of events which led eventually to the downfall of the Hungarian independence movement and the bitter repression which followed it. What is of particular interest is that an officer in the *Honved* (National Guard), Mor (Maurice) Than, produced a proposal for adhesive postage stamps on July 3rd 1848. Essays were printed by the Magyar Kereskedelmi Bank in Budapest but the independence of Hungary was crushed before the scheme could be implemented.

The 'stamp' proposed by Mor Than was a 1 krajczar (kreuzer) denomination and featured the Hungarian coat of arms surmounted by the crown of St Stephen. Ears of wheat were shown in the side panels while the inscription read 'MAGYAR ALLADALMI POSTA' (Hungarian Post).

BATAVIA

A postal service known as the 'land-mail' operated on the Dutch island of Batavia in the 1840s, and type-set labels were used for this service in 1845–6. The design bore a three-line inscription in Dutch meaning 'Carried by land-mail—to pay, due—Batavia.' The amount of the postage and the date were inserted in manuscript in the space provided. There were several different types of these labels, varying in the lettering and setting of the inscriptions. The labels did not prepay postage and for this reason may be regarded as the forerunners of today's postage due labels. The land-mail service reverted to hand-struck marks in 1847.

POSTAL STATIONERY

While adhesive postage stamps were undreamed of much before the 1840s and consequently took a considerable time to win acceptance, postal stationery was a different subject altogether.

The envelopes and wrappers adopted by various countries as a means of indicating the prepayment of postage were, after all, not so very different physically from the covers on letters in the 'pre-adhesive' period. Indeed, the hand-struck postage stamps used for almost three centuries before the Penny Black had demonstrated that prepayment of postal charges was quite feasible, if not particularly popular. The only difference between the hand-struck postage stamps of pre-1840 times and the postal stationery which appeared from then onwards was the fact that the former was stamped at the time of posting, whereas the latter was sold to the customer already stamped, though some time might elapse before it was actually put into service.

It is in this light that the introduction of postal stationery should be seen. The idea of selling to the public envelopes, letter-sheets and wrappers on which the postage was already indicated was revolutionary; the idea of prepaying postage was not.

NEW SOUTH WALES

It appears the Governor of New South Wales had been watching the development of postal reform in Britain very closely and had borrowed from Rowland Hill the idea of stamped stationery. Bearing in mind the remoteness of New South Wales in the days of sailing ships (a six-month journey was average) it seems doubtful whether the postal reform movement in Britain could have had much influence on the approval granted in November 1838 for the release of prepaid envelopes. The idea seems to have originated with James Raymond, the colony's Postmaster General, and the fact that his proposals were implemented in November of that year indicates that the scheme had been under way for some time prior to that.

The stamps consisted of embossed albino replicas of the Great Seal of New South Wales with a circular band inscribed 'GENERAL POST OFFICE NEW SOUTH WALES'. Envelopes bearing this stamp were sold for 1 s 3 d a dozen or singly for 2 d each and were valid within the limits of the Sydney twopenny postal area. The public were permitted to have their own envelopes and sheets impressed with this stamp at the rate of 1 s 8 d for twenty-five impressions. The response of the public to this scheme was disappointing and, in a bid to increase the popularity of stamped stationery, the Post Office reduced the price in 1841 to 8 s per 100 (or slightly under a penny each). Nevertheless the stamps continued to be utilized infrequently and used examples are scarce compared with the 'stampless' covers of the period. These embossed stamps continued in use long after 1850 when New South Wales introduced adhesive stamps and they are even referred to in a Postal Act of 1857. An oval embossed stamp, showing the Great Seal but inscribed 'GENERAL POST OFFICE SYDNEY', was used simultaneously on news-wrappers. Since newsbands were ripped off and discarded when the newspaper was opened it is not surprising that used wrappers in general (or the stamps provided for specific use on them) should be relatively scarce. Yet it seems curious that no example of the New South Wales embossed wrapper of the 1840s should have come to light until 1961. The embossed stationery of New South Wales, incidentally, gave rise to some of the earliest commemorative items—stamped postcards released belatedly in 1889 to celebrate the golden jubilee and depicting reproductions of the Great Seal stamp of 1838. Sadly, the centenary of the world's first stamped stationery was allowed to pass unnoticed and neither stamps nor stationery were released by Australia to mark the occasion in 1938.

FINLAND

Postal stationery was adopted in several European countries before adhesive stamps. First and foremost in this category come Finland and Russia which both introduced stamped envelopes in 1845—fully a decade before they embraced adhesive stamps. Finland's envelopes were issued in denominations of 10 and 20 kopeks, distinguished by stamps impressed in the bottom left-hand corner, in black and rose respectively. The stamps consisted of an upright oval containing the Finnish arms and the inscription 'PORTO STEMPEL' (Postage Stamp) with the denomination in a ribbon beneath the oval. The main interest of these envelopes lies in their watermarks, no fewer than seventeen different types being identified. These watermarks were papermakers' marks appearing once in each sheet. Thus the majority of envelopes encountered are unwatermarked, while the watermarked examples usually show only a portion of the device. Paper, manufactured by J.C. Frenckell & Son and such companies as Tervakosi and Juvankosi, was employed and most of the watermarks incorporated the emblems, initials or names of these firms. A relatively small quantity of envelopes was produced on wove paper but the bulk of them appeared on laid paper. A total of 67,500 of the 10 k and 12,500 of the 20 k was issued between 1845 and 1850 when a new design, featuring the coat of arms in a horizontal oval and inscribed in Cyrillic as well as the Roman alphabet, was introduced. Reprints of these items were produced in 1893, but may be easily distinguished by the use of different paper, ink and different shapes to the flaps of the envelopes. In addition, however, bogus envelopes were manufactured in the late nineteenth century. Apart from minor differences in the details of the stamps, these stamps were in new colours (rose for the 10 k and green for the 20 k) and appeared on the back flaps of large-sized envelopes.

RUSSIA

Russia's first stamped stationery was provided in 1845 for use in the city of St Petersburg. Like the Finnish envelopes these envelopes bore the national coat of arms impressed in one corner, but only one denomination (5 kopeks) was provided. The coat of arms was surounded by a circular band inscribed in Cyrillic S.P.B. (St Petersburg) Gorodskaya Pochta (City Post) and at the foot 'postage 5 k, envelope 1 k'. The stamps were impressed in shades of blue on greyish-white paper of a rough texture. The envelopes were hand-made and vary considerably in size. The St Petersburg stationery is relatively scarce either mint or used : only 4,000 were sold in 1845, some 26,000 in 1846 and 40,000 in 1847–8. The same stamp was used on letter sheets issued in 1846.

Much more plentiful, however, are the envelopes used in St Petersburg between 1848 and 1868. The stamps were identical to the first issue, but the shapes of the envelopes differed radically and can be identified without any difficulty from the scarcer variety of 1845–8.

A similar type of stamped envelope was released in Moscow in 1846, the main difference lying in the inscription 'Moskov' instead of 'S.P.B.'. Although the Moscow stamps were of the same value, a different colour, vermilion, was used. The Moscow envelopes are comparatively rare: only 6,000 were produced and the bulk of these were destroyed at the end of 1846. A new printing with the stamp in scarlet was issued in 1847, but likewise failed to win popularity and is thus fairly scarce today.

Postal stationery for general use throughout the Russian Empire did not appear until 1848. In that year envelopes in denominations of 10 k black, 20 k blue and 30 k carmine were issued. The stamps appeared on the back flaps of the envelopes and were typographed with the imperial coat of arms in albino embossing. Around the top was the inscription in Cyrillic '10 kop. postage' and round the foot '1 kop. for the envelope' in an abbreviated form. Several different types of these stamps have been recorded, with broad or narrow letters in the inscriptions and with broad or narrow tails to the eagle in the coat of arms. This type of envelope remained in use, with variations, until 1868. Later varieties, distinguished by the 'knife' (or shape of the flaps of the envelopes), are still relatively easy to find, especially in used condition.

THURN AND TAXIS

The postal system organized throughout Germany by the Counts of Thurn and Taxis was responsible for many innovations in that part of the world, not the least being in the use of postal stationery. Although Bavaria has the honour of releasing the first adhesives (1849), Thurn and Taxis led the way with a stamped envelope three years earlier. I must confess that this item is something of a mystery to me. Scant reference is made to the early postal stationery of Thurn and Taxis in most philatelic works, and then only the embossed envelopes of 1861–6 are listed. In 1846, however, an envelope was produced under the auspices of Thurn and Taxis. These envelopes were intended for local use in Wurttemberg, and were confined to the cities of Stuttgart, Heilbronn, Ludwigsburg, Ulm and Reutlingen. They were sold for 1 ½ kreuzers and were in use till 1852 when adhesive stamps were introduced. The envelope bore an impressed stamp inscribed in Gothic script 'Frankirter Stadt Brief' (Franked Town Letter) in red within a chamfered double-lined frame. There is no further information available, unfortunately, concerning this envelope and its period and place of use.

Adhesive stamps were not adopted by Thurn and Taxis till 1852.

CHAPTER V

THE 1850s: THE DEVELOPMENT OF THE POSTAGE STAMP

By the end of the first decade of the adhesive postage stamp, this convenient device had extended to no more than nine countries, while postal stationery of some form or another was in use in four others.

It often seems a mystery that stamps and stationery were so slow to catch on. The reasons for this were that the world in the middle of the nineteenth century was still relatively unsophisticated and there was a certain element of distrust, by the public and governments alike, of prepayment of postage. Secondly, the general level of literacy in Europe—not to mention the other continents—was low and the desire for postal communication not very strongly developed. Thirdly, relatively few countries possessed a developed postal system at that time. Fourthly, and probably the most important reason of all, there were very few international agreements on the handling of mail and thus such stamps as did exist were confined to the country of origin. Their validity stopped short at the frontiers of the issuing country.

By the end of the 1840s, however, enormous social and economic progress was being made all over the world and the need for international communications was increasing rapidly. In the decade from 1850 to the end of 1859 no fewer than seventy-one countries adopted adhesive stamps and by 1860 the use of stamps had spread across the world into every continent. This decade witnessed the first tentative steps towards international postal agreements. Admittedly these consisted mainly of direct treaties and conventions between two countries and the day when a Universal Postal Union could come into being was still a long way off.

NEW SOUTH WALES

On New Year's Day 1850 the first adhesive stamps appeared in Australia. New South Wales, which had introduced prepaid postal stationery in 1838, released its first adhesive stamps on January 1st 1850. As early as December 1848 proposals had been made for the establishment of uniform postal rates within the colony and these culminated in an 'Act to Establish a Uniform Rate of Postage and to Consolidate and Amend the Law for the Conveyance and Postage of Letters' which came into effect on January 1st 1850. One of the clauses in this Act envisaged the issue of adhesive stamps.

These were produced in Sydney and have long been popularly known as the 'Sydney Views' from their motif based on the Great Seal of the colony, showing the figure of Australia greeting a band of convicts just arrived at the penal settlement of Botany Bay. The colony's motto inscribed below the vignette has often been a puzzle to philatelists. *Sic fortis Etruria crevit* (In this way Etruria grew in strength) is a quotation from Virgil.

The stamps consisted of 1 d, 2 d and 3 d values, each being engraved by a different craftsman although using the same basic design. The earliest version of the 1 d was engraved by Robert Clayton and may be recognized by its clear impression and the absence of clouds in the background. Subsequently the plate was re-engraved by H. C. Jervis and clouds added to the designs. The 2 d was the work of John Carmichael, a deaf-mute who is said to have refused to sign a government bond agreeing to complete the work by a certain date. The authorities had to accept his word—which he honourably kept. In April 1850 Carmichael's plate was entirely reworked by H. C. Jervis, and then again in September of that year. The fourth engraving of the 2 d plate was made by Jervis in April 1851; Jervis himself was responsible for the 3 d stamps. Apart from the extensive re-engraving of these stamps they showed various degrees of wear and were also produced by Carmichael and Jervis; these, in turn, gave way to the beautifully engraved stamps of Perkins Bacon, recess-printed in the colony in 1856, and the De La Rue typographed stamps of 1862–5.

VICTORIA

The neighbouring colony of Victoria was to have begun issuing stamps simultaneously and preparations by Thomas Ham, the government printer, were made in 1849 to this end. New Year's Day was a public holiday in Melbourne and the post offices were closed, so the stamps could not be released till January 3rd, although the *Melbourne Argus* of January 1st stated that

194 *New South Wales, 1 d, 'Sydney View', 1850*

195 *Spain, 6 reales, 1850*

196 *New South Wales, 2 d, 'Laureated Queen', 1851*

194

195

196

they were available. The first stamps of Victoria are known to collectors as the 'Half-Lengths', because of their portrait of Queen Victoria. The 1 d and 3 d stamps were engraved by E. Wilson (whose initials appear at the foot of the design) and the 2 d by Thomas Ham (hence the initials TH in the bottom corners). Transfers were then made from the steel dies.

During the decade in which these stamps were current, three printers were involved in their production: Thomas Ham (1850–4) J. S. Campbell & Co. (1854–9) and Campbell & Fergusson (1854–8). The stamps were released imperforate, but 3 d stamps of the Campbell or Campbell & Fergusson printings were roulleted 7 to 8 ½ at the General Post Office in Melbourne or perforated 12 by Robinson of Melbourne in 1859–60.

A new design, known as the 'Queen Enthroned', was introduced for the 2d in December 1852. Initially recess-printed by Ham, it was subsequently lithographed by Campbell or Campbell & Fergusson and underwent numerous changes in paper, shade and lithographic transfer between the end of 1852 and 1856. In the decade up to 1860 Victoria made use of Campbell & Fergusson and S. Calvert for other stamps, including an octagonal shilling stamp (July 1854) and the so-called 'woodblocks' of 1854–9. In his period Perkins Bacon of London recess-printed 1 d and 6 d stamps bearing full-length portraits of Queen Victoria on the throne. It is interesting to compare the treatment of this subject by the local printer and the recognized 'Old Masters' of stamp production. Perkins Bacon's design was at least a passable likeness of the queen, and the subtle use of their characteristic engraved background lent solidity and dignity to the design. Various locally produced stamps appeared

up to 1870, when De La Rue provided a plate for 2 d stamps.

SPAIN

Although the Home Office of the provisional government of General Espartero, asked the Spanish Postmaster General in 1843 to establish a system for the prepayment of postage ... 'as already adopted in some civilized countries of Europe', six years elapsed before this came into effect. On October 24th 1849 a royal decree of Queen Isabella II authorized the issue of postage stamps for the prepayment and registration of correspondence. The preamble to this decree referred to the method of franking letters '... invented in England and recently introduced into France'. The Home Secretary, the Count of San Luís, advocated the use of adhesive stamps to indicate prepayment and proposed that lower rates of postage should be applicable to prepaid letters in order to encourage people to prepay the postage.

The postal rate on unpaid letters was 1 real (8 cuartos) while that on prepaid letters was fixed at 6 cuartos. Double letters (i.e. those of a heavier weight) were rated at 15 c if unpaid and 12 c if prepaid. At the same time rates for registered letters were fixed at 10 to 25 reales depending on weight, the cost including postage and registration. Between the end of October 1849 and the date on which the stamps were actually introduced, several lengthy decrees and proclamations regarding the use of the forthcoming stamps were published. Among other details these gave copious instructions to the public on how to use the stamps. They were to be placed on the top left-hand corner of the letter (though this was often ignored in practice), and the stamps could only be used on mail circulating within the kingdom. Prepaid letters at this time could be sent abroad only to Italy, and these had to have the amount of postage indicated in manuscript.

The stamps themselves were designed and engraved by Bartolomeo Coromina and lithographed at the Government Printing Works in Madrid, where all Spanish stamps (with the exception of certain issues of the National State in 1936–9) have been produced ever since. Two designs were used, the 6 c showing a profile of the queen facing left and the other denominations using a similar profile facing right. The denominations were 6 and 12 c for ordinary letters and 5, 6 and 10 r for registered mail.

211, 195

Fear of forgery induced the Spanish authorities to change the designs of the stamps at annual intervals (the only years when new issues did not appear were 1857–9 and 1863). Between January 1850 and June 1870 Spain produced a total of 285 different stamps, involving twenty-nine distinct designs and several types of overprint (the latter resulting from the republican period 1868–70). This unparalleled prolificity contributed much to the early unpopularity of Spanish stamps with collectors, though Spain's output in the classic period seems modest by present-day standards.

The first stage in the reduction of postal rates came in November 1852, when it was proposed that letters posted in Madrid for delivery within the city boundaries should be charged at 1 cuarto (single) and 3 c (double letters). Accordingly stamps of these denominations, featuring the city's coat of arms, were introduced in April 1853. A curious feature of these stamps was that they were typographed in bronze—the first occasion on which metallic ink was employed in stamp production.

197 *New South Wales, 5 d, 1855*
198 *New South Wales, 1 d, 1856*
199 *New South Wales, 2 d, 1862*
200 *Victoria, 1 d, 'Half Length', 1850*
201 *Victoria, 1 s, 1854*
202 *Victoria, 2 d, 'Queen Enthroned', 1852*
203 *Victoria, 1 d, 1856*
204 *Victoria, 6 d, 1854*
205 *Victoria, 1 d, 1857*
206 *Victoria, 3 d, 1860*
207 *Victoria, 6 d, 1860*
208 *Victoria, 2 d, 1863*
209 *Victoria, 2 d, 1870*
210 *Victoria, 5 s, 1867*

197

198

199

200

201

204

205

206

207

208

209

210

211

212

CORREO INTERIOR

FRANCO. 3 CUARTOS.

214

* CORREOS *

FRANCO 2. C⁵

215

· CORREOS ·

4 CUARTOS ·

CORREOS

4. CUARTOS.

218

219

220

221

222

223

224

225

The homely features of Isabella II 226, 227
decorated the majority of Spanish stamps
up to the time of her abdication in 1868.
Apart from the Madrid locals, however, the 212-222
series of 1854 featured the coats of arms of 215
Castile and Leon, while low value stamps
of 1867 (5 and 10 milesimas de escudo)
depicted the numerals of value. Stamps of 222
the republican period, released in 1870, bore
the full-face portrait of a female symbolizing 223
Spain. Official stamps, with denomination
in weights rather than values, appeared in 224, 225
1854–5.

SWISS FEDERAL ISSUE

The previous chapter dealt with the postage
stamps introduced by the cantons of
Geneva, Basle and Zurich between 1843
and 1849 and the transitional issues of
Geneva and Zurich in 1849–50, following
the assumption of control by the Federal
postal department. Federal issues did not
make their appearance until May 1850 when
the 2 ½ rappen stamps, inscribed 'ORTS
POST' or 'POSTE LOCALE' (German and
French for 'local post'), were introduced.
These stamps, like the other Swiss stamps
up to 1854, were lithographed by the photo-
graphic firm of Durheim in Bern and printed with a black frame and the Swiss emblem
(a white cross on a red background) in the
centre. The Swiss cross may be found with
or without a black frame-line, while the
paper varied considerably in shade and
thickness. These stamps were gradually
extended to the various cantons which had
not previously issued stamps.

A proclamation dated September 23rd
1850, published by the Federal postal
administration, announced the release on
October 1st of a new series of stamps,
known to collectors as the 'Rayons', from the
inscription. The proclamation stated that

from October 1st '... the administration shall sell at the local post offices stamps for the franking of letters intended for Switzerland only, for the first radius, blue stamps at 5 rappen; for the second radius, yellow stamps, at 10 rappen; for the third and fourth radius, also for letters weighing more than half an ounce, sufficient stamps for the value of the franking must be affixed. Stamps on letters for foreign countries are not accepted as of any value.'

229 The stamps referred to in this proclamation were the 5 and 10 rappen inscribed 'RAYON I' or 'RAYON II', to denote the radius or distance. On January 1st 1852 15 rappen stamps in vermilion and inscribed 'RAYON III' were added to the series. The first printings of the 15 rappen had small figures of value, but in April 1852 the design was redrawn with larger numerals. The Rayon stamps were superseded in September 1854 by a series engraved by Vogt of Munich and initially embossed by J. G. Weiss in that city, but subsequently printed in Bern. The stamps, featuring the seated figure of Helvetia, are popularly 228 known as the 'Strubbelis' (tousle-haired) on account of the flowing locks of the female figure. The size of the stamps was reduced in 1862 and Helvetia altered in pose and 230 general appearance. An interesting feature of the early Swiss stamps was the inclusion of silk threads in the paper as a security device. In the series of 1862–7 this gave way to a cross impressed in the paper as a kind of watermark.

AUSTRIA AND THE GERMAN STATES

Germany in the middle of the nineteenth century was no more than a geographic term which described Austria, Prussia and

226 *Spain, 2 reales, error of colour (blue instead of red), 1851*

227 *Spain, 12 c, with frame inverted, 1865*

226

227

thirty-seven other kingdoms, principalities, duchies and free cities. Various attempts at the unification of Germany were made from 1815 onwards and, indeed, a loose Federal organization existed, with a Parliament at Frankfurt-am-Main, under the headship of Austria. This Confederation had virtually no political power but it was a first step towards the unity of the German states. In 1818 the *Zollverein* (customs union) was formed under the leadership of Prussia and paved the way for the standardization of tariffs and currencies in Germany. In March 1850 the majority of German states came close to unification under Prussia. Bavaria and Wurttemberg, however, remained aloof and Austria threatened war unless Prussia backed down. By the Convention of Ollmutz in November 1850 Prussia gave way. Twenty years were to elapse before a Germany united without Austria was to come into being.

Although the rivalry of Austria and Prussia put back the cause of German unity that year, in one respect at least this cause made signal progress. On April 6th representatives of Austria and Prussia signed a postal treaty, agreeing standard postal rates and foreshadowing the introduction of adhesive stamps in both states. In accordance with this treaty Austria (and her Italian dominions in Lombardo-Venetia) began issuing stamps on June 1st. Saxony joined the German-Austrian Postal Union and introduced adhesive stamps on June 29th, but Prussia did not issue stamps till November 15th.

AUSTRIA

Austria's stamps featured the Imperial arms and were inscribed across the top 'KK POST-STEMPEL' (Royal and Imperial postage stamp). Those stamps used in Austria, Hungary, Galicia and Dalmatia were inscribed in denominations from 1 to 9 kreuzer, while those used in Lombardo-Venezia (Austrian Italy) bore values from 5 to 45 centesimi. Corresponding denominations in each series used the same colours. From then until the loss of Lombardo-Venezia in the Seven Weeks' War of 1866 the stamps of the Hapsburg Empire were **231** uniform in design. In 1858 the embossed profile of the Kaiser Franz Josef was introduced. The stamps were devoid of inscription other than the value (by this time altered to soldi in Lombardo-Venezia, kreuzer currency being retained everywhere else).

New sets in 1861 and 1863 respectively **232, 235** featured the emperor's profile and the Imperial arms. After the establishment of the Dual Monarchy in 1867 (according the Magyars of Hungary equal rights with the Germans of Austria) the value was tactfully abbreviated to kr, which could be inter- **233** preted as kreuzer or krajczar in German and Magyar districts respectively. Austria also issued special stamps for newspapers, the majority of which portrayed Mercury. **234, 238**

SAXONY

Saxony's first stamp, released on June 29th 1850, was the celebrated red Three Pfennigs, intended for the prepayment of postage on **236** newspapers—hence its great scarcity, since most used copies would have been discarded with the wrappers. This stamp, designed and typographed by J. B. Hirschfeld of Leipzig, obviously owed a great deal to the only German stamps then in existence—the kreuzer stamps of Bavaria released barely seven months earlier. The numeral design, with the value in words in the side panels,

the name of the country at the top and the word FRANCO at the foot—all shaped the style of the Bavarian *Schwarzer Einser*. A further thirteen months elapsed, however, before Saxony extended adhesive stamps to cover postage in general. C. C. Meinhold then recess-printed a series portraying King Frederick Augustus II in
240 denominations from ½ to 3 neugroschen (12 pfennigs equalled one neugroschen). The stamps were printed in black on various
242 colours of paper. A new 3 pf newspaper stamp, featuring the coat of arms of Saxony, was introduced simultaneously.

The accession of King John I in August 1854 necessitated a new definitive series, released in June 1855 in a similar style to the preceding series but with the new king
241 facing left instead of right. The last series used by Saxony was typographed by Giesecke & Devrient of Leipzig, with the Saxon arms embossed in the centre. This
243, 244 series, ranging from 3 pf to 5 ngr, was introduced in July 1863 and remained in use four years. Saxony, like many other German states, backed the wrong side in the Austro-Prussian War of 1866 and paid the penalty by being forced to join the North German Confederation.

PRUSSIA

In some respects the stamps of Prussia
249 paralleled those of Saxony, in that a recess-printed series portraying King Frederick William IV was superseded in the 1860s by a typographed series, with the Prussian arms
245 embossed in the centre. These stamps, produced by the Prussian State Printing Works in Berlin, had no connection with the issue of Saxony; yet it is interesting to note how the stamps of the German states tended to follow similar patterns, all but

228 *Switzerland, 15 r, 'Strubbeli', 1854*

229 *Switzerland, 5 r, 'Rayon I', 1850*

230 *Switzerland, 30 c, 'Helvetia', 1862*

231 *Austria, 2 k, 1858*

232 *Austria, 15 k, 1861*

233 *Austria, 25 k, 1867*

234 *Austria, 6 k, 'Red Mercury', newspaper stamp, 1856*

235 *Austria, 3 k, 1863*

236 *Saxony, 3 pf, newspaper stamp, 1850*

237 *Austrian Italy, 10 c, 1850*

238 *Austria, 1 k, newspaper stamp, 1867*

239 *Austria, 9 k, with Andreaskreuz, 1850*

240 *Saxony, 3 ngr, Frederick Augustus II, 1851*

241 *Saxony, 5 ngr, John I, 1855*

242 *Saxony, 3 pf, newspaper stamp, 1851*

243 *Saxony, ¹/₂ ngr, 1863*

244 *Saxony, 2 ngr, 1863*

228

229

230

231

232

233

234

235

236

237

238

240

241

242

243

244

245

246

247

248

four of them—and the postal system operated by the Counts of Thurn and Taxis **246** —using embossed arms types in the 1860s.

SCHLESWIG-HOLSTEIN

On the day that Prussia released her first stamps the duchies of Schleswig and Holstein produced a combined issue, typographed at Altona by Köbner and Lemkuhl with the ducal arms embossed in the centre. These duchies, with a German population but under the personal rule of the king of Denmark, had been governed virtually as Danish provinces, despite the protests of the people and the objections of the German Confederation. In 1848 an insurrection broke out in Schleswig and led eventually to the intervention of German federal troops. By the Protocol of London, signed in May 1852, the duchies were handed back to Denmark. Philatelically the brief period of independence was marked by the 1 and **250** 2 schilling stamps of 1850. Although inscribed with the initials of both duchies these stamps could only be released in Holstein since, by that time, the Danes had re-occupied Schleswig. These stamps are commoner mint than used, since the bulk of the stock was seized by the Danish authorities and subsequently disposed of to stamp dealers in Copenhagen. They were withdrawn from use at the end of August 1851 and a further thirteen years elapsed before Schleswig-Holstein returned to the stamp album.

HANOVER

The last of the German states to begin issuing stamps in 1850 was the kingdom of Hanover, which made its philatelic debut

245 *Prussia, 4 pf, 1858*

246 *Prussia, 3 pf, 1865*

247 *Hanover, 2 gr, George V, 1859*

248 *Hanover, ¹/₂ gr, 1860*

on December 1st. Considering the close links between the Hanoverian and British courts at this time it seems strange that more than a decade should pass before Hanover emulated Britain in the matter of adhesive postage stamps. Ernst August, king of Hanover, was also Duke of Cumberland and uncle of Queen Victoria. The Salic Law of inheritance debarred Victoria from succeeding to the throne of Hanover, but close ties were maintained even after the crowns were separated, and a link with Britain was the appearance of the British lion and unicorn flanking the coat of arms on the first stamps of Hanover.

Hanover did not enter the German-Austrian Postal Union until June 1st 1851 and therefore the 1 gutengroschen stamp of December 1850 possessed local validity only. This stamp, featuring the numeral of value surmounted by the coat of arms, was typographed in black on greyish-blue paper by Senator Culemann. A similar design, but with a solid instead of dotted background to the numeral, was adopted in July 1851 for 1 ggr stamps and a series in denom-
252 inations of $^1/_{30}$, $^1/_{15}$ and $^1/_{10}$th of a thaler. At this time a thaler consisted of 24 gutengroschen (local currency) or 30 silbergroschen (Prussian currency). Thus the stamps designed for use on external mail had their values expressed in fractions of a thaler to conform to the Prussian monetary system. The curious dual currency system used in Hanover in this period is further illustrated by the stamp introduced in April 1853 for use on news-wrappers. In the centre it was inscribed '3 PFENNIGE' (equal to a quarter of a gutengroschen) while across the top was the inscription 'EIN
253 DRITTEL SILBERGROSCHEN' (a third of a silbergroschen). From October 1st 1858 the currency of Hanover was regularized at the thaler of 30 new groschen, each

249 *Prussia, 1 sgr, 1850*

250 *Schleswig-Holstein, 1 sch, 1850*

251 *British Guiana, 4 c, 'Cottonreel', 1850*

252 *Hanover, $^1/_{10}$ th, 1851*

253 *Hanover, 3 pf, newspaper stamp, 1853*

249

250

251

consisting of 10 pfennigs, and this led to the release of a 3 pf stamp in 1863 inscribed 'DREI ZEHNTEL' (three tenths) instead of 'EIN DRITTEL' (one third).

Ernst August was succeeded by his son King George V in 1851, but eight years elapsed before his portrait appeared on the stamps of Hanover. Stamps of 1, 2, 3 and 10 gr were typographed by Culemann between 1859 and 1861; originally imperforate, these stamps (other than the 10 gr) appeared in 1864–5 with an arc roulette. In 1860, ½ gr stamps featuring a crowned posthorn appeared. In the Seven Weeks' War of 1866 the Hanoverians were routed by the Prussians at Langensalza and in October, Hanover was forcibly incorporated in Prussia, whose stamps were used thereafter.

BRITISH GUIANA

Like many other British colonies in the mid-nineteenth century, British Guiana had an external postal service operated as a branch of the General Post Office in London. In 1850 there were two post offices in the country, situated at Georgetown in the county of Demerara and at New Amsterdam in the county of Berbice. These offices were controlled by deputy postmasters appointed by the British Postmaster General. Until 1856 mail from British Guiana going abroad was despatched either unpaid, or with the prepaid postage indicated by means of hand-struck stamps. From 1856 to 1860 (when control of the external posts was transferred to the colonial authorities) British stamps were used and may be identified by the numeral obliterators A03 (Georgetown) and A04 (New Amsterdam).

At the beginning of 1850 E.T.E. Dalton, deputy postmaster of Demerara draw up a plan for an internal mail service. The

scheme was submitted to the Governor in April and shortly afterwards approved, a sum of $ 2,400 being voted for the service as an experiment. Nineteen receiving offices were established in connection with the service and rates of postage fixed at 4, 8 or 12 cents depending on the distance of the receiving offices from Georgetown. The *Official Gazette* of June 15th 1850 contained details of the service which came into operation on July 1st.

The service had been conceived and put into operation within a few months. There was thus little time in which to prepare postage stamps and consequently the first issue was primitive in the extreme. Joseph Baum and William Dallas, proprietors of the *Royal Gazette* newspaper and printers to the government, were entrusted with the production of the stamps. These were typeset within a circular frame of printer's rule and bore the inscription 'BRITISH GUIANA' with the value across the centre. The stamps were printed in black on different coloured paper.

On March 1st 1851 a local service within the city of Georgetown was started up, the charge for local letters being 2c. A stamp of this denomination was therefore printed in the same design. It seems curious that little was known of this stamp for many years; it did not come to the attention of philatelists till 1877, and for many years thereafter its authenticity was questioned. In 1890 a document written by Dalton came to light, dated March 11th 1851, in which he stated that 'this month the Georgetown Penny Post commenced from which some small revenue may be expected'.

The 'Cottonreels' as these stamps are popularly known were initialled by various postal officials prior to issue—E. T. E. D(alton), E. D. W(right), J. B. S(mith), H. A. K(illikelly) and W. H. L(orimer).

The subsequent history of Guianese stamps down to the 1880s consists of a mixture of local and London issues, reflecting the slow and infrequent communications between England and South America at that time.

In April 1851 it was proposed that a uniform rate of postage be introduced irrespective of distance. Consequently a flat rate of 4 c per single letter was levied and, at the same time, a charge of 1 c on newspapers (hitherto carried free) was adopted. Stamps of these denominations were ordered from England in a somewhat casual fashion. Dalton gave the order to a local firm of stationers, Richardson & Colebeck, and they passed it on to Waterlow & Sons of London who had no previous experience of stamp production. Waterlows lithographed the stamps in black on surface-coloured paper. The design was relatively simple and consisted of the colony's emblem, a sailing ship, and the Latin motto (from Horace) *Damus petimusque vicissim* (we give and seek in return). The engraver who prepared the plates misspelled the second word *patimus* (we suffer), thus perpetrating the world's first philatelic error of inscription.

A new, more substantial and ornate design which featured the colonial emblem, but with the motto correctly spelled, was introduced the following year and from then until 1934 this emblem continued to be the sole or major feature of the Guianese definitive stamps.

Waterlows produced new 'ship' designs for British Guiana in 1853–9, 1860, 1863–4 and 1866. In between, however, there were several local makeshifts on which space does not permit a detailed account. Suffice it to say that among the type-set provisionals produced by the *Royal Gazette* in this period was the celebrated One Cent Black on

261
262

257

Magenta of 1856. The only authenticated example of this stamp has a romantic pedigree—discovered by a schoolboy, Vernon Vaughan, in 1873 and sold by him for 6 shillings, passing through the collections of Count Ferrary and Arthur Hind, and being sold in 1970 by Frederick Small for the record sum of $280,000. The 4 c stamp of this issue, in black on blue or magenta paper, is commoner but nevertheless ranks among the world's great rarities.

George Melville produced 1, 2 and 4 c type-set provisionals at the *Royal Gazette* office in October 1862. The ship, which came from the stock cut used in the heading of shipping notices, was not used on this occasion and the centre of these stamps was left blank. The inscription 'BRITISH GUIANA POSTAGE' and the value was arranged on the four sides, surrounded by rows of printer's ornaments which differed considerably in pattern and layout.

Nine countries made their philatelic debut in 1851—ten if we include Trinidad which had had a local issue (the Lady McLeod stamp) four years previously. Significantly only half of these were in Europe, the remainder all being in the Western hemisphere.

SARDINIA

The year began with the first issues of Sardinia, which went on sale on New Year's Day. The kingdom of Sardinia in fact extended far beyond that island and included the duchy of Savoy and other districts on the north-western mainland of Italy. Those who aspired to Italian unity looked to Sardinia and its ruler, King Victor

Emmanuel II, to achieve the *Risorgimento*. The kingdom of Sardinia in the mid-nineteenth century was the most progressive of the Italian states and it is hardly surprising that it should have been the first to adopt adhesive stamps. It has often been claimed that Sardinia pioneered postal prepayment by means of stamps—in the form of the letter sheets of 1818 impressed with the *Cavallini* or little horsemen, but as this mark denoted the payment of a fiscal rather than postal duty it is not strictly relevant in this context.

256   The first stamps consisted of 5, 20 and 40 centesimi, lithographed by F. Matraire at Turin. Three years later the same designs were used for these denominations, but embossed on coloured paper. This experiment did not prove successful and the issue of October 1853 was quickly superseded by a form of compromise in which the king's profile was embossed in colourless relief, with the frames lithographed as before.

263   The last series used by Sardinia followed the same basic design but had a typographed instead of lithographed frame. New values of 10 and 80 c and 3 lire were added to the typographed series between 1858 and 1861. 1 and 2 c stamps inscribed 'GIORNALI STAMPE' (journals and printed matter)

264   with the numeral of value embossed in the centre were introduced in 1861. The shades of the Sardinian stamps varied considerably and numerous errors of omitted, double or inverted embossing abound.

These stamps were used in other parts of Italy between 1859 and 1862, following the campaigns of that period which led to the unification of the peninsula under Sardinia. In addition, Matraire produced stamps in similar designs, portraying King Victor Emmanuel, for use in the Neapolitan provinces (1861) and the kingdom of Italy itself (1862).

TUSCANY

In the middle of the last century Italy was a conglomeration of petty kingdoms and principalities, many of whom were directly or indirectly under Austrian control. In this category came the grand duchy of Tuscany whose ruler, Leopold II, had only quelled his rebellious subjects in 1848–9 with the aid of a large Austrian army. Commercially Tuscany (capital Florence) was tied to Austria and in December 1850 a postal treaty between the two countries was signed, which later formed the basis of an Italo-Austrian Postal Convention, stabilizing postal rates and regulations between the states and Austria. This treaty envisaged the introduction of adhesive stamps and these duly appeared on April 1st 1851.

The electrotypes were manufactured by M. Alessandri of Florence, from engravings by Giuseppe Niderost, and the stamps typographed by F. Cambiagi at the Grand Ducal Printing Office in Florence. The denominations consisted of 1 and 2 soldi, 2, 4 and 6 crazie. In July 1851, 1 and 9 crazie stamps were introduced.

The following year stamps valued at 1 quattrino were introduced for postage on newspapers and a 60 crazie for foreign correspondence. All of these stamps bore a common design featuring the Marzocco (Tuscan) lion holding a shield emblazoned   254 with the Florentine fleur-de-lis. The stamps were printed on bluish or greyish paper with a sheet watermark of Tuscan crowns. Stamps on white unwatermarked paper are proofs which, nevertheless, may sometimes be found in postally used condition.

Between 1854 and 1859 a circular stamp inscribed 'BOLLO STRAORDINARIO PER LE POSTE' (extraordinary stamp for the post) was in use to defray a tax on newspapers. This stamp, sold for 2 soldi, was introduced in retaliation for the action of the neighbouring duchy of Parma which taxed political journals emanating from Tuscany at the rate of 9 centesimi. From October 1st 1854 the Tuscan stamp had to be affixed to any newspapers and periodicals entering the grand duchy from any state taxing Tuscan papers.

Between 1857 and 1859 a new sheet watermark was employed, consisting of a network with the inscription 'II E RR POSTE TOSCANE' applied diagonally. Stamps with this watermark had a relatively short life, on account of the political upheavals in Tuscany in 1859. Leopold II was forced to abdicate on July 21st 1859 and was succeeded by his son, Ferdinand IV, who reigned for only twenty-seven days before he was deposed. By popular vote Tuscany then joined the Sardinian Confederation.

In November 1859 Sardinian currency was introduced in Tuscany and this necessitated a new series of stamps which appeared on January 1st 1860. The stamps, in denominations from 1 centesimo to 3 lire, corresponded with the contemporary series of Sardinia. The stamps had the same frame and inscription as the previous series but featured the arms of the House of Savoy in place of the Marzocco. Although in use for a relatively short time these stamps are far scarcer mint than used, and the three lire (now catalogued by Stanley Gibbons at $10,200 (£5,000) mint and $5,100 (£2,500) used) ranks as Italy's most valuable stamp.

DENMARK

Until 1849 the postal services of Denmark were in the hands of private individuals who charged the public at varying rates and whose operations were confined to fairly limited areas. In May of that year, how-

254 *Tuscany, 1 crazia, Lion, 1851*

255 *Tuscany, 3 lire, Arms of Savoy, 1860*

256 *Sardinia, 40 c, Victor Emmanuel II, 1851*

257 *British Guiana, 4 c, 1856*

254

255

256

257

ever, the Danish government decided to nationalize the posts. Indemnities (in some cases quite heavy) were paid to the former postal operators and a national postal administration established. At first postage continued to be prepaid in cash and this fact noted by means of manuscript endorsement or hand-struck marks. At this time the postage on a letter within the city of Copenhagen was fixed at 2 rigsbank skillings and at 4 rbs for a letter to or from the outer suburbs. On March 11th 1851 the postal rates were revised so that 2 rbs continued to be the local Copenhagen rate, while the 4 rbs rate was extended to cover the rest of the country. Unpaid letters were henceforth charged at the rate of 6 rbs. A 4 rbs stamp in brown was introduced on April 1st 1851 and a 2 rbs value in blue four weeks later. The 2 rbs stamp had the value inscribed in the centre with the inscription 'KGL. POST FRIMAERKE' (Royal Post Stamp) in a circular band. On the 4 rbs the inscription was rendered in full 'KONGELIGE POST FRIMAERKE' on three sides of the design with the value at the foot and the royal emblem—sword and sceptre surmounted by a crown—in the centre.

The production of these stamps was unusually complicated in a bid to defeat the would-be forger. The designs were engraved on steel by M. W. Ferslew of Copenhagen. First burelage or a network of brown wavy lines was applied by recessprinting to the paper by Ferslew, then the stamps were typographed probably by H. H. Thiele. Printings of these stamps were certainly made by Thiele in 1852–4, differing in the shade and sharpness of the burelage. The plates for the 2 and 4 sk stamps were entirely redrawn by A. Buntzen in October 1854. In these designs the 2 sk conformed to the 4 sk in format and design, and in both cases the value was now rendered by the abbreviation 's'. Electrotypes were taken from the Buntzen engravings and the stamps typographed by Thiele, using the same paper and burelage as before. New printings were made by Thiele in 1858 differing from the preceding issue by the spandrels, which were composed of wavy lines instead of dots. Hand-made paper was used until June 1862 when smooth, machine-made paper was introduced for the 4 s value. With the exception of a few private perforations gauging 12 or 13, the stamps of Denmark were imperforate until 1863, when rouletting was adopted, and 8 and 16 sk values were added to the series in 1857.

King Christian IX ascended the throne in 1863, but the change of ruler was not reflected in the stamps. Instead, a new design, also featuring the royal Danish emblems, was introduced in May 1864 in denominations from 2 to 16 sk, to be superseded by the famous crowned numeral design of 1870 which remained in use, with numerous variations, till 1905. From 1851 to 1933 all Danish stamps, with few exceptions, were produced by Thiele.

Following the lead of Austria, Prussia, Saxony and Hanover, two other German states began issuing adhesive stamps in 1851, viz Baden and Wurttemberg. Both of them signified their adherence to the German-Austrian Postal Union in the stamps which they issued, and since these stamps incorporated in their inscriptions the date on which the Union came into being, it has been argued that these were the world's first commemorative stamps. As the stamps remained in use for a considerable time, and in fact, were the only stamps of the respective states at that time, they have therefore to be regarded as definitives and not commemoratives in the modern sense.

258 Baden introduced a series on May 1st, consisting of 1, 3, 6 and 9 kreuzer. The stamps, engraved by C. Naumann and typographed by Hasper of Karlsruhe, were printed in black on different coloured paper. The designs featured the numeral of value prominently in the centre, with BADEN and 'Freimarke' in Teutonic script at top and bottom and the minuscule inscription referring to the German-Austrian Postal Union in the side panels. The 9 k was normally printed on dull rose paper, but a few examples have been found on the green paper normally reserved for the 6 k. Between 1853 and 1858 the colour of the paper used for printing the 1 and 6 k changed once and that of the 3 k changed on two occasions. A new design, featuring the

267 grand ducal coat of arms, was adopted in 1860 for a series typographed in various colours on white paper. This series underwent changes in perforation and re-appeared in 1862–4 with an unshaded background to

268 the arms. Both versions, however, continued to refer to the Postal Union by including the word 'POSTVEREIN' in the right-hand vertical panel. In October 1864

269 a new arms design was introduced in which the word 'FREIMARKE' was substituted for 'POSTVEREIN'. Separate issues for Baden came to an end in 1871, when the grand duchy became part of the recently formed German Empire.

WURTTEMBERG

Wurttemberg, which began using adhesive stamps on October 15th 1851, adopted a similar frame arrangement of the inscriptions and the same wording, the sole difference being that the name of the king-

258 *Baden, 3 k, 1851*

259 *Wurttemberg, 3 k, 1851*

260 *Wurttemberg, 6 k, 1857*

261 *British Guiana, 4 c, 1853*

262 *British Guiana, 4 c, 1860*

263 *Sardinia, 40 c, 1855*

264 *Sardinia, 1 c, newspaper stamp, 1861*

265 *Denmark, 4 s, 1864*

266 *Denmark, 2 rbs, 1851*

267 *Baden, 3 k, 1860*

268 *Baden, 18 k, 1862*

269 *Baden, 1 k, 1868*

270 *Wurttemberg, 9 k, 1869*

258

259

260

261

262

263

264

265

266

267

268

269

270

271

272

273

274

275

276

277

dom was rendered in upper and lower case lettering. In the centre, however, the numeral of value was set in a diamond-shaped frame, instead of the circle used by Baden. Like Baden, these stamps were typographed in black on various coloured papers, the same colours being used for corresponding denominations of the Baden-sian series; but unlike Baden, Wurttemberg introduced a higher denomination of 18 kreuzer the following year for registered letters carried up to fifty German miles. 259

Wurttemberg was not as faithful as Baden to the memory of the Postal Union, dropping the 'commemorative' inscription from the design introduced in 1857. This series featured the royal coat of arms embossed in colourless relief with the frame typographed in colour on white paper. The plates were manufactured in Bern, Switzerland, and the printing carried out at the Ticket Printery of the State Railway Commission in Stuttgart. A curious feature of 260 this series was the orange silk thread enmeshed in the paper as a security device. Silk thread paper was adopted by Bavaria in 1849 and also appeared on the Swiss series of 1854 which was produced by the same printers, Weiss of Munich; but credit for the invention of this security measure must go to Britain, whose embossed 10 d and 1 s stamps of 1847–8 bore a fine silk thread in the so-called 'Dickinson paper'.

The arms stamps of Wurttemberg underwent numerous changes of paper, perforation and colour, remaining in currency until January 1869, when they were replaced by the 270 small numeral design. Along with Bavaria, Wurttemberg continued to issue ordinary postage stamps after the formation of the Empire in 1871. This privilege survived until 1902, and even later stamps for government correspondence or municipal mail were kept until 1920 and 1924 respectively.

271 *Hawaii, 1 c, Princess Victoria Kamamalu, 1871*
272 *Hawaii, 2 c, Kamehameha IV, 1864*
273 *Hawaii, 5 c, Kamehameha V, 1866*
274 *Hawaii, 6 c, Kamehameha V, 1871*
275 *Hawaii, 18 c, Mataio Kekuanaoa, 1871*
276 *Canada, 10 c, Prince Albert, 1859*
277 *Canada, 3 c, 'Small Cents', 1870*

Although American commercial penetration of Hawaii in the early nineteenth century was extensive, this Polynesian archipelago in the northern Pacific was allowed to continue as a native kingdom, with its own customs and laws, until the end of the century. This curious dual system was reflected in the postal services operating in the middle of the century. Two political factions existed at this time : one backed by the missionaries, argued in favour of free postage to encourage literacy among the islanders; the other, backed by the traders, urged the introduction of a proper postal service which, to be efficient, had to be paid for.

An Act establishing a postal service was passed by the Hawaiian Assembly as early as 1846, but nothing was done to implement this until 1850, when a subsequent Act laid down an external postal rate of 10 c per letter (reduced the following year to 5 c on the introduction of adhesive stamps).

The post office established in September 1851 was not under government control, but was farmed out to Henry M. Whitney, a printer and stationer of Honolulu who published a newspaper, *The Commercial Advertiser*. It is not known whether the first stamps were printed there, or at the office of *The Polynesian*, the government paper. The stamps were type-set and printed in September 1851, being placed on sale early the following month. *The Polynesian* of October 4th mentioned the three denominations of 2 c, 5 c and 13 c. The lowest value prepaid the newspaper rate while the
278   5 c represented the letter rate. The 13 c
279   stamp denoted the prepayment of three separate fees : 5 c Hawaiian postage, 6 c United States postage and 2 c ship letter fee for conveying the letter from Hawaii to

278 *Hawaii, 2 c, 'Missionary', 1851*

279 *Hawaii, 5 c, 'Missionary', 1852*

280 *Hawaii, 13 c, 'Missionary', 1852*

281 *Hawaii, 2 c, Inter-island Post, 1859*

282 *Hawaii, 5 c, Kamehameha III, 1853*

278

279

280

281

282

America. All three stamps were inscribed in upper and lower case lettering 'Hawaiian Postage', though the 13 c was re-issued in 1852 with the inscription amended to 'H.I. & U.S. Postage'.

280

On account of the fact that the majority of the known examples of these stamps were subsequently discovered on correspondence from American missionaries they have acquired the sobriquet of 'Missionaries'. These stamps are all major rarities, especially the 2 c denomination for which there was little use, since the inland service which it was intended to represent did not materialize till eight years later. The stamps were printed in blue on extremely thin, brittle paper and this accounts for the fact that few of the Missionaries are in perfect condition.

282

The primitive Missionaries were superseded in 1853 by intaglio designs by Holland of Boston, USA, bearing rather crude portraits of King Kamehameha III. These stamps, in denominations of 5 and 13 c, were inscribed 'Honolulu Hawaiian Is'. The 13 c stamp went so far as to show the breakdown of the postage, being inscribed in the side panels 'HAWAIIAN-5 Cts' and 'UNITED STATES-8 Cts'.

During the 1850s there was protracted debate in the Hawaiian Assembly on the vexed question of the internal postal system. The system of free transmission of mail on Oahu and between that island and the others was greatly abused by natives and American traders alike, but was extremely inefficient and uncertain. From time to time attempts were made to reform this idealistic, though corrupt system, but it was not until 1858 that Joseph Jackson, Whitney's successor, managed to get his recommendation regarding inter-island postage accepted by the Assembly. Even then there was a bitter fight over this issue,

between *The Polynesian* (in favour of postage) and *The Commercial Advertiser* (which opposed it). Inter-island postage was formally introduced on August 1st 1859, stamps of 1 and 2 c value being type-set in 281 an austere numeral design for this purpose. An interesting feature of these stamps was their inscriptions in both English and Hawaiian, though the value was rendered in English as well as denoted prominently by figures. This was in sharp contrast to the lithographed 2 c of 1861–3 and the handsome recess-printed series of 1864–91, 271-275 both of which bore the value in Arabic numerals but also with the Hawaiian equivalent in words. These stamps, like the remaining issues under the kingdom, portrayed various members of the Hawaiian royal house whose names, like Princess Kamamalu, Princess Likelike, Queen Kapiolani or King David Kalakaua, have a musical quality in tune with their exotic homeland.

CANADA

From 1763, when the colony was annexed 284,276,277 after the Seven Years' War, Canada's postal administration was under the control of the General Post Office in London.

From 1827 to 1851 Thomas Stayner was Deputy Postmaster General for Canada, which at that time was confined to the present-day provinces of Ontario and Quebec. The other provinces had the status of separate colonies, and in postal matters had their own deputy postmasters general responsible direct to the GPO in London. A Post Office Act was passed in August 1850 transferring the control of the postal services from London to the local authorities. This Act came into effect on April 7th 1851. In connection with this transfer of authority, adhesive stamps were envisaged. Hitherto prepayment of postage had been indicated by means of handstruck marks, usually in the form of a numeral 3, showing the inland letter rate of 3 d.

The introduction of adhesive stamps, however, had been contemplated at an earlier date, and a resolution urging this step was passed by the Canadian Legislative Assembly: 'That postage stamps for prepayment be allowed and that Colonial stamps be engraved'. This resolution was approved on May 25th 1849.

A considerable time elapsed between that date and implementation of the resolution. In February 1851 Sandford Fleming produced designs for 3 d and 1 s stamps both featuring the beaver, Canada's national emblem. These essays were intended for lithographic reproduction. This method of printing did not commend itself to the postal officials, who thereupon placed the contract for the production of the first stamps with the New York firm of Rawdon, Wright, Hatch & Edson who had already been recess-printing postage stamps for nine years. Fleming's beaver design was retained for the 3 d stamp printed in New York and first placed on sale on April 23rd 1851. It has been claimed that this stamp was the first in the world to depict an animal, but in so doing, Canadian philatelists ignore the Basle Dove (1843) and the St Louis Bears (1845) which also depicted fauna. Nevertheless in its proper rather than heraldic approach to the subject, the Threepenny Beaver represents a significant landmark in stamp design—the forerunner of the pictorialism which was not fully established till forty years later.

The other stamps in the series portrayed Prince Albert the Prince Consort (6 d) and Queen Victoria (12 d), the latter based on

283 *Canada, 3 d, Beaver, 1851*

284 *Canada, 12 d,*
mint pair from bottom of sheet, 1851

285 *Canada, 12 ¹/₂ c, 'Large Cents', 1868*

148

283

284

285

the famous portrait by Edward Chalon. The inscription on the top value—TWELVEPENCE—alluded to the fact that the term 'shilling' had a different interpretation in different parts of North America. The anomalous position of Canadian currency in the mid-nineteenth century was reflected in the denominations added to the series in 1855–7. The 10 d stamp was inscribed 10 cy (currency) and 8 ½ stg (sterling), while the 7 ½ d stamp not only bore the abbreviated values 7 ½ cy and 6 stg but was inscribed 'CANADA PACKET POSTAGE SIXPENCE STERLING'. These stamps prepaid the postage on letter to Europe via British packet boats, originally set at 10 d and reduced to 7 ½ d in 1856. The 7 ½ d stamp used the Chalon portrait, similar to that on the discontinued 12 d, but the 10 d bore the portrait of Jacques Cartier, discoverer of Canada. Though this choice was perfectly justifiable it marked a departure from the established tradition of portraying the queen or some heraldic device. Bearing in mind, however, that the New York printers had portrayed Washington and Franklin on the earliest stamps of the United States there was thus an incipient tradition in North America for using historic personalities as stamp subjects.

In August 1857 Canada introduced a ½ d stamp, bearing a profile of the queen. This stamp prepaid the postage on newspapers, but was also useful in making up other postal rates in combination with the existing denominations. This completed the basic series of Canadian stamps. During the period from 1851 to 1859 these stamps underwent numerous variations in paper and shade, while perforation was introduced in 1858. The same five designs were retained for the decimal series of July 1859 following the introduction of the dollar of 100 cents. In May 1858 Rawdon, Wright, Hatch & Edson changed their name to the American Bank Note Co. and this name henceforward appeared as an imprint in the sheet margins of these stamps. These stamps, in denominations from 1 to 17 cents, remained in use until 1868, when the so-called 'Large Cents' series was introduced throughout the newly constituted Dominion of Canada.

The adhesive stamps of Canada had an interesting, though mysterious, prelude in the form of a stamped envelope apparently produced by R. W. Kelly, postmaster of New Carlisle, on his own initiative. This envelope bore an impressed stamp containing the words 'Three Pence' in cursive script, within a rectangular border of printer's ornament. Only one example of this curiosity has so far come to light and is believed to have been used in the transitional period between April 7th and 23rd when the adhesives were introduced.

NEW BRUNSWICK AND NOVA SCOTIA

Two of the maritime colonies in British North America, New Brunswick and Nova Scotia, followed Canada's lead and released adhesive stamps in 1851. In both cases Post Office Acts the previous year had paved the way for postal reforms, including uniform rates of postage and the encouragement of prepayment by means of adhesive stamps. The postal administrations in these colonies became independent of the General Post Office in London on July 6th 1851 and the proclamations published simultaneously on that date both announced the release of stamps. The order for stamps on behalf of both colonies was placed through the agency of a stationer, Trelawney Saunders of London, with the firm of Perkins Bacon in June 1851. Perkins Bacon evidently lost no time in putting the commission into effect, since they were able to report to Saunders on August 7th that they had despatched consignments of stamps by rail to Liverpool the previous day, to connect with the British packet boat bound for North America. The stamps reached their respective destinations in time for release on September 1st 1851.

Each colony issued stamps in denominations of 3 d, 6 d and 1 s in a diamond-shaped format—the first stamps ever produced in this shape. The designs, incorporating the floral emblems of the United Kingdom and the royal crown, were identical in every respect save the name of the colony and the insertion of a mayflower instead of a rose on the issues of Nova Scotia. Since both colonies had double-barrelled names, the words occupied the upper side panels of the frame, with the value in words and POSTAGE in the lower corners. For the sake of economy the plates used for the stamps of both colonies were manufactured from the same original master die, transfer rollers being employed to lay down subsidiary dies on which the requisite inscriptions could be engraved prior to making the plates. Nova Scotia required a 1 d stamp for local letters and a stamp of this value was introduced in May 1853. This stamp had a distinctive design, featuring the Chalon portrait of Queen Victoria in a diamond-shaped frame, the whole enclosed in a square tastefully embellished with engine-turned ornaments. Perkins Bacon entrusted the production of this stamp to one of their employees, H. Smith, who turned out 654,000 in the space of three weeks—a record output for that time, but one in which quality inevitably suffered, since the 1 d stamp did not

286 *New Brunswick, 1 s, 1851*
287 *Nova Scotia, 1 d, 1853*
288 *Nova Scotia, 10 c, 1860*
289 *Trinidad, 1 d, Britannia, 1851*
290 *Brunswick, 3 sgr, 1852*

286

287

288

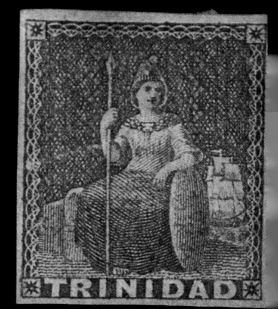

289

come to the usual high standards of this firm.

The pence issues of New Brunswick and Nova Scotia varied considerably in shade according to the different printings required; but the chief interest of these stamps 305,288 lies in the fact that bisection or quartering was resorted to in order to make up the different postal rates.

In 1860 both colonies adopted Canadian decimal currency and new sets of stamps became necessary. In both cases the contract was awarded to the American Bank Note Co., in New York. The Nova Scotian series, ranging from 1 to 12 ½ cents, adopt-301 ed portraits or profiles of Queen Victoria, 303 but New Brunswick, on the instigation of its Postmaster General, Charles Connell, went wholeheartedly pictorial with five designs. Two featured the queen and the youthful Prince of Wales (later King 304 Edward VII) in Highland dress. Communications, internal and external, were alluded to on the 1 c and 12 ½ c stamps, which 299 featured a locomotive and the paddle-300 steamer *Washington* respectively. For the place of honour, on the much-used 5 c 302 stamp, Connell reserved his own portrait—an action which sparked off bitter controversy in the colony and precipitated his resignation as Postmaster General. A 5 c portraying the queen was hurriedly prepared and put on sale about July 18th; in the interim 5 c letters were prepaid in cash and accordingly hand-struck, or made use of bisected 10 c stamps. A 2 c stamp, which also bore a portrait of the queen, was subsequently added to the series in 1863.

Both New Brunswick and Nova Scotia ceased to issue their own stamps in March 1868, following the introduction of the 'Large Cents' stamps of the Dominion of Canada.

TRINIDAD

Mention has already been made of the 289,306,307 'Lady McLeod' stamp, used to prepay letters between Port of Spain and San Fernando in 1847, but this was a purely private venture. In the year that the Lady McLeod stamps first appeared the Governor of Trinidad, Lord Harris, wrote to the Secretary of State for the Colonies, proposing a properly organized postal system and the opening of nine post offices in the main towns of the island. It was anticipated, however, that such a service would inevitably run at a loss and its introduction was delayed for four years pending negotiations between the colony and the Treasury in London, as to the apportionment of this deficit. In preparation for the introduction of the service, stamps were ordered from Perkins Bacon in 1848. These were recessprinted in the design of Britannia seated on bags of sugar, subsequently used also for the earliest Perkins Bacon issues of Barbados and Mauritius. These stamps bore no denomination, it being intended that the difference in value should be indicated by the colour, but when the stamps were eventually put on sale on August 14th 1851, both purple-brown and blue colours were used indiscriminately as penny stamps. Uniform penny postage was introduced on that date, inland post offices being opened at San Fernando and Port of Spain, while the police stations took on this role elsewhere.

Britannia on her sugar bags remained the sole design for the stamps of Trinidad throughout the entire classic period. During the thirty-two years in which it was current, however, it underwent a number of important changes: from blue to white paper (1854), the locally lithographed versions running to five distinct printings

(1852–60), the design redrawn to include the value, in words, at the foot of the design (1859), the introduction of perforations (1859–60), the transfer of the contract from Perkins Bacon to De La Rue (1862) and the appearance of the Crown CC watermark (1863). Until 1869 Trinidad got by with only four denominations, 1 d, 4 d, 6 d and 1 s, but in that year De La Rue produced a large-format 5 s, using their celebrated surface-printing process, and bearing the diademed profile of Queen Victoria. Nevertheless Britannia remained popular as the motif of the lower denominations (with the exception of the Queen's Head series of 1883–4) right down to 1935, when bi-coloured pictorials became the order of the day.

The year 1852 was another bumper one in the early development of philately, with no fewer than four countries introducing adhesive stamps on New Year's Day alone. A further six adopted adhesive stamps during the course of the year, and includ-ed the first French colony and the first Asian state to do so.

BRUNSWICK

Two German states and the postal system operated by the Count of Thurn and Taxis adopted adhesives during January 1852. The first of these was the duchy of Bruns-wick which joined the German-Austrian Postal Union on January 1st and on that day introduced stamps in denominations of 290 1, 2 and 3 silbergroschen. They were engraved by Karl Petersen on woodblocks and typographed by Johann Heinrich Meyer of Brunswick on yellowish-white paper with reddish-brown gum. The only variety of note in this series was the 2 sgr bisected and used as 1 sgr. An example of this bisect, on cover bearing the postmark of Holzminden, was in the collection of Count Ferrary. The series was short-lived, being replaced in March 1853 by similar designs printed in black on coloured paper, in the manner which was then customary in many of the other German states. Smaller denominations of ¼ and ⅓ sgr were added to the set in March 1856. Both the 1 and 2 sgr of this series have been recorded bisected.

In 1857 Brunswick issued a fractional 308 stamp for internal postage and, therefore, inscribed in the local currency of gute-groschen. The stamp, sold for one gute-groschen, consisted of four portions each bearing a crown and the value ½ ggr Fractions of all kinds may be found: ¼ ggr on local letters, ¾ ggr on letters to rural communities, and so on, according to the mileage. Originally this stamp was printed in black on brown paper, but a printing in brown on white paper was also produced, though never issued for postal duty.

The currency of Brunswick was originally based on the thaler of 24 gutegroschen, each of which consisted of 12 gutepfennige. The thaler of 30 silbergroschen was used on mail going beyond the ducal frontier. In 1858 the currency of the duchy was reform-ed to the thaler of 30 neue silbergroschen, each equal to 10 neue pfennige. This explains why the ½ ggr stamp of 1863 was also inscribed FÜNF PFENNIG. The 309 colours of the 1 and 3 sgr stamps were changed in 1861, and rouletting was intro-duced for the ½, 1, 2 and 3 sgr values in 1864. Brunswick's last series appeared in 1865 and consisted of an upright oval design with the white horse emblem embossed in the centre, in the manner of the other German states' issues.

Four days after Brunswick the grand duchy of Oldenburg began issuing stamps, although, like Brunswick, it had joined the German-Austrian Postal Union on New Year's Day. The stamps were lithographed by Gerhard Stalling of Oldenburg and featured the grand ducal coat of arms above the value expressed in fractions of a thaler. To confuse the issue the equivalent in local currency was given in ribbons placed vertically in the frame. Thus the $1/30$ thaler stamp was also inscribed 2 $2/5$ grote and 1 silbergroschen, the $1/15$ thaler had 4 $4/5$ grote and 2 sgr, and the $1/10$ thaler had 7 $1/2$ grote and 3 sgr. These stamps prepaid the postage on town letters, inland letters and correspondence destined to other parts of Germany respectively. In January 1855 a fourth denomination, for franking printed matter and newspapers, was released: the $1/3$ sgr, which bore the local value of 4 schwaren in the side ribbons.

In January 1858 Oldenburg adopted the thaler of 30 groschen and consequently issued a new series in this currency. The stamps did not appear until July 1859 and consisted of $1/3$, 1, 2 and 3 gr values, lithographed by Stalling and featuring the coat of arms in a small upright design. Initially the stamps were printed in black on coloured paper, but two years later different colours on white paper were substituted. Again Oldenburg followed the German pattern by issuing an upright oval series in 1862 with the arms embossed in colourless relief. Like many of the other issues in this *genre* the series of 1862 was printed at the Prussian State Printing Works in Berlin. Both Oldenburg and Brunswick joined the North German Confederation in 1867 and ceased to issue distinctive stamps at the end of that year.

The postal service as a monopoly of the state is a relatively modern concept, and private postal services survived through much of the nineteenth century. Such a one, though on the grand scale, was that operated by the Counts of Thurn and Taxis, a princely family of the Holy Roman Empire which had organized postal services in many parts of Europe since the fifteenth century. By the mid-nineteenth century, however, many of the former kingdoms and principalities of central and western Europe had shaken off or purchased the monopoly of Thurn and Taxis. The postal stationery issued by the Thurn and Taxis administration for use in Wurttemberg in 1846 has already been noted. In 1851 Wurttemberg terminated its agreement with Thurn and Taxis and introduced its own stamps.

After the loss of the posts in Wurttemberg, the Thurn and Taxis service continued to operate in the north German districts comprising the principalities of Hessen-Kassel, Lippe-Detmold and Lippe-Schaumburg, the grand duchy of Saxe-Weimar-Eisenach, the principalities of Schwarzburg-Sondershausen and Reuss, Gotha in the duchy of Saxe-Coburg-Gotha, the duchy of Saxe-Meiningen, as well as maintaining post offices in the free cities of Hamburg, Bremen and Lubeck. In southern Germany the postal service operated in the principalities of Schwarzburg-Rudolstadt, Hohenzollern-Hechingen and Hohenzollern-Sigmaringen, the duchy of Nassau and part of Saxe-Meiningen, Coburg in the duchy of Saxe-Coburg-Gotha, the grand duchy of Hessen-Darmstadt and the free city of Frankfurt-am-Main, the last-named being the headquarters of the service.

Adhesive stamps were introduced on January 29th 1852, those used in the north being inscribed in silbergroschen currency, while those in the south employed kreuzer currency. Both sets featured the numerals of value prominently, the northern series having inscriptions set in four sides of a rectangular frame, whereas the southern series had a circular frame containing the inscriptions. In both cases the word 'Freimarke' (postage stamp) was featured in prominent lettering, while in tiny Germanic script appeared the legend 'Thurn und Taxis' and an abbreviation signifying the German-Austrian Postal Union of 1850 to which the Thurn and Taxis service became a signatory in May 1851.

Both sets were typographed by C. Naumann of Frankfurt. The sets ranged from ¼ sgr to 3 sgr and from 1 to 9 kr. The original sets were printed in black on various coloured papers but in 1859–61 new sets, printed by Naumann from dies engraved by F. M. Kepler, were made in different colours on white paper. Higher denominations of 5 and 10 sgr and 15 and 30 kr were issued at this time. Various denominations changed their colours between 1862 and 1864. Prior to 1865 all the stamps of the Thurn and Taxis service were released imperforate, but in July of that year colourless rouletting gauging 16 was introduced. The following year, as an aid to separation, the rouletting was applied in colour. The 1 sgr is known without rouletting vertically between pairs, while the 3 kr is known rouletted partly in colour and partly albino.

On January 28th 1867 a treaty was signed between Prussia and the Count of Thurn and Taxis, whereby the latter sold his postal service to the Prussian postal administration for 3,000,000 thalers. At the time of the treaty the Thurn and Taxis network had 302 post offices and agencies serving an estimated population of 3,400,000. The working of the service had been sadly dis-

293
294
310

291 *Oldenburg, ¹/₁₀ th, 1852*

292 *Oldenburg, ¹/₃ gr, 1859*

293 *Thurn and Taxis, 3 sgr, 1852*

294 *Thurn and Taxis, 6 k, 1852*

295 *Parma, 5 c, 1852*

296 *Modena, 10 c, 1852*

297 *Papal States, ¹/₂ b, 1852*

298 *Papal States, 2 b, 1852*

291

292

293

294

295

296

297

298

rupted by the war between Austria and Prussia in June-August 1866 and it never quite recovered from this upheaval.

THE PAPAL STATES

Three of the political entities in the Italian peninsula also adopted adhesive stamps in 1852. The first of these, whose stamps appeared on January 1st, was the Papacy (usually known to philatelists as the Roman States, the Papal States or the States of the Church). In 1852 the Pope (Pius IX) still wielded considerable secular power, governing not only Rome itself but a number of surrounding towns and districts. The revolution of 1848, however, had seriously undermined his power and it was largely due to Austrian intervention that the Pope had been restored to his dominions. As in other parts of Italy, the 1850s were an uneasy time for the rulers of the petty states, faced with increasing agitation for unification under the House of Savoy.

A series of stamps, in denominations 297 from ½ to 7 bajocchi, was typographed 298 in black on coloured paper by Doublet & 312 Decoppet of Rome. The stamps featured the papal emblems of crossed keys and triple tiara with the inscription 'FRANCO BOLLO POSTALE'. Different frames were used for each denomination. In July stamps of 50 b and 1 scudo were added to the series, while a 8 b value appeared in October. During the fifteen years in which they were current these stamps varied considerably in shade. The temporal dominions of the Pope were severely curtailed in the campaigns which culminated in the establishment of the kingdom of Italy in 1860, but the Pope continued to govern Rome for a further decade, backed up by a garrison of French troops.

Commercially, however, Rome could not continue in splendid isolation and in 1867 Italian currency was adopted. The stamps were re-issued in September of that year with values expressed in centesimi, and printed in black on coloured glazed paper. Perforation was introduced for those stamps issued between March 1868 and October 1870. Napoleon III was forced to evacuate his garrison from the Eternal City in 1870 as a result of the Franco-Prussian War, and this left the Pope defenceless. Rome was promptly occupied by Italian troops and annexed to Italy. The government of the kingdom was transferred from Florence to Rome. Relations between the Church and the Kingdom were understandably strained and it was not until 1929 that the Pope was permitted secular authority, confined to the Vatican City State which has issued its own stamps since that date.

MODENA AND PARMA

In northern Italy the two little duchies of Modena and Parma also adopted stamps in 1852, both introducing this measure on June 1st, with sets of five stamps in denom- 295 inations of 5, 10, 15, 25 and 40 centesimi. 296 Both issues were typographed in black on coloured paper and both adopted the ducal coat of arms as the central motif. Furthermore, in both cases the name of the duchy was rendered cryptically at the top, and the value given at the foot, with ornamentation in the side panels. Modena's stamps were inscribed 'POSTE ESTENSI', alluding to the fact that the ruling family was named Este. Parma's stamps bore the legend 'STATI PARM', an abbreviation which was more easily identifiable.

In addition Modena had a 1 lira stamp, printed in black on white paper. The chief

interest of Modena's stamps lies in the numerous errors and varieties in the inscriptions, which hardly reflected to the credit of Messrs Rocca, Rinaldi & Algeri who manufactured the electrotypes. The stamps of Parma were relatively free from mistakes of this sort, though the 15 c is known in *tête-bêche* pairs. The 5, 15 and 25 c stamps were re-issued in 1853–5 in various colours on white paper. The Duchess Marie-Louise, second consort of Napoleon Bonaparte, became regent of Parma in 1854 and three years later a new series was released in denominations of 15, 25 and 40 c. Again the Bourbon fleur-de-lis formed the central motif but the inscription was expanded to 'DUC. DI
313 PARMA PIAC. ECC.' (Duchy of Parma, Piacenza and so on).

The second War of Independence, which resulted in the unification of Italy under the House of Savoy, had important repercussions on the philately of both duchies. Mixed franking of Sardinian and Parmesan stamps is known on letters dated between August 1859 and January 1860. Stamps of Modena in the same period were cancelled with a nine-bar obliterator containing the coat of arms of Savoy, and conversely Sardinian stamps are recorded with Modonese cancellations between June and October 1859. In both states the ruling families were deposed by popular movements. Pending their absorption into the new kingdom of Italy both states had provisional governments which issued their
314 own stamps. Those of Modena were in-
315, 316 scribed 'PROVINCIE MODONESI' and bore the arms of Savoy while those of Parma were inscribed 'STATI PARMENSI' in a functional design incorporating the figure of value. The stamps of Sardinia were substituted in Modena and Parma in 1860 and those of Italy two years later.

299 *New Brunswick, 1 c, Locomotive, 1860*
300 *New Brunswick, 12 1/2 c, Steamship, 1860*
301 *New Brunswick, 2 c, Queen Victoria, 1863*
302 *New Brunswick, 5 c, Connell, 1860*
303 *New Brunswick, 5 c, Queen Victoria, 1860*
304 *New Brunswick, 17 c, Prince of Wales, 1860*
305 *Nova Scotia, 1 c, 1860*
306 *Trinidad, 4 d, Britannia, 1859*
307 *Trinidad, 5 s, 1869*

300

302

305

306

307

308

309

310

311

312

313

314

315

316

Prior to the 1880s the French colonies made use of a general series of stamps; in the classic period this consisted of the Eagle series inscribed 'Colonies de l'Empire Français'. Even so, this series did not come into use until 1859 and prior to that date only hand-struck postal markings were employed. There was, however, one notable exception to this—the Indian Ocean island of Réunion, which issued its own stamps between 1852 and 1860.

Why Réunion should have been the only French colony to do so is something of a mystery. This remote colony could scarcely be regarded as one of the more important of the French overseas possessions, either in terms of population or commerce. Perhaps the people of Réunion were emulating their neighbours in Mauritius—likewise a remote Indian Ocean island, which had had the distinction of issuing the first British colonial stamps in 1847.

Be that as it may, 15 and 30 centimes 317, 318 stamps were authorized by a decree of M. Doret, governor of Réunion, on December 10th 1851, and this came into force on January 1st 1852. The stamps were type-set in small sheets containing four subjects, each of which varied in slight detail from the others. M. Lahuppe of St Denis, the island's capital, as responsible for producing the stamps. Only one consignment was printed, consisting of 7,500 of each denomination. No postmarks were used, though a few copies have been recorded with pen-cancellations. The stamps were inscribed 'Ile de la Réunion' at the top, and 'Timb.-Poste' and the value at the foot. The centre of the design in each case was made up of fancy printer's ornament. Following the introduction of the French colonial general series in 1859 the distinctive stamps of

308 *Brunswick, ⁴/₄ ggr, 1857*

309 *Brunswick, 1 gr, 1865*

310 *Thurn and Taxis, 30 k, 1859*

311 *Oldenburg, 1 gr, 1862*

312 *Papal States, 4 b, 1852*

313 *Parma, 15 c, 1859*

314 *Modena, 20 c, Cross of Savoy, 1859*

315 *Parma, 20 c, 1859*

316 *Modena, 10 c, newspaper stamp, 1859*

Réunion were suppressed. They had long been a thing of the past when philatelists discovered their existence and though their authenticity was at first doubted they were soon regarded as major rarities. This encouraged the Belgian dealer, J. B. Moens to produce passable imitations, said to have been composed from the original type, but lacking the proper kind of paper. Subsequently four other reprints or outright forgeries of these rare stamps were produced, though only the Moens version of 1864 is likely to confuse the debutant stamp collector.

THE NETHERLANDS

Prior to 1890 (when the operation of the Salic Law debarred the succession of the Dutch Queen Wilhelmina to the grand ducal throne of Luxembourg) the kingdom of the Netherlands and the grand duchy of Luxembourg were joined in a personal union under one ruler. William III came to the throne as king and grand duke respectively in 1849 and the following year important postal reforms were carried out in both his dominions. Postal rates were reduced and made uniform. Curiously enough, at this stage no provision was made for adhesive stamps, although the practice was well established elsewhere in Europe by this time. It was with great reluctance that the Dutch authorities were pressed by Parliament to take the decision to issue stamps. The Post Office felt that the cost of producing stamps would not be justified! Other arguments put forward at the time were that the use of stamps would be too complicated for the general public and that prepayment of postage would offend the recipient.

317 *Réunion, 15 c, 1852*

318 *Réunion, 30 c, 1852*

319 *Netherlands, 5 c, William III, 1852*

320 *Luxembourg, 10 c, 1852*

321 *Barbados, 1/2 d, block of four, 1852*

317

318

319

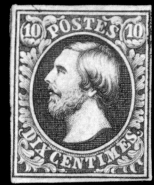

320

321

At length the government gave way and agreed to introduce adhesive stamps, although this measure was delayed until New Year's Day 1852. On that date three stamps,

319 in denominations of 5, 10 and 15 cents, were introduced. The stamps were simply inscribed 'POSTZEGEL' (postage stamp) and bore the long-haired profile of the king. J. W. Kaiser engraved the dies and the stamps were recess-printed at the Mint in Utrecht. The initial series remained in use for twelve years, undergoing various changes in shade, paper and gum, while the plates were extensively retouched. Kaiser also engraved a series in the same denominations which appeared in 1864, using an older, balder profile of the king. The earliest printings of these stamps were made at the Utrecht Mint, but from 1866 the work was handled by Johann Enschede en Zonen of Haarlem.

Enschede, however, did not enjoy a monopoly of Dutch stamp production, since a series of low value stamps, featuring the national coat of arms, was typographed by Virey Brothers of Paris between 1869 and 1876. Nevertheless the higher denominations were recess-printed by Enschede.

32, 333 A new set, from 5 to 50 c, was released in October 1867 and portrayed the king facing left. Though in use only until 1872 this series underwent numerous changes in perforation and paper, while two dies (differing in the shape of the numerals) were used for each value. A novel feature of this series was the use of gold metallic ink for the 50 c—the first occasion on which this

334 device was used. Low values, featuring the coat of arms, appeared in 1869.

LUXEMBOURG

The introduction of stamps in the grand duchy lagged behind Holland by some nine months. The stamps, when they appeared on September 15th 1852, were no less enigmatic, being inscribed merely 'POSTES' at the top. Jacques Wiener designed the

320 10 centimes and 1 silbergroschen stamps which were recess-printed by Schmidt-Bruck of Luxembourg. The use of the French language in conjunction with German currency and the portrait of the Dutch monarch puzzled many of the early stamp collectors, but this combination illustrates the curious political and economic situation of Luxembourg in the mid-nineteenth century. The 10 c stamp prepaid local letters, while the 1 sgr stamp prepaid letters destined to countries of the German-Austrian Postal Union.

Naumann of Frankfurt typographed an

335 arms series in denominations from 1 to 40 c released between 1859 and 1863. Originally released imperforate, these stamps appeared in 1865 with a roulette form of separation. The name of the country was rendered

336 'G. D. de Luxembourg' on the arms series, in upper and lower case lettering on the low values and in capitals on the higher denominations.

BARBADOS

Bearing in mind how revolutionary the idea of cheap postage had been in Britain in 1840, and that thirty years elapsed before the basic rates were in any way reduced, it is all the more creditable that the colony of Barbados should have introduced a ½ d rate as early as April 1852. An Act of the colonial legislature was passed the previous September establishing an inland post on the island and this came into effect six months later. In the interim John Walker, Colonial Secretary of Barbados, visited London and negotiated direct with Perkins

Bacon for a supply of stamps recess-printed in the Britannia design already used for Trinidad and Mauritius. A plate was prepared using the Britannia die, with the name of the island inserted at the foot, and quantities of stamps run off in blue (1 d) and greyish-slate (2 d). Subsequently 321 stamps in green (½ d) were also produced and consigned to Barbados in time for release on April 15th 1852. The original consignment of 1 d and 2 d stamps, however, was lost at sea in the wreck of the S. S. *Amazon*. Little use was found for the greyish-slate stamps most of which were officially bisected and used as 1 d stamps between August and September 1854 during a temporary shortage of that denomination. A brownish-red 4 d was introduced in 1855. Stamps in slate or slate-blue, probably intended as 2 d stamps, were also printed, but as they were too close to the 1 d stamp in colour they were never issued to the public.

The earliest stamps were produced on paper with a pronounced bluish tinge; from 1855 onwards pure white paper was adopted. These undenominated stamps remained in use until 1873 and in the intervening years underwent changes of various sorts. Perforation was adopted in 1860 and a star watermark in 1870. During this period also the colours of the stamps varied considerably. A similar Britannia design, with the name BARBADOS in a curve across the top and the value, in words, at the foot, was 337 introduced in 1858 for 6 d and 1 s stamps, but was extended to the other denominations between 1873 and 1878, when the contracts had passed to De La Rue. A consignment of 1 s stamps, printed in blue instead of black, was produced by Perkins Bacon by mistake. These stamps, which would have easily been confused with the penny stamp, were never issued. Most of them were subsequently destroyed, though a few pen-cancelled examples have survived.

SCINDE

On July 1st 1852 the first stamps of Asia made their appearance. A great deal of mystery still surrounds these stamps, especially in regard to the place of manufacture. By the middle of the nineteenth century, large parts of Asia had come under European influence. It is a little surprising, however, that the part of this great continent in which stamps made their debut should have been a district which had only recently come under European rule. The district of Sind or Scinde (now part of West Pakistan) was conquered by Lord Napier of Magdala in 1850 and a rudimentary postal system known as a 'Dawk' introduced the following year. The introduction of adhesive postage stamps in this remote outpost of empire was due mainly to the far-sightedness of its first governor, Sir Bartle Frere who seems to have acted upon his own initiative and arranged the production of half anna-stamps.

His requests made to the government of British India for more adequate postal facilities fell on deaf ears. In his memoirs he later wrote: 'So, as we believed that post offices were not luxuries, we got the stamps manufactured by De La Rue & Co. and they were issued to stamp-vendors and Government officials ... and every police officer and native district collector of land revenues, customs, etc., was ordered to receive and forward with his own official papers to his immediate official superior all letters bearing these mysterious stamps of the British Government or rather of the Great Company, the Honourable East India Company. Thus every Government office in Scinde became a district post office for stamped letters and the first official who had a real post office at hand sent to it all the stamped letters which he and his subordinates had collected ... The system worked well and of course very cheaply for we got a complete network of post offices and postal lines all over the country without expense.'

Undoubtedly the success of Frere's experiment led the Indian government into introducing postage stamps two years later, and the 'Scinde Dawks' as they are popularly known, were then withdrawn from sale, though examples have been recorded in use as late as 1857. The reference to De La Rue is puzzling, since no mention of the Scinde stamps can be found in the archives of that company and it was not, in fact, until 1854 that De La Rue became involved in stamp printing. The stamps themselves are quite unlike anything ever produced by De La Rue. The first issue consisted of small red circular wafers, of the type used to seal envelopes, with the talismanic emblem of the East India Company embossed within a belt inscribed 'SCINDE DISTRICT DAWK'. Subsequently the stamps were 324 embossed in blue or white in sheet format, so that multiples are known. The stamps of Scinde were suppressed in October 1854, on the introduction of the general series throughout British India.

PORTUGAL

Like its neighbour Spain, Portugal in the mid-nineteenth century was ruled by a woman, Donna Maria II, who had ascended the throne in 1834 at the age of fifteen. From the outset, her reign was beset by civil wars and uprisings and it was not, in fact, till the emergence of the Duke of Saldanha at the head of a coalition ministry

in 1851 that peace returned to that troubled country. During his five years in office Saldanha instituted many important reforms, not the least of which affected the postal services.

Adhesive stamps were introduced on July 1st 1853. The stamps, in denominations of 5, 25, 50 and 100 reis, were design- 323 ed and engraved by Francisco de Borja Freire and recess-printed, with the queen's profile embossed, at the Mint in Lisbon. The inscription consisted of the word 'CORREIO' (posts) at the top and the value at the foot. The initials of the designer and engraver appear on the neck of the bust. Each denomination had a different frame in various fancy shapes. Two versions exist of the 5 r, the second of which, from a worn die, gives the impression of the queen's head being somewhat smaller. All four denominations varied considerably in shade. At the time of the issue of these stamps numeral obliterators were also introduced, ranging from 1 (Lisbon) to 219 (Villa Real de Santo Antonio)—that being the total number of post offices functioning in Portugal in 1853.

Donna Maria did not live very long to see her profile on stamps. She died in November 1853 and was succeeded by her eldest son, Dom Pedro V. Borja Freire 322 engraved new dies with similar frames and a profile of the young king substituted. The Pedro series was not issued until 1855, remaining in use for seven years. The initial printings showed the king with straight hair, but subsequent printings of the 5 and 25 r stamps showed him with curly hair. Two versions of the 25 r of this printing exist, with single or double lines in the network patterns in the corners. As before, numerous shades of these stamps have been recorded, while the 25 r changed from blue to rose in 1858.

Pedro and two of his brothers died in 1861 during a cholera epidemic. A third
338 brother, Dom Luiz, who was absent from the country at the time, succeeded to the throne and reigned till 1889. Again Borja Freire adapted the frames of the preceding series to an embossed profile of the new king, this time facing left, for a series released between 1862 and 1864. A 10 r value was added in 1863. Two types of the 5 r of this series exist, differing in the position of the numerals in relation to the ornament in the bottom left-hand corner.

A new series, designed and engraved by C. Wiener, was introduced in 1866. The king's profile was embossed as before, but the frame was typographed. The series of 1866–70 was distinguished from the issue
339 of 1870–84 by the value labels, which were curved at the ends in the former series and with straight ends in the latter. In 1867 perforation was introduced, although experiments with an unusual form of cross-roulette (*perce en croix*) were made on this series about the same time. Stamps with this roulette were despatched to Madeira and are thus regarded by collectors as distinctive to that island.

CHILE

Although Brazil began issuing stamps in 1843, as we have seen, a further decade elapsed before this example was followed by any other country in Latin America. In the 1840s Chile relied on British post offices in Valparaiso, Caldera and Coquimbo, and the services of the Pacific Steam Navigation Company, for mail communications along its lengthy coastline and to other countries. An internal mail service, however, had been established in Spanish colonial times and it was in connection with

322 *Portugal, 25 r, Pedro V, 1855*

323 *Portugal, 5 r, Maria II, 1853*

324 *Scinde, 1/2 anna, 1852*

325 *Chile, 20 c, Columbus, 1853*

326 *Cape of Good Hope, 4 d, triangular, 1853*

322

323

324

325

326

this service that it was decided, in 1852, to introduce adhesive stamps.

Unlike Brazil, Chile went to Britain for its first stamps, commissioning Perkins Bacon to produce 5 and 10 centavos stamps. Early philatelists were puzzled by the identity of the personage portrayed on them and there was much conjecture over the meaning of the word 'COLON' inscribed above the portrait, some saying that it indicated the carriage of mail to the port of Colon, while others considered it to be an abbreviation for *Colonia* (colony). However, the Ordinance which instituted adhesive stamps stated clearly that Christopher Columbus was to be portrayed on the stamps and 'Colon' was merely his name rendered in Spanish. Columbus was, in fact, portrayed on all Chilean stamps prior to 1910.

Perkins Bacon used an attractive engine-turned background for this design. The same background subsequently served for the first issues of New Zealand and South Australia produced two years later. The stamps were shipped out to Chile in April 1853 and came into use on July 1st. Almost to the end of the classic period this handsome design sufficed for the stamps of Chile and during that period it provided plenty of philatelic interest. In accordance with the normal Perkins Bacon practice the plates were sent out to the country and further consignments of the stamps were recess-printed locally by Narciso Desmadryl. Desmadryl also produced a lithographed version of the 5 c, from transfers taken from the Perkins Bacon plate. In addition printings of the 5 c were made in 1855 by H. C. Gillett and between 1856 and 1862 at the Post Office in Santiago. Perkins Bacon also produced 5 c stamps from an entirely new plate; these stamps may be distinguished from the 1853 printings by

the larger numeral watermark. In January 1862 1 and 20 c values were added to the series. These and a new printing of 10 c stamps were produced by Perkins Bacon; the new 10 c stamps may be distinguished from the earlier version by the larger numeral watermark. A new style of numeral watermark was adopted in 1866 for 5 c stamps printed at the Santiago Post Office from Perkins Bacon plates; again the size and shape of the numeral watermark distinguished the stamps of 1866 from preceding issues.

The first major change in Chile's stamps came in 1867 when a somewhat similar design was recess-printed in denominations of 1, 2, 5, 10 and 20 c by the American Bank Note Co. of New York. Although remaining current for more than a decade this series provided none of the varieties so characteristic of the Perkins Bacon series.

CAPE OF GOOD HOPE

The prepayment of postage by means of adhesive stamps was authorized as early as 1846 and two years later Perkins Bacon were asked to prepare dies and plates for 1 d and 2 d stamps for the Cape of Good Hope. Shortly afterwards, however, these instructions were countermanded and a further four years elapsed before the subject of adhesive postage stamps was resurrected. In August 1852 the Cape authorities again approached Perkins Bacon and commissioned the 1 d and 4 d stamps in the celebrated triangular format. Rough sketches in triangular and pentagonal design were forwarded by Charles Bell, the Surveyor-General of the colony, who believed that the use of abnormal shapes would facilitate the sorting of mail by the largely illiterate native employees of the post office.

William Humphrys engraved Bell's triangular design featuring the seated figure of Hope and the stamps, in denominations of 1 d and 4 d, were recess-printed by Perkins Bacon. The stamps were shipped out to South Africa and placed on sale on September 1st 1853. Anchor watermarked paper with a pronounced bluish tinge was used at first, but white paper was introduced in 1855. At this time the series was augmented by 6 d and 1 s denominations. The 4 d stamp, normally printed in various shades of blue, has also been recorded in black, but nothing is known about this stamp. The Black Fourpence may have been an essay of some sort, but it seems to have been gummed and put into circulation in the normal way. About seven examples have so far been recorded, one of which is in the Mosely Collection at the British Museum. In 1863 the Perkins Bacon contract expired and subsequent printings of the Cape triangulars were made by their rivals, De La Rue, using the original plates. De La Rue printings may be identified by the differences in shades (early printings) and by the somewhat fuzzy appearance of the later printings made from unclean or worn plates.

In the interim, however, a shortage of the London-printed stamps in 1861 was met by the locally improvised 'woodblocks'. The term 'woodblock' is actually a misnomer, since the stamps were typographed from metal stereos, but their comparatively crude appearance was akin to that achieved by engraving on wood, hence the nickname. Errors of colour were caused by the insertion of a stereo of the wrong value in the plate. This gave rise to the 1 d blue and 327 the 4 d red, when the normal colours should have been the reverse.

Not surprisingly, De La Rue were not long in reverting to their more traditional

327 *Cape of Good Hope, woodblock pair showing 4 d error of colour, 1861*

328 *Tasmania, 1 d, 1853*

329 *Tasmania, 4 d, 1853*

330 *Tasmania, 2 d, 1855*

331 *Philippine Islands, 5 c, Isabella II, 1854*

327

328

329

330

331

style of printing, and in 1864 they introduced the rectangular Hope design. Like the triangulars these stamps were designed by Charles Bell. Though lacking the aesthetic qualities of their predecessors the rectangulars were destined to have a long life, surviving in a number of cases as late as 1902.

TASMANIA

Of the six Australian states, three—Tasmania, New South Wales and Victoria—were granted representative government in 1855-6. The first of these had made remarkable progress after the end of the penal settlement in 1852 and rapidly overtook its more sophisticated neighbours on the Australian mainland. Inevitably this progress included a reorganization of the postal administration and culminated in the Act of 1853 authorizing the introduction of adhesive postage stamps. Like New South Wales and Victoria, Tasmania relied heavily on local talent in this matter. C. W. Coard engraved plates for 1 d and 4 d stamps, each subject on the plates of twenty-four stamps being engraved individually. H. and C. Best, proprietors of the *Courier* newspaper in Hobart, recess-printed the stamps which were put on sale on November 1st 1853. The 1 d rate covered letters within the island itself, while 4 d prepaid the postage to the Australian mainland. Both stamps featured a profile of Queen Victoria which can only be described as a crude parody of the royal effigy. The 1 d stamp had a rectangular frame and the 4 d an octagonal frame, both containing the inscription 'VAN DIEMENS LAND' and the denomination in words. Van Diemens Land was the name bestowed on the island in 1742 by Abel Tasman, in honour of the then Governor-General of the Dutch East Indies Company. When the island attained responsible government in 1855 the name was changed in honour of the explorer who discovered it, though this change was not reflected on the stamps for a further three years.

Between 1853 and the end of 1855 the locally produced stamps were subject to a number of changes of paper, shade and state of the plates, the latter wearing out rapidly and requiring a certain amount of re-engraving. These stamps were regarded as little more than a stopgap, for as early as May 1853 the colonial authorities had begun negotiations, through the Colonial Office in London, with Perkins Bacon for a supply of stamps. The negotiations dragged on for eighteen months and it was not until August 1855 that the Perkins Bacon stamps were put into circulation on the island. The stamps, in a large upright format, bore the Chalon portrait of the queen, with an engine-turned background and the name VAN DIEMENS LAND across the top. The stamps were recess-printed in denominations of 1 d, 2 d and 4 d, imperforate, on paper bearing a large star watermark. The plates were shipped out to Tasmania where Messrs Best printed stamps in these designs between 1856 and 1870. Perkins Bacon produced 6 d and 1 s stamps, inscribed 'TASMANIA', in 1858 and, as before, subsequent printings were made in the colony. Apart from the changes of colour, paper and watermark in the long period in which they were current, the stamps of Tasmania are chiefly of interest to philatelists on account of the ingenious methods used to separate them. Between 1864 and 1870 pin-perforation, serrated perforation, oblique roulette, cross-roulette and a very rough roulette (probably performed with a spurrowel) were employed by various postmasters, in addition to more orthodox forms of perforation carried out by J. Walch and Sons of Hobart and R. Harris of Launceston. Perforation of these stamps was taken over by the government at Hobart in 1871 and 6 d and 1 s denominations of this series continued to be issued as late as 1892.

Of the three countries to adopt stamps in 1854 it is significant that none of them was in Europe (where the idea was now well established). On the other hand, all three countries were located in the more remote parts of the world—two in Asia and one in Australia.

THE PHILIPPINE ISLANDS

The Philippine Islands, that were the most advanced of the Spanish overseas possessions, lagged some four years behind the mother country, introducing adhesive stamps on February 1st 1854. The first issue consisted of 5 and 10 cuartos and 1 and 2 reales stamps portraying Queen Isabella II. They were merely inscribed 'CORREOS' (posts), with the date 1854 Y 55 to denote that the stamps were valid for postage during that period only. The stamps were printed in Manila from locally engraved plates and thus (if we uphold the theory that the Scinde Dawks were of British origin) may be regarded as the first stamps to be produced in Asia. Numerous stamps of the same values were lithographed locally between June 1855 and the end of 1863, their common feature being the singularly unflattering profiles of Queen Isabella.

The inscription 'CORREOS INTERIOR' was included on stamps issued between 1859 and 1863 and the 1 r stamps released in February 1863 were inscribed 'PLATA F' (*plata fuerte* = strong silver currency) to differentiate them from values prepaid in

331
343
344

332 *Netherlands, 10 c, 1854*

333 *Netherlands, 10 c, 1867*

334 *Netherlands, 1 1/2 c, 1869*

335 *Luxembourg, 1 c, rouletted, 1870*

336 *Luxembourg, 12 1/2 c, 1859*

337 *Barbados, 1 s, 1866*

338 *Portugal, 5 r, Luiz, 1862*

339 *Portugal, 5 r, 1867*

340 *Cape of Good Hope, 1 d, rectangular, 1864*

341 *Tasmania, 1 s, 1858*

342 *Tasmania, 1 d, 1864*

343 *Philippine Islands, 5 c, 1861*

344 *Philippine Islands, 5 c, 1859*

345 *Philippine Islands, 3 1/8 c, 1864*

346 *India, 1/2 a, 1856*

347 *India, 8 p, 1860*

10 C

POSTZEGEL

NEDERLAND

10 CENT.

333

NEDERLAND

½ CENT

334

G.D. de Luxembourg

1   1

1 CENTIME

G.D. DE LUXEMBOURG

12½   12½
centimes

336

BARBADOS

ONE SHILLING

337

CORREIO

5 REIS

REIS   5   5

PORTUGAL   CORREIO

5   REIS   5

340

341

342

343

344

345

348

349

0

351

352

353

354

355

356

357

358

359

360

361

debased local currency. Stamps for use in Cuba and Puerto Rico followed in 1855 and were also permitted for use in the Philippines; such stamps can only be distinguished by means of the postmark, showing the names of Manila, Cavite or other Filipino towns. A new series, with values inscribed in centimos de peso, was released in January 1864. The stamps, which were typographed by the Sociedad del Timbre, Madrid, were in the curious denominations of 3 $^1/_8$, 6 $^2/_8$, 12 $^4/_8$ and 25 c, made necessary by the introduction of a metric currency in that year. The four denominations were equivalent to the 5 and 10 cuartos and 1 and 2 reales of the preceding issue. Queen Isabella's deposition in Spain resulted in the overprint of various obsolete stamps 'HABILITADO POR LA NACION' (valid for the nation) under the authority of the provisional government. Following the formal abdication of the queen in 1870, stamps portraying the female allegory of Spain were released, in denominations of 5, 10, 20 and 40 centimos de escudo, the unit of currency having been changed yet again.

345

WESTERN AUSTRALIA

In 1852 a proclamation published by the Governor of the colony, Commander Charles FitzGerald, regulated the postal service within Western Australia and laid down rates for inland and local letters. No mention was made in this proclamation regarding adhesive stamps and, in fact, hand-struck markings continued in use for a further two years. Nevertheless it was in that year that the colonial autorities made contact with Perkins Bacon, via Edward Barnard, Agent General for the Colonies in London, and ordered one million penny stamps. This requisition actually stipulated

348 *Norway, 2 s, 1867*

349 *Cuba and Puerto Rico, 10 c, 1868*

350 *New Zealand, 2 d, local printing, 1855*

351 *New Zealand, 2 d, worn plate, 1862*

352 *New Zealand, 6 d, perforated, 1864*

353 *St Helena, 6 d, 1856*

354 *St Helena, 2 d, 1868*

355 *Finland, 5 p, 1866*

356 *Mecklenburg-Schwerin, $^4/_4$ s, 1864*

357 *Mexico, 1 p, Hidalgo, 1864*

358 *Uruguay, 180 c,
Montevideo Sun, tête-bêche pair, 1858*

359 *Uruguay, 12 c, 1864*

360 *Uruguay, 1 c, 1866*

361 *Uruguay, 5 c, 1866*

the design of the proposed stamps, 'the
362 device of which is to be a Black Swan upon
a coloured ground. ...' This distinctive
bird, which gave its name to the original
settlement of the Swan River, was the
emblem of the colony and, as such, was to
appear on all the postage stamps down to
1913 (except for the series of five high
values in 1902).

Perkins Bacon prepared the 1 d stamps,
recess-printed entirely in black, and shipped
them out to Australia in August 1853,
thereby anticipating the Ordinance of the
Legislative Council passed in May 1854
which announced that stamps would be
introduced on August 1st of that year. As
this stamp proved to be quite inadequate to
cover the various postal rates in the colony
a local expedient was resorted to. H. Sam-
son, the government printer at Fremantle
made a lithographic transfer from the swan
motif of the 1 d stamp and pasted them on
to thick card at regular intervals. Octag-
363 onal (4 d) and oval (1 s) frames were then
prepared and pasted on to the cards round
the swan motifs. The work was extremely
intricate and it is hardly surprising that a
number of prominent varieties arose in
which the letters of the frames were distort-
ed. One frame on the sheet of 4 d stamps
was inserted upside down and this gives
364 rise to the so-called 'Inverted Swan' error.
Very few of these errors have been recorded.

A. Hillman lithographed 2 d and 6 d
stamps in 1857 in a similar design. The
first printings of these stamps were imperforate, but various forms of rouletting were
applied to the series in 1858–9. New 2, 4
and 6 d stamps were printed in the colony
in 1860 from plates made by Perkins Bacon.
These were imperforate at first but subsequently various forms of roulette and
perforation were used. Perkins Bacon
printed further quantities of 1, 2, 4, 6 d and

362 *Western Australia, 1 d, 'Black Swan', 1854*

363 *Western Australia, 1 s, 1854*

364 *Western Australia, 4 d,
'Inverted Swan' error, 1854*

362

363

364

1 s stamps in 1861, distinguishable from the earlier stamps and the local printings by their colours and perforations. De La Rue printed these stamps from 1864 onwards, at first on unwatermarked paper and then, from 1865, on Crown CC paper. These handsome stamps remained in use till the 1890s.

INDIA

The example set in Scinde by Sir Bartle Frere soon came to the notice of the postal authorities in Calcutta and in 1853 a Commission was appointed to examine the possibility of extending adhesive stamps to the territory of British India as a whole. Experiments in the production of stamps by embossing (the method which had been adopted for the Scinde Dawks) were made in 1853, but abandoned on the grounds that the process was too slow and laborious. Via the Board of Inland Revenue in London, an approach was made to De La Rue (then engaged in producing their first adhesive stamps, the Receipt stamps of 1853) and eventually this firm secured a contract to print Indian stamps, the beginning of a long association which was to last unchallenged until 1926.

In the meantime, however, experiments in local production culminated in a series of 365, 366 three stamps, (½, 1 and 4 annas), lithographed by Captain H. L. Thuillier at the Surveyor-General's office in Calcutta. A fourth denomination of 2 annas was pro- 367 duced simultaneously at the Calcutta Mint. The printing of these stamps took place in the summer of 1854 and the stamps were first placed on sale on October 1st of that year. Three distinct dies were used in the preparation of both the ½ and 1 a stamps, but it was the 4 annas indigo and red stamp which has provided the greatest variety and interest to philatelists, since four dies were used for the head and two for the frame, often in different combinations. From the combination of Head Die I and Frame Die I comes Asia's most famous error, the so-called 'Inverted Head', resulting from the sheets being inserted in the press upside down after the frames had been printed. Possibly only one sheet of this error escaped undetected, since barely a score of examples have been recorded. They include the remarkable cover, now in the Tapling Collection at the British Museum, which bears two examples of the inverted error side by side.

A standardized design, typographed by De La Rue in denominations of 4 and 8 a, was introduced in October 1855. Further denominations were added from 1856 onwards. The last of these was an 8 pies 346 value in purple issued in May 1860, after the postal administration had been taken over by the Crown; it was intended primar- 347 ily to prepay the soldiers' letter rate to England. In the aftermath of the Indian Mutiny the administration of India passed out of the hands of the East India Company on November 1st 1858 and Lord Canning was appointed the first of a long line of viceroys. No changes appeared in the stamps until 1865, and then only in the adoption of a watermark featuring an elephant's head. The 8 pies stamp of the watermarked series was at one stage sold for 9 p and may be found with various unofficial surcharges of NINE or NINE PIES.

The half-ounce letter rate from India to Britain via Marseilles was fixed at 6 a 8 p and came into effect from August 15th 1863. The 6 a fiscal stamp used on foreign bills was pressed into service as a postage stamp while India waited for supplies of the new denominations. The words FOREIGN and

BILL, which appeared at the top and bottom of the design, were cut off, and the stamps overprinted POSTAGE in green. These stamps were used on letters in conjunction with the 8 p stamp. New 4 a stamps, as well as the 6 a 8 p denomination, were introduced between 1866 and 1867. The dies for several Indian stamps were re-engraved between 1868 and 1878, mainly in the features of the queen's profile and diadem, but it was to be some years after the proclamation of Victoria as Empress of India in 1877 that any significant change was made in the stamps of the country.

NORWAY

Three countries, in different parts of the globe, introduced stamps on New Year's Day 1855. In July 1854 the united kingdom of Norway and Sweden decided to issue adhesive stamps. Curiously enough it was Norway, rather than her more highly developed and more affluent neighbour Sweden, which implemented the resolution first. Uniform rates of postage came into effect on January 1st in Norway, a letter weighing one *lod* being charged 4 skilling. A stamp of this denomination, featuring the lion rampant coat of arms, was engraved by N.A.H. Zarbell and typographed by Wulfsberg of Christiania (Oslo) on paper bearing a lion watermark. This stamp was released imperforate, though examples are known with unofficial rouletting.

368   A new series, ranging from 2 to 8 skilling, was released in 1856. The stamps, typographed by P. A. Nyman at the Swedish Government Offices in Stockholm, bore a profile of King Oscar. These stamps remained in use for several years after Oscar's death in 1859. Under his successor, Charles XV, the coat of arms motif was

365 *India, ¹/₂ a, 1854*
366 *India, 2 a, 1854*
367 *India, 4 a, 1854*
368 *Norway, 4 s, Oscar I, 1856*
369 *Cuba and Puerto Rico, 1 r, 1855*
370 *South Australia, 1 d, 1855*
371 *South Australia, 4 d, 1867*

365

366

367

368

369

370

371

reverted to, in a series of 2, 3, 4, 8 and 24 sk stamps issued between 1863 and 1866. These stamps were originally produced on paper with a watermark of wavy lines in the margins of the sheet, with lions in each corner. Thus the majority of stamps are found without any trace of the watermark. This set was lithographed by C. F. Schwenzen of Christiania. A somewhat similar design, but produced typographically, was used for a series printed by Petersen of Christiania in 1867–8. The 2 sk and some of the 4 sk stamps of the Petersen series may also be found with the marginal watermark, but the majority of the stamps of this issue were printed on unwatermarked paper. This issue continued in use till 1871. Though outside the 'classic' period discussed in this book, the Posthorn and Numeral design, introduced in 1872, is worthy of mention since it has endured down to the present day, undergoing numerous changes in currency, perforation, paper, watermark and method of printing in the course of that time, and holding the world record for philatelic longevity.

CUBA AND PUERTO RICO

Although adhesive stamps had made their appearance in the Philippines in 1854, the Spanish government decided that it would be simpler if one uniform series of stamps was in use throughout the colonial territories. Accordingly a series was introduced on January 1st 1855 which was intended for use not only in the Philippines but also in Cuba and Puerto Rico in the West Indies. The stamps portrayed Isabella II and were similar in design to those currently used in Spain, but with values rendered in the colonial currency of the real plata fuerte (strong silver). The series consisted of ½,

1 and 2 r stamps, but between 1855 and 1860 the 2 r stamps were surcharged Y¼ in Cuba for use on Havana local mail. The surcharge indicated the equivalent of a quarter of a strong silver real, the rate of the local mail service, the Y being the abbrevation for 'Interior', used instead of 'I' to avoid confusion with the numeral 'I'.

A new ¼ r value was introduced in 1862 to replace the surcharged stamps. The design showed Queen Isabella facing to the left, instead of to the right as on the previous issues, and in 1864 a new series was released with a similar portrait in a different frame. The set consisted of ¼, ½, 1 and 2 r values. Two years later the ¼ r value was re-issued overprinted 66 to denote the year of issue. The following year perforation was adopted.

The currency of the Spanish Caribbean colonies was changed in 1866 to the peseta of 100 centimos de escudo, and 5, 10, 20 and 40 c stamps were released in that year. The currency was again changed, in 1871, to the peseta of 100 centimos de peseta, and this resulted in a new series of 12, 25, 50 c and 1 p. As in Spain and the Philippines, stamps were overprinted in 1868–9 to indicate their validity under the provisional government, being superseded in 1870–1 by stamps bearing female allegories of the republic. Separate issues for Cuba and Puerto Rico did not materialize until 1873.

SOUTH AUSTRALIA

In the early 1850s the British colony of South Australia made several notable improvements in communications—a regular bi-monthly mail service linking with Singapore and Sydney (1853), the introduction of uniform rates of postage and postal

treaties with neighbouring colonies (1854)—
all of which paved the way for the release of
adhesive stamps on January 1st 1855.
During 1854 a contract for 1 d, 2 d, 6 d and
1 s stamps had been placed with Perkins
Bacon in London and a consignment was
duly shipped to the colony. The shilling
stamps, printed in violet, were never issued
since it was felt that the colour might be
confused with the dark blue of the 6 d
denomination. The majority of the 500,000
shilling stamps were destroyed in 1857, but
a few examples have survived.

The stamps were recess-printed in Perkins
Bacon's inimitable manner, the background
being similar to that already used for Chile
and soon also to be used for New Zealand.
William Humphrys engraved the profile of
Queen Victoria from a drawing by Henry
Corbould. Between 1856 and 1858 further
printings of these stamps (and shilling
stamps in orange) were made by the
Government Printer at Adelaide using the
Perkins Bacon plates. The local printings
differ markedly in shade from the London
printing. Rouletting as a means of separation was adopted in 1858. At first the
stamps thus rouletted were those of the
1856–8 local printings, but between 1860
and 1869 new printings in different shades
were also rouletted. Finally, between 1867
and 1871, stocks of obsolete imperforate
stamps, or stamps which had already been
rouletted, were perforated in various gauges.
Examples are known which are perforated
horizontally and rouletted vertically. South
Australia was the last of the Australian
colonies to adopt perforation ; its convenience to the user, however, was far
outweighed by the exceeding complexity
of the perforations, with their myriad
combinations and permutations of different
gauges, and this continued to be a feature
of South Australian stamps down to 1913

when they were superseded by the Commonwealth issues.

New values were added to the series in
1860–7. Two designs were used to produce
4 d and 2 s stamps (1867) and 9 d and 10 d
stamps (1860–6). The 10 d was created by
printing the 9 d in yellow instead of lilac
and surcharging it with the new value in
words. The same expedient was adopted
in 1868 when the 4 d was printed in blue
instead of purple and surcharged to convert
it to a 3 d denomination.

BREMEN

By the mid-1850s stamps had extended to
most of the principal German states. The
first of the free cities, however, did not
introduce stamps until 1855 and the others
followed at a considerably later date. The
important seaport of Bremen adopted
stamps on April 10th 1855. Prior to that
date the cosmopolitanism of Bremen was
reflected in the existence of post offices and
postal agencies of France, Berg, Hanover,
Prussia and Thurn and Taxis at one time or
another, in the city. The agreement with
the Counts of Thurn and Taxis was terminated in 1855 and Bremen assumed sole
responsibility for its own postal arrangements. Bremen's first stamp consisted of a
3 grote value, printed in black on either
horizontally or vertically laid blue paper.
Those of the earliest printing, on horizontal
paper, may be found with a lily watermark
covering four stamps. There were three
different types of the 3 grote stamp. They
vary in the shape of the central ornament at
the foot of the stamp below the EM of
BREMEN. All three types are found with
and without a broken line under the words
'STADTPOST AMT'.

Bremen's international character was reflected in the complicated currency used there. The basic unit was the gold thaler (equivalent to 3.32 marks), which was divided into 72 grote. But for foreign mail routed via Great Britain a currency based on 22 grote equal to 10 silbergroschen was used. This explains why stamps in denominations of 5 and 7 grote and 5 silbergroschen were introduced between 1856 and 1861. Until 1861 stamps were issued imperforate, but that year they were produced with a form of roulette known as *perces en scie* (saw-tooth). Between 1861 and 1864, 2 and 10 grote and 5 silbergroschen stamps were issued perforated 13. All of Bremen's stamps were lithographed by G. Hunkel of Bremen and featured the key emblem in various different frames.

After the Seven Weeks' War of 1866, Bremen joined the North German Confederation and ceased issuing its own stamps on December 31st 1867.

SWEDEN

As early as 1847 Peter Martenson proposed in the Swedish riksdag the adoption of postal reforms on British lines, and the introduction of adhesive stamps. Procrastination in the Swedish parliament, however, delayed the introduction of this measure for eight years. Martenson died of cholera in 1854, though not before he had seen important steps taken which led to the issue of Sweden's first stamps. Postal rates were reorganized in 1853–4, paving the way for adhesive stamps which were introduced on July 1st 1855.

Sweden's stamps in the classic period may justifiably be regarded as the world's most aristocratic stamps, since their production was entrusted to a nobleman, Count Per Ambjorn Sparre who had secured a contract in 1851 to produce Sweden's banknotes. All the stamps of Sweden, from 1855 to 1871, were typographed by Count Sparre or his associates, G. and E. Scheutz. The first series consisted of 3, 4, 6, 8 and 24 skilling stamps depicting the triple crown emblem of Sweden. Little use could be found for the lowest denominations, other than for supplementary postage on mail going abroad, and the majority of the printing was subsequently destroyed. Normally printed in green, the 3 sk gave rise to one of the world's most celebrated errors, the 3 sk in yellow. The only known example of this error was discovered by a schoolboy, Georg Wilhelm Backman, in 1885 on a letter from Nya Kopparberget to Romfartuna. Backman sold the stamp to a Stockholm dealer for 7 kronor, and lived to see this unique item change hands for about $10,200 (£5,000) in 1937 when King Carol of Romania purchased it. The stamp is thought to have been sold in 1950 for $55,080 (£27,000). The stamp is now known to have been printed in 1857 when a 3 sk cliché was inserted by mistake in a plate of the 8 sk. It is not known whether this mistake was detected at the time, but as a result of Sweden's adoption of decimal currency the following year new stamps in öre values were released, and the last printing of the 8 sk must therefore have had a short life. The öre series, from 5 to 50 ö, were in the same designs as the preceding series. Additional denominations of 3, 17 and 20 ö were released between 1862 and 1866 in a new design showing the lion couchant of Sweden. Two types exist of the 3 ö, differing in the shape of the ornament in the top right-hand corner of the frame. A government issue of local stamps, for use in Stockholm, was made in 1856.

The most conservative country in the classic period, so far as the release of new designs was concerned, was New Zealand which, in a period spanning almost twenty years, made use of one design. For the 1 d, 2 d 374 and 1 s stamps, introduced on July 18th 1855, Perkins Bacon used the Chalon portrait of Queen Victoria on a background similar to that already adopted by South Australia. The combination was an exceptionally pleasing one, so it is hardly surprising that it survived in use for so long. To the collector, however, the Chalon Heads or Full Faces, as they are popularly known, present many problems of classification. Perkins Bacon's London printings have a full rich colour which distinguish them readily from the subsequent printings, made in New Zealand. The first local printing, by J. Richardson of Auckland, was made on blue paper. In 1857 Perkins 350 Bacon star watermarked paper was used for a printing of 1 d stamps, but in a dull orange shade which is quite different from 351 the original dull carmine. Subsequent printings by Richardson were made on unwatermarked paper and include a 6 d brown, added to the series in 1859. Experiments with various forms of rouletting or perforation were made in this period.

John Davies took over the printing contract in 1862 and subsequent issues were produced by him at the General Post Office in Auckland. Davies used paper watermarked with a large star similar to that used by Perkins Bacon. Again the shades of the stamps are an important guide to classification. Only the first printings by Davies were imperforate, those from June 1862 onwards being perforated or rouletted in various ways. A small printing of certain denominations was

372 *Sweden, Stockholm local stamp, 1856*

373 *Sweden, 24 s, 1855*

374 *New Zealand, 1 d, London printing, 1855*

375 *Bremen, 5 g, 1856*

376 *Finland, 5 k, 1856*

377 *Danish West Indies, 3 c, 1855*

378 *Mecklenburg-Schwerin, 5 s, 1856*

372

373

374

375

376

377

378

made in 1862 on distinctive pelure unwatermarked paper. A 3 d value was introduced the same year. In 1864 a watermark consisting of the letters NZ was adopted, though further printings of all denominations were made on star paper from then 352 until 1867. These later star watermarked stamps can be distinguished from their predecessors by means of their different gauge of perforation. Further combinations of paper, perforation, shade and watermark continued to characterize the Chalon Head stamps of New Zealand until 1874 when they were superseded by a series typographed in Wellington, from dies manufactured in London by De La Rue.

DANISH WEST INDIES (VIRGIN ISLANDS)

Four years after the mother country, adhesive stamps were extended to the Danish West Indies (now the United States Virgin Islands). In view of the great importance of the islands to postal communications in the West Indies and Latin America, it is surprising that adhesive stamps were so long in being adopted. At that time most of the mail to and from the Caribbean area was routed through the British postal agency in St Thomas, the chief island of the group. Mail handled by this agency bore hand-struck marks and British adhesives were not introduced until 1865.

377 The stamp released by the Danish colonial authorities in November 1855 was a 3 cents value, intended for local, internal mail. The stamp was typographed by H. H. Thiele of Copenhagen in various shades of carmine or crimson, on hand-made paper covered with a burelage of brown-orange or orange-yellow wavy lines. When the sheets of stamps arrived in the colony it was found that the climate had caused them to stick together. They were immersed in water to soak them apart, and then dried and regummed. This accounts for the various types of gum found on unused specimens, ranging from white to deep brown. The stamps with white gum were those which did not require to be soaked apart and examples are comparatively rare.

A new type of white paper was used after 1866. It is easily distinguished from the earlier hand-made paper. The 3 c stamps, in a design which closely resembled the contemporary Danish series, continued in use till 1873, when a crowned numeral design, also on the Danish model, was adopted. In the late 1860s a postal service operated by Robert Todd between St Thomas, La Guaira and Porto Cabello on the coast of South America used distinctive stamps depicting a steamship. These stamps were local in status and are therefore omitted from the standard stamp catalogues, but possess considerable interest to students of Caribbean philately.

ST HELENA

The South Atlantic island of St Helena, in the middle of the nineteenth century, was an important port of call for shipping plying between Europe and South Africa. After the Suez Canal was opened in 1869 St Helena's importance declined considerably, but in its heyday the island gave anchorage to as many as a thousand ships each year. In 1854 the letter rate from the island to Britain was 6 d per half ounce. No local mail service existed and therefore, when adhesive stamps were being considered, 6 d was deemed to be the only denomination required. Perkins Bacon recess-printed a stamp of this value, using a new profile of Queen Victoria against a background which was comparatively coarse by Perkins Bacon standards. The stamps were shipped out to the island and were put on sale on New Year's Day 1856. At first they were imperforate but perforations were introduced 353 in 1861.

Two important changes came about in 1863. The contract to print the stamps passed to De La Rue, who continued to use the Perkins Bacon plate till 1894. New postal rates, ranging from 1 d for soldiers' letters to 1 s for half-ounce letters to Britain, were introduced in 1863, thereby necessitating new stamps. However, in an example of official parsimony unparalleled 354 anywhere else in the world, St Helena continued to make use of the 6 d stamp, printed in various colours and surcharged with new values in words or figures.

It says a very great deal for the quality and standards of the original Perkins Bacon workmanship that the 6 d plate could have lasted in use for almost forty years. During that period variety was added by changes in colour, the use of first Crown CC and then Crown CA watermarks, and a host of different gauges of perforation. Throughout that period the only unsurcharged stamps were the 6 d which continued in various shades of blue till 1889 when the colour was changed to grey. In fairness it should be stated that St Helena could not afford the luxury of new stamp designs and the high cost which that entailed. It is significant that sizeable quantities of the various issues were subsequently destroyed, the numbers surcharged having greatly exceeded the actual requirement. Throughout the nineteenth century the greatest need continued to be for 6 d and 1 s stamps.

FINLAND

Although Finland throughout the nineteenth century was administered as a dependency of Russia, it possessed considerable autonomy, not the least being in postal matters, and was often far in advance of Russia in this field. The stamped stationery of 1845 has already been mentioned; ten years later the lead of the other Scandinavian countries in adopting adhesive stamps was followed by Finland. An Imperial manifesto of February 1856 permitted the issue of stamps in the grand duchy of Finland for use on foreign as well as domestic correspondence. C. M. Mellgren engraved dies for 5 and 10 kopek stamps showing the 376 Finnish arms in a horizontal oval. The value inscribed in the Roman and Cyrillic alphabets was placed at the sides of the oval. The stamps were typographed at the Stamped Paper Office of the Finnish Treasury, on laid or wove paper, by means of a small hand-press, producing a single impression with each stroke. Narrow strips of paper were used to print two rows of ten stamps in a *tête-bêche* setting. Few post offices possessed postmarks prior to 1859 and thus the majority of the stamps are found with cancellation effected by pen-strokes.

A new series was released in January 1860, featuring the coat of arms in an upright frame with the value in Roman and Cyrillic lettering as before. The stamps were typographed on tinted paper and several prominent shade varieties have been recorded. A curious method of separation was adopted for this series. Altogether five different types of serpentine roulette were used, varying in length shape and size of 'teeth'. The stamps consisted of 5 and 10 k denominations, but following the change to the markka of 100 penni in 1866, stamps of

355 5, 8, 10, 20 and 40 p in the same design were issued. A similar design, but with a rectangular instead of oval frame round the coat of arms, was used for the 1 m value. This series remained in use till 1875. During the nine years of their currency these stamps varied considerably in shade, paper and serpentine roulette. Stamps with missing teeth are relatively common and are worth much less than perfect specimens.

MECKLENBURG-SCHWERIN

From Mecklenburg-Schwerin, which began issuing stamps on July 1st 1856, came a novel device in the form of a schilling stamp divided into four quarter-schilling portions. Perhaps the idea for this unusual stamp was inspired by the bipartite stamps of Geneva (the so-called 'Double Geneva'), though each quarter formed a tiny stamp on its own, and there was no band or inscription joining the four quarters into a single entity, as in the Genevan stamps. At
378 the same time 3 and 5 s stamps in a more orthodox format were issued. The stamps all featured the bull's head emblem of the grand duchy and were typographed at the Prussian State Printing Works from dies engraved by Otto of Güstrow. Though Otto never had the honour of actually printing the stamps for his own country, it is interesting to note that he printed the first stamps of the Transvaal some thirteen years later.

The stamps of Mecklenburg-Schwerin were originally imperforate but various forms of rouletting were used from 1864
356 onwards. A new four quarter shilling stamp, with a plain instead of shaded background, was released in 1864 and two years later a 2 s denomination was added to the series. The grand duchy joined the North German Con-

federation in 1867 and ceased to issue its own stamps.

CORRIENTES

The first of the states of the Argentine Confederation to issue stamps was Corrientes which introduced a 1 real stamp in August 1856. The stamp, depicting the goddess Ceres, was a blatant imitation of the contemporary French series perpetrated by Matthew Pipet who engraved the die for the Corrientes State Printing Office. The instability of the currency used in Corrientes was reflected in the continual changes of denomination on the stamps. The original 379 issue was inscribed 'UN REAL M. C.', the real M. C. being worth 50 centavos in paper money. The stamp was re-issued in February 1860 with the value tablet crossed out by hand and was sold for 3 centavos fuertes ('strong' or silver centavos). Between 1860 and 1871 the stamps were printed in black on paper of various colours, with the value tablet completely erased from the design. Initially they were printed on blue paper and sold for 3 centavos, but in January 1864 the colour was changed to green and the stamps sold for 5 centavos. This was reduced to 2 centavos in February 1864. The colour was changed again to lemon-yellow in 1867, but the value remained at 2 centavos. The colour changed yet again, between 1873 and 1878, and two years later the stamps of Corrientes were suppressed by the central government.

MEXICO

Almost a decade after stamps were provided by the United States Post Office, the idea spread south of the Rio Grande. Much of the external postal traffic of Mexico in the mid-nineteenth century was handled by the British post offices in Tampico and Vera Cruz, yet it is surprising that it took so long for stamps to be adopted by the Mexican postal administration. The first series, released on August 1st 1856, consisted of ½, 380 1, 2, 4 and 8 reales values printed in sheets of sixty with the stamps set wide apart. The design showed Miguel Hidalgo, the patriot of the War of Independence, with CORREOS MEXICO at the top and the value in words at the foot. When second settings of the 1 and 2 r stamps were made in larger sheets than before, the stamps were set close together and there were considerable variations in shade. Many of the higher denominations were bisected and used at half their face value.

A curious feature of Mexican stamps from 1856 to 1883 was the overprint of district names as a security measure. In 1864 the date and a consignment number were also added to the overprint. Most district offices, on sending stamps to places under their control, overprinted numbers on the stamps corresponding to numbers on their invoices, in addition to the consignment number overprinted at Mexico City. Such numbers are termed sub-consignment numbers. This cumbersome system continued officially till 1882 but in some districts the practice continued till 1886.

The colours of the first Hidalgo series were changed in 1861. Three years later the American Bank Note Co. recess-printed a 357 new series for Mexico. The stamps were similar in design to the previous issue. These stamps could only be released in the districts of Monterey and Saltillo, held by the republicans at that time. Napoleon III took advantage of the American Civil War and the civil disorders in Mexico to make

379

380

381

382

the Archduke of Austria, Maximilian, Emperor of Mexico. The republican government had run into serious financial difficulties and France, a major creditor, landed troops and rapidly overran the country. Maximilian's reign was short-lived; he fled from the capital in 1867 and in May of that year was executed by a republican firing squad at Queretaro. During his reign Mexico had a series of stamps featuring the eagle emblem. Subsequently a lithographed series portraying the Emperor Maximilian was introduced in August 1866, with values inscribed in decimal currency of 7, 13, 25 and 50 centavos. Later printings of the Maximilian stamps were recess-printed between October 1866 and April 1867.

After the withdrawal of French troops and the downfall of Maximilian the republic was restored under Benito Juarez. The first stamps issued by the new republic consisted of the 1861 Hidalgo series overprinted 'MEXICO' in Gothic lettering. An entirely new series portraying Hidalgo was released in September 1868, lithographed in denominations of 6, 12, 25, 50 and 100 c. There were two versions of each denomination, showing either a thin figure of value without a stop or a thick figure of value with a stop. Both versions are known either imperforate or perforated in various gauges. The combinations of district name, consignment and sub-consignment numbers and date add considerably to the complexity of these stamps. In 1867–8 local issues were made in Chiapas, Chihuahua, Cuernavaca and Guadalajara.

URUGUAY

The stamps of Uruguay had been in use for eight years before the name of the country appeared on them. This in itself was not unusual in the nineteenth century, but what makes the early stamps of Uruguay stand out is the fact that the first issues were inscribed with the mode of conveyance, while subsequent issues bore the name of the capital city rather than the country.

A common feature of all Uruguayan stamps from 1856 to 1864 was a chubby-faced sun surrounded by rays. The first series, consisting of 60 and 80 centavos and 1 real denominations, were inscribed 'DILIGENCIA', denoting that mail thus franked would be transported by *diligencias* (stagecoaches). This was confirmed in an official notice, published a fortnight after the stamps were put on sale, stating that letters sent to the provinces by *diligencia* should be properly checked at the agencies or the head office. The stamps were lithographed by Mege & Willems of Montevideo. The 80 c value was created by erasing the value on 60 c transfers and inserting the new denomination. The same procedure was followed with the 1 r, the entire value tablet instead of the numerals being erased. New 60 c stamps were issued a year later, from entirely new transfers in a slightly redrawn design. Additional denominations of 120, 180 and 240 c were released in March 1858 in a somewhat larger design inscribed 'MONTEVIDEO' at the top and 'CORREO' (posts) at the side. One example (formerly in the Ferrary Collection) has been recorded of the 180 c in the colour of the 240 c stamp. The layout of the sheets of the 120 and 180 c stamps was peculiar, consisting of seventy-eight stamps in thirteen rows of six. Moreover, each sheet contained one inverted stamp, thus creating *tête-bêche* varieties.

A smaller version of the Montevideo Sun series was lithographed in July 1859 with thin figures and values in centesimos. In 1861–2 a similar series, but with thick

381

382

383, 384

358

figures, was produced. Mege & Willems
359 printed a low value series in 1864 consisting
of 6, 8, 10 and 12 c denominations, featuring
the national coat of arms and inscribed
'REPUBLICA ORIENTAL' (Eastern Republic). As yet the name of the country
itself was not regarded as sufficiently important to appear on stamps. A further two
years elapsed before the stamps bore the
name. The series of 1866 was printed in
Britain, but instead of going to Perkins
Bacon or De La Rue, the Uruguayan authorities approached the Scottish firm of
Maclure, Macdonald in Glasgow. The
360 stamps, in numeral designs from 5 to 20 c,
361 were lithographed in Glasgow and shipped
out to Uruguay imperforate. Subsequent
consignments were perforated in London
prior to shipment or perforated by Mege
& Willems in Montevideo. Apart from
the numerous variations in perforation these
stamps bristle with errors, particularly in
the spelling of the word 'CENTESIMOS'
which formed a continuous background of
tiny lettering on the 5 and 10 c values.

The numeral series was put on sale on
January 10th 1866, but this did not prevent
the release ten days earlier of a totally unnecessary and highly speculative series of
provisional surcharges, regarded in retrospect as one of the earliest attemps by a
postal administration to contrive the market
artifically for the sake of revenue from
collectors.

NEWFOUNDLAND

The fourth of the British colonies in North
America to adopt stamps, Newfoundland,
followed the example of New Brunswick
and Nova Scotia in commissioning Perkins
Bacon to print its stamps, released on New
Year's Day 1857. Two factors influenced

385 *Newfoundland, 3 d, 1857*
386 *Newfoundland, 1 d, 1857*
387 *Ceylon, 1 d, 1857*
388 *Natal, 3 d, 1859*
389 *Ceylon, 4 d, strip of four, 1859*

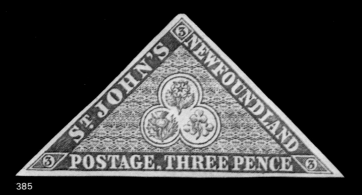

385

386

387

388

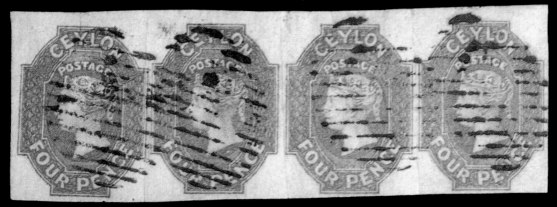

389

the choice of design—the verbose inscription which included not only the name of the colony but also its chief town, and economy in the production which was beginning to be almost obsessive with Perkins Bacon. The problem of cramming the inscription 'ST JOHN'S NEWFOUND-

386 LAND' and the value expressed in words on to the stamps was solved fairly ingeniously by William Humphrys who engraved the dies. The need for economy, dictated partly by the limited resources of Newfoundland and partly by the policy of Perkins Bacon, resulted in the 1 d stamp being adapted from the design of the New Brunswick and Nova Scotia series. The 3 d

385 was triangular in format and obviously leaned heavily on the Cape of Good Hope triangulars for inspiration. The remaining

393, 394 denominations of 2, 4, 5, 6½, 8 d and 1 s were in an upright format with the heraldic flowers of the United Kingdom on an engine-turned background reminiscent of the stamps of Chile, South Australia and New Zealand. The earliest printings were on thick paper but thin paper was adopted in 1860 and the following year the colours of the stamps were changed. A curious feature of Newfoundland's early stamps was the use of a uniform colour for the majority of denominations—scarlet-vermilion (1857), orange-vermilion (1860) and rose-lake (1861).

The monotony of the early issues gave way, in 1866, to refreshing pictorialism in a series ranging from 2 to 24 cents, recess-printed by the American Bank Note Co. of New York. Each design had an irregular frame-line. Different portraits of Queen

96, 397 Victoria graced the 12 and 24 c, while her
395 late Consort, Prince Albert, appeared on
90-392 the 10 c. Codfish, seal and fishing schooner formed the subjects of the 2, 5 and 13 c values. A 1 c stamp featuring the Prince of

Wales (later King Edward VII) in Highland 398 costume was added to the series in 1868. This attractive series, with its mixture of local publicity and royal portraiture, set the 399 pattern for Newfoundland's stamps down to 1947 when the colony joined the Confederation of Canada.

CEYLON

An Ordinance made in May 1854 in Ceylon announced changes in postal rates which foreshadowed the introduction of adhesive stamps. The Acting Postmaster General of the island, Mr G. G. Fraser, wrote to London requesting a supply of 60,000 of the embossed 6 d stamp then used in Britain. He asked that the stamps be overprinted CEYLON. Although this application was approved by the Colonial Office it was rejected by the Board of Inland Revenue at Somerset House, where the 6 d stamp was printed. Subsequently the requisition for 6 d stamps was passed to Perkins Bacon who utilized the background of their Pacific Steam Navigation Co. stamps, in conjunction with a sensitive profile of the queen by Humphrys, to produce some of the most handsome stamps from the classic period. A consignment of 60,000 stamps was shipped to Ceylon in August 1855 and arrived at Colombo the following December. For this reason many of the older catalogues and philatelic textbooks give 1855 as the year of issue of the first Ceylonese stamp, but in fact it was not put on sale until April 1st 1857. The inordinate delay is inexplicable, especially since there was considerable agitation in the island's newspapers urging the introduction of the stamps. A 1 d stamp in a similar design 387 was issued in August 1857, both stamps being produced on blued paper. White paper was used for later printings, as well as for 2 d, 5 d, 10 d and 1 s stamps released in the same year.

Contrary to the usual custom, the contract for Ceylon's first series was shared with another printer, De La Rue, who typographed a ½ d stamp issued in October 1857. This was De La Rue's first contract awarded through the Crown Agents. Although they were by this time also printing stamps for India it seems curious that they should have been asked to print the Ceylon ½ d.

400

389 Perkins Bacon recess-printed 4 d, 8 d, 9 d, 1 s, 9 d and 2 s stamps in an irregular frame (subsequently used also for Tasmania), with a profile of Queen Victoria. The earliest printings of these stamps were imperforate, though the ½ d, 1 d and 2 d are known rouletted unofficially. Perforation was adopted in 1861, various gauges being used. De La Rue took over the Perkins Bacon plates in 1862; De La Rue printings may be recognized by the smooth unwatermarked paper and different gauge of perforation.

In September 1864 a 10 d denomination was added to the series. It was recessprinted by Perkins Bacon but perforated by De La Rue. Between 1863 and 1867 De La Rue reprinted the series on paper watermarked Crown CC. The 1867 printings were made on a distinctive hand-made paper.

In 1866 De La Rue brought out the first two values of a new series, using their typographical process. The 1 d and 3 d stamps bore profiles of Queen Victoria engraved by Joubert de la Ferté. The Ceylon 'Pence' series continued to the end of the classic period, being superseded by an entirely typographed set produced by De La Rue in 1872 following the conversion of the island's currency to the rupee of 100 cents.

NATAL

Between 1845 and 1850 two postal services were organized in the South African colony of Natal, by the military garrison and by the Pietermaritzburg newspaper *The Natal Witness* respectively. Both services were suppressed in 1850 when the colonial government instituted a regular service linking Pietermaritzburg and Durban. Hand-struck markings were used to indicate prepayment of postage until May 1857 when a series of locally produced adhesives was introduced.

The first stamps of Natal were embossed in relief on paper of various colours. The dies, engraved in London by William Wyon, were similar to those then in use for stamping legal documents, and were struck by Messrs May and Davis at the Natal Treasury in Pietermaritzburg, the denominations being 1 d blue, 3 d pink, 6 d green, 9 d blue and 1 s buff. The 1 d changed colour to rose in 1859, to avoid confusion with the 9 d denomination, and two years later the embossed design was revived for 1 d on buff paper, as a result of a temporary shortage of the stamps which by that time were being supplied from London.

Perkins Bacon were commissioned to produce 1 d and 3 d stamps and these were put into circulation in 1859. These stamps reproduced the Chalon portrait of Queen Victoria against a background of vertical engine-turning. A 6 d denomination in this design was added to the series in 1861. De La Rue took over the printing contract in 1863 and produced these stamps, recognizable by the Crown CC watermark (the Perkins Bacon issues were either unwatermarked or bore a small crown watermark). As usual De La Rue soon switched to their favourite process of surface-printing, for a 1 s stamp introduced in 1864, but the recess-printed Chalon Heads continued to

388

be used as late as 1895 for certain denominations. In 1867 the Chalon series was released with the overprint POSTAGE in various styles and sizes of lettering. This was done to prevent the public using the stamps indiscriminately for revenue purposes and vice versa. The 1 d stamp, in yellow instead of lake, was intended for fiscal use, but conversely is thought to have been postally used in 1869.

PERU

As early as March 1851 the Postmaster General of Peru, M. A. Davila, proposed to his Government that the adoption of adhesive stamps would be of assistance to members of the public wishing to send letters abroad and would also simplify the services of the couriers of Lima and Callao. On May 16th of that year Davila received a letter from the Ministry of the Government sanctioning his proposals and instructing him to take the matter further with the Treasury Department. Nevertheless a further six years elapsed before Davila's proposals were implemented. Eventually the Peruvian Council of Ministers passed decrees on October 19th 1857 authorizing the use of stamps. A further six months elapsed before Peru began issuing its own stamps, but in the interim the Postmaster General introduced an experimental measure on a modified postal system operating between Lima and Chorillos only. In connection with this service he obtained a quantity of stamps from the agent of the Pacific Steam Navigation Company. These stamps, in denominations of 1 real blue and 2 reales brown-red, had been ordered by the steamship company from Perkins Bacon in London but had not yet put them into service. Davila published a circular on November 23rd 1857 announcing that these stamps would be available from December 1st onward for correspondence between Lima and Chorillos.

A few of these stamps were subsequently used by the company and may be recognized by the oval numeral obliterators. The stamps used by the Peruvian Post Office bore the names of Lima and Callao, the former being found with or without a date. The stamps featured a steamship in a transverse oval surrounded by engine-turning. The denomination given in reales and onza de peso surmounted the oval and the initials of the company PSNC appeared in the corners. These stamps are known in other colours on various types of paper but though prepared for use were never actually issued.

The experiment having proved successful the Peruvian Post Office prepared a set of stamps in denominations of 1 dinero, 1 peseta and ½ peso, lithographed by Emilio Prugue of Lima and introduced on March 1st 1858. The stamps featured the Peruvian arms. In the plate of one hundred of the 1 peseta stamps the first five subjects were ½ peso stamps by mistake. This gives rise to the ½ peso in rose-red instead of yellow. *Se-tenant* pairs of the ½ peso and 1 peseta stamps are among the major rarities of Peru. Modified designs of the arms series were issued in 1859–60 and in 1862 a new version of the 1 d was produced in which the frame was lithographed and the coat of arms embossed in colourless relief. The stamps of 1858–63 were inscribed 'PORTE FRANCO' (postage free) and the name of the country was not incorporated until 1866 when a new series was recess-printed by the American Bank Note Co. The currency was reformed on the basis of the peso or sol of 100 centavos. The recess series, in denominations of 5, 10 and 15 c, featured vicuñas in a natural setting—an early example of pictorialism. Nevertheless 1 dinero stamps in the embossed arms series continued in use, the colour being changed from red to green in 1868.

The last issue made by Peru in the classic period consisted of 5 c stamps released in 1870. The design featured the national arms surmounted by a locomotive, with the inscription 'CHORILLOS LIMA CALLAO' round three sides of the frame. This stamp was intended for use on letters conveyed by the recently inaugurated railroad between the three cities named. As a result, it has sometimes been claimed that this stamp was a commemorative issue but such was not the case.

This stamp was lithographed with the arms and locomotive embossed in colourless relief as before. This technique, unique to the Peruvian stamps of 1862–73, was effected on a Lecocq machine imported from Paris. The Lecocq machine printed stamps one at a time on a continuous band of paper about 24 mm wide. Thus blocks or multiples other than pairs or strips of these stamps are unknown.

RUSSIA

Few countries can have approached the decision to release adhesive stamps as cautiously as Russia. Stamped stationery had been introduced in St Petersburg in 1845 but a further thirteen years elapsed before Russia saw fit to use adhesives. It was, in fact, left to the grand duchy of Finland (see page 202) to pioneer adhesive stamps in the Tsarist Empire. On December 10th 1857 according to the Julian calendar (December 20th in the Western or Gregorian calendar) Russia finally took the plunge and issued a 10 kopek stamp featuring the Imperial

390 *Newfoundland, 2 d, Codfish, 1866*
  (with imprint of American Bank Note Co.)

391 *Newfoundland, 5 c, Seal, 1866*

392 *Newfoundland, 13 c, Schooner, 1866*

393 *Newfoundland, 4 d, 1862*

394 *Newfoundland, 6 d, 1862*

395 *Newfoundland, 10 c, Prince Albert, 1866*

396 *Newfoundland, 12 c, Queen Victoria, 1866*

397 *Newfoundland, 24 c, Queen Victoria, 1866*

398 *Newfoundland, 1 c, Prince of Wales, 1868*

399 *Newfoundland, 6 c, Queen Victoria, 1870*

400 *Ceylon, 1/2 d, 1857*

401 *Natal, 1 d,* POSTAGE *overprint, 1869*

402 *Peru, 2 r, Pacific Steam Navigation Co, 1857*

403 *Peru, 1 p, 1863*

404 *Peru, 5 c, 1866*

405 *Peru, 10 c, 1866*

406 *Russia, 5 k, 1863*

407 *Naples, 1/2 t, Victor Emmanuel II, 1861*

390

391

392

393

394

395

396

397

398

399

400

401

402

403

404

405

406

407

408

409

410

411

412

413

414

415

416

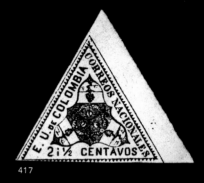

417

418

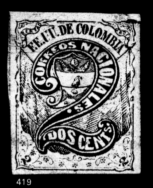

419

420

421

422

423

arms. The stamp, designed by F. M. **425** Kepler, was typographed at the Imperial Government Printing Works and was originally released imperforate. Some ten days later stamps perforated 14½ or 15 were put on sale, and 20 and 30 k values at the same time. The stamps bore a numeral watermark, consisting respectively of the figures 1, 2 or 3. Contrary to normal practice this watermark was formed by a thickening of the paper. The stamps were typographed in two colour combinations, with the double-headed eagle embossed in colourless relief. This attractive design, with variations, remained in use in Russia until the Revolution of 1917; indeed, the 'arms' stamps of Imperial Russia survived well into the Bolshevik period, being sold in April 1922, for example, at one hundred thousand times face value during the inflation of that time.

Unwatermarked paper was adopted in October 1858 and in 1864–5 the design was redrawn to include a background network. A sheet watermark extending over eight stamps was introduced in 1868. New designs for lower denominations were produced in the same period. A 5 k stamp, **406** prepaying local correspondence in Moscow and St Petersburg, was issued in July 1863. Inscribed 'Marka Gorod Pochti' (town postage stamp) this stamp was typographed in black and blue and featured the Imperial eagle. A month after its release it was authorized for general use and was withdrawn from circulation at the end of the year. A new design, for 1, 3 and 5 k stamps, was released in July 1864. As before the Imperial eagle was depicted, this time in an oval frame, with prominent numerals of value in the corners. These low denomination stamps underwent the same changes of paper, shade and perforation as the higher values.

In the mid-nineteenth century, Naples and its surrounding district formed part of the Bourbon Kingdom of the Two Sicilies. The postal services of Naples and its island counterpart, Sicily, were administered separately and both issued their own stamps for a brief period before the Bourbons were ousted in favour of Italian unity.

The first stamps of Naples appeared on New Year's Day 1858 and were recess-printed by Gennaro de Maio of Naples. The paper was hand-made and watermarked with the Bourbon fleur-de-lis repeated forty times in each sheet. The designs featured the arms of the kingdom: the horse of Naples and the three legs with the head of Medusa for Sicily, together with the three fleur-de-lis of the Bourbon family. The 426 ½, 1 and 2 grana denominations were in a square format, while the 5, 10, 20 and 50 g values were rectangular. The arms were surmounted by various shaped frames, each bearing the words 'BOLLO DELLA POSTA NAPOLETANA' (stamp of the Neapolitan Post). The dies were engraved by Giuseppe Masini who inserted secret marks in the frames consisting of the letters of his name. There were three plates of the 2 g, one only for the 50 g and two for each of the other denominations. Two types of paper were used and some values may be found printed on both sides of the paper.

King Ferdinand II died on May 22nd 1859 and his eldest son succeeded him as Francis II. Garibaldi invaded Sicily in May 1860, crossing the Straits of Messina shortly afterwards and deposing Francis on September 7th. A provisional government for Naples and Sicily was set up in November and remained in power for two years before the erstwhile kingdom was

424 *Peru, 1 d, 1858*

425 *Russia, 10 k, 1858*

426 *Naples, 1 g, 1858*

427 *Naples, ¹/₂ t, Trinacria, 1860*

428 *Naples, ¹/₂ t, Cross of Savoy, 1860*

429 *Buenos Aires, 5 p, 'Barquito', 1858*

430 *Argentina, 15 c, 1858*

424

425

426

427

428

430

429

absorbed by Italy. Two stamps were issued during the early days of the provisional government. They were of ½ tornese value and were intended to prepay the postage on newspapers. The first of these stamps is known as the *'Trinacria'*, after the three-legs emblem which it depicted. It was made up of the ½ g plate with the G erased and a T inserted in its place by hand. Each stereo on the plate was altered individually.

After the occupation of Naples itself, the stamp was again altered. This time the centre was erased and replaced by the Cross of Savoy, again by hand on each stereo. The stamps of Naples were superseded in February 1861 by the stopgap issue for the Neapolitan Provinces. This series, printed by F. Matraire in Turin, portrayed King Victor Emmanuel II in designs similar to those of Sardinia but with values in Neapolitan currency.

BUENOS AIRES

A decree of June 27th 1857 reorganizing the postal services in the Argentinian state of Buenos Aires, led the way to the introduction of adhesive stamps in April 1858, following the example set by neighbouring Corrientes. The stamps, popularly known as *'Barquitos'* (little ships) featured a steamship in a horizontal oval with the inscription ·CORREOS BUENOS AIRES' in the upper and lower frames and the value in the side panels. Denominations of 2, 3, 4 and 5 pesos were typographed at the Banco y Casa de Moneda in Buenos Aires. In October 1858 a 4 reales stamp was produced by slightly altering part of the inscription on the 4 p denomination so that the abbreviation PS read RS. At least one stamp in the plate was left unaltered, thus producing the error of the 4 p in the colour of the 4 r

stamp. The 5 p plate was converted to produce 1 p stamps by erasing the final CO in CINCO and attempting to alter the first two letters so that it appeared like UN. Some curious hybrid varieties occurred in the process. The plate of the 4 r was again altered by erasing the CUA of the abbreviated word CUATᵒ. The resulting inscription 'Tᵒ rˢ' was passed off as 1 peso. Most of these stamps were so poorly printed anyway that it would have been difficult to decipher the value intended, had this not been clear from the colour used.

These improvisations were superseded in September 1859 by a new design featuring the head of Liberty with a similar frame to the preceding series. Stamps in denominations of 4 r and 1 and 2 p were produced. These stamps vary considerably in appearance, on account of the rapid deterioration of the plates. In November 1862 the colour of the 1 and 2 p stamps was changed, from blue to red, to red and blue, respectively. The political autonomy of Buenos Aires was curtailed in 1859 but its postal administration continued to be separate until 1862 when stamps of the Argentine Confederation replaced the states' issues.

Stamps inscribed 'CONFEᵒⁿ ARGENTINA' (Argentine Confederation) were produced by the centralist government at Rosario and released two days after Buenos Aires issued its first stamps. Carlos Riviere lithographed the stamps in denominations of 5, 10 and 15 centavos and showed the clasped hands and rising sun emblem of the Confederation. The original series was printed with small figures of value, but in January 1860 similar stamps were released with larger figures. The 10 and 15 c with larger figures, though prepared for issue, were never actually put on sale. A new series in the same three denominations was introduced in January 1862. The stamps were inscribed 'REPUBLICA ARGEN-TINA', reflecting the change from a federal to a unitary republic, and this inscription has appeared on the country's stamps ever since.

The 1862 series, lithographed by R. Lange of Buenos Aires, featured the national arms in a circular device. Numerous variations in shade and printing have been recorded in this series. In the first printings the C of CENTAVOS was broad and there was an accent over the U of REPUBLICA. One stamp in every sheet of the 15 c had no accent over the U, and in later printings it was also absent from all the 5 and 10 c stamps. The 15 c is also known in *tête-bêche* pairs, the first stamp in the second row of each sheet having been accidentally inverted. Towards the end of 1863 successive printings of the 5 c stamps caused considerable wear on the plates. Stamps from the worn plates have almost none of the fine lines in the background and seem to lack corners.

In April 1864 a further series of 5, 10 and 15 c stamps was issued. Recess-printed at the Casa de Correos, the stamps differed in the frame designs but all three portrayed

Bernardino Rivadavia who, in 1826, had become the first president of Argentina. The Rivadavias were in use until 1873 and during that relatively long period were subject to many changes of perforation and shade. The paper used varied from medium to very thin or very thick, while ribbed and carton paper were also used occasionally. While the Rivadavia stamps were still current, a new set of 5, 10 and 15 c values was recess-printed by the American Bank Note Co., portraying Rivadavia, Belgrano and San Martin respectively. Rivadavia's portrait on the 5 c was entirely redrawn in printings of this stamp that were produced subsequently.

MOLDAVIA AND WALLACHIA

The first stamps to appear as a result of radical political change were issued in 1858. In the aftermath of the Crimean War the Danubian principalities of Moldavia and Wallachia were granted autonomy, though still owing nominal allegiance to the Turkish sultan. Postage stamps were introduced in Moldavia in July 1858 shortly after the principality became independent. At that time Turkey itself did not have stamps, and Russia, the 'protector' of the principalities, had been using stamps for a few months only. On the other hand, Austrian post offices functioned in the larger towns and cities of the principalities, so the use of stamps was familiar to the commercial section of the population at least.

The issue of stamps for internal postage was authorized in May 1858 and during the early part of July a quantity of stamps, in denominations of 27, 54, 81 and 108 parales, was produced by means of hand-stamps bearing a circular device showing the bull's head emblem of Moldavia and a posthorn. The inscription 'Porto Skrisori' was rendered in Cyrillic.

Comparatively few of the Moldavian Bulls were printed. They were produced in sheets of thirty-two containing eight *tête-bêche* pairs. The small hand-press had only a single die and small working surface, and as a result the printer was obliged to turn the paper round before he could add the last rows of stamps. New postal rates in November 1858 led to a series of 5, 40 and 80 p stamps in a rectangular design featuring the same motifs as before. They were inscribed 'PORTO GAZETEI' (newspapers) or 'SCRISOREI' (letters) in Roman lettering, though the value was shown in Cyrillic. All denominations are known in *tête-bêche* settings.

The European powers recognized Prince Alexander as joint ruler of both Moldavia and Wallachia in 1861 but separate postal administrations were maintained until the following year. The stamp-producing equipment was then transferred from Jassy 431 to Bucharest and a new series, for use in both principalities, was issued in June 1862. The stamps featured the bull's head of Moldavia and the eagle of Wallachia. The value was now rendered in Roman lettering. These stamps were withdrawn from use at the end of December 1864 and superseded by the first stamps of Romania on New Year's Day 1865.

CÓRDOBA

Last of the Argentine states to introduce 435 stamps was Córdoba which produced 5 and 10 c stamps in October 1858, in the wake of Buenos Aires and the Argentine Confederation. The stamps featured the province's coat of arms and were lithographed in sheets of thirty by Larsch of Buenos Aires. There was, however, little use for these stamps, following the gradual extension of the Federal issues, and genuinely used copied are rare. Three major varieties occurred in each sheet of the 5 c value. These consisted of a full stop after CEN, the omission of the first O in CORDOBA, and a topless 5. Apart from these major varieties almost every stamp in the sheet bore constant distinguishing flaws. The colour of the 5 c value varied considerably from pale to deep blue, and the paper used for both values tended to vary from one part of the sheet to another. Usually it appears to be laid, with clearly marked ribbing, but stamps from the edge of the sheet often look as though they had been printed on a form of wove paper. Values

of 15, 20 and 50 c and 1 peso are completely bogus.

After an average of five or six new countries a year, 1859 proved to be a bumper year for new issues. Nine postal administrations adopted adhesive stamps, four of them choosing New Year's Day to mark their philatelic debut. Of these two were the German free cities of Hamburg and Lubeck.

HAMBURG

The important international status of the port of Hamburg is reflected in the fact that, prior to 1859, the stamps of six postal administrations—Schleswig-Holstein, Hanover, Prussia, Thurn and Taxis, Denmark and Mecklenburg—were used there. At an earlier period both France and Britain had maintained post offices in the city.

The common design of Hamburg's first stamps, by C. G. Hencke, featured the triple-towered coat of arms surmounted by figures of value. The seven denominations ranged from ½ to 9 schillings and were typographed by T. G. Meissner. New 436 values of 1¼ and 2½ s in similar designs, 410 lithographed by C. Adler, appeared in February 1864. The shades of these stamps, particularly the 1¼ s, varied enormously. The nine values of the series were gradually reprinted with perforations between 1864 and 1865. The colour of the 7 s was changed from orange to mauve in February 1865. Examples of this stamp in mauve without perforations are known, though the stamp was not regularly issued in this state. Imperforate examples of the 3 s are known also, but these were in a different shade of blue from that of the 1859–64 imperforate series.

A new design was introduced for the 1¼ s value in 1866 and a 1½ s stamp added at the same time. These two stamps were typographed by Meissner in the 1859 design and released in May 1867. The stamps of Hamburg were withdrawn at the end of that year, when the city joined the North German Confederation. An un-denominated stamp in lilac-brown was, however, permitted for local use in Hamburg. These stamps, sold for half a schilling, remained in use in Hamburg till January 1872 when the stamps of the German Empire were introduced.

LUBECK

Lubeck's first stamps were lithographed by H. G. Rathgens of Lubeck in denomina-
437 tions of ½, 1, 2, 2½ and 4 schillings on paper bearing a watermark of myosotis flowers. A curious error is the 2 s stamp with the erroneous inscription 'ZWEI EIN HALB' normally found on the 2½ s de-nomination. Unwatermarked paper was adopted for ½ and 1 s stamps issued in April 1862. These stamps featured the double-headed eagle of Lubeck, with the numerals of value placed prominently in the four corners.

The movement towards uniformity in the design of the stamps used in the German states was felt in Lubeck in 1863 when an
411 oval design, with the eagle embossed in the centre, was typographed at the Prussian State Printing Works in the same five de-nominations. Like Hamburg, Lubeck is-sued a 1¼ s stamp in 1864; this stamp resembled the embossed series closely in design, but was lithographed locally by Rathgens in various shades of brown. A 1½ s stamp was typographed in Berlin and released in December 1865, again fea-

431 *Moldo-Wallachia, 30 p, 1862*
432 *Moldavia, 80 p, 'Bull', 1858*
433 *Moldavia, 81 p, 'Bull', 1858*
434 *Sicily, 1 g, 'Bomba Head', 1859*
435 *Cordoba, 10 c, 1858*
436 *Hamburg, 3 s, 1859*
437 *Lubeck, 4 s, 1859*

431

432

433

34

435

turing the double-headed eagle, but within an octagonal frame. This stamp, like the series of 1863, was rouletted, whereas the locally printed stamps were imperforate. Lubeck likewise ceased to have its own stamps on joining the North German Confederation.

SICILY

Stamps had been issued in Naples, the mainland portion of the dominions of King Ferdinand II, in January 1858. Exactly a year later separate issues for the island of Sicily (also under his rule) were released. Whereas the Neapolitan stamps had featured the coat of arms of the Kingdom of the Two Sicilies, those of Sicily itself bore the bearded profile of the king. Ferdinand, 434 nicknamed Bomba from his disconcerting habit of bombarding his unruly subjects into submission, is said to have been so vain that he could not bear to see his features obliterated on the stamps and, as a result, an ornamental device like a picture frame was concocted to cancel the stamps without marring his countenance. It is unlikely that the king expressed any personal wish in this matter; a similar device had, in fact, been adopted in Spain in 1850 for the same purpose of avoiding unnecessary lese-majesty. The 'Bomba Heads', as the Sicilian stamps are popularly known, were recess-printed by F. Lao of Palermo in denominations of ½, 1, 2, 5, 10, 20 and 50 grana (1 grano = 2 centesimi). Three plates were made for the 1 and 2 gr, two plates for the ½ and 5 gr and one plate for the 10, 20 and 50 gr, the resulting stamps differing in minor details. A wide range of shades is known for all but the 10 gr denomination, a fact which is all the more remarkable when it is considered that the stamps were is use for a comparatively short period.

Bomba died in 1859 and was succeeded by Francis II whose throne was rapidly taken from him the following year as a result of the War of Independence. Sardinian, and subsequently Italian, stamps were substituted in 1861. Apart from a number of prominent retouches the short-lived stamps of Sicily provided several major errors. Of the ½ gr in cobalt instead of yellow only two examples have so far been recorded. Two sheets of the 1 gr are known to have been passed through the press twice, thus creating clear double prints. In addition constant re-entries on the sheets gave rise to the double impression varieties of the 1 and 50 gr values.

VENEZUELA

The sixth country in South America to issue stamps was Venezuela which introduced a series in denominations of ½, 1 and 2 reales on January 1st 1859. The stamps, 414 lithographed in the United States, featured the national coat of arms. The American printings may readily be identified by their fine impression. Subsequently the plates were sent to Caracas and further printings made by H. G. Neun. The Neun printings were very much coarser in appearance. Examples of the American and Neun printings are known on greenish or bluish paper, respectively, but these are thought to have been essays.

In August 1861 Neun lithographed a series of low value stamps in denominations of ¼, ½ and 1 centavos (12½ centavos 438 = 1 real). Like its predecessor, this series featured the coat of arms, but in a wider format. An entirely new series, showing an eagle and the inscription FEDERACIÓN 412 VENEZOLANA (Venezuelan Federation) was released in 1863–4 in values from ½ c to 2 r. The stamps of this series vary considerably in shade. In 1865 a printing of the ½ r was made from a retouched die in which the words MEDIO REAL were taller and thinner than in the original version.

Between 1864 and 1870 Felix Rasco of Caracas lithographed a series from ½ c to 413 2 r featuring the coat of arms in an octagonal frame inscribed 'CORREO DE LOS EE. UU. DE VENEZUELA' (Posts of the United States of Venezuela) with the value, in words, at the foot.

COLOMBIA

Venezuela's neighbour, Colombia, began issuing stamps some seven months later introducing 2 ½, 5, 10 and 20 centavos and 439 1 peso stamps in August 1859. Lithographed by Ayala and Medrano of Bogotá they featured the coat of arms of the Granadine Confederation, as the country was then known. The 5 and 20 c values are known in *tête-bêche* combinations and there was a wide range of shades in all denominations. A similar design was used for 5, 10 and 20 c stamps released in June 1860.

In 1861, under President Tomás de Mosquera, the country's name was altered 415 twice; first to the United States of New Granada and then to the United States of Colombia. That year a revolutionary faction from Bogotá released a set of stamps bearing the title ESTADOS UNIDOS DE 416 NUEVA GRANADA for use in southern and eastern districts of Colombia. The name Colombia first appeared on stamps issued in 1862, and until 1886 the stamps were also inscribed E. U. (abbreviation for 'Estados Unidos'—United States). This abbreviation was dropped when Colombia became a centralized republic and the autonomy of her component states was se-

438 *Venezuela, ¹/₄ c, 1861*

439 *Colombia, 2 ¹/₂ c,*
   Granadine Confederation, 1859

440 *Bahamas, 1 d, Interinsular, 1859*

441 *Bahamas, 6 d, 1861*

442 *French Colonies, 20 c, 1859*

443 *Romagna, ¹/₂ b, 1859*

438

439

440

441

442

443

verely curtailed. Between 1865 and 1886, however, many of the states were encouraged to issue their own stamps and in some cases these survived as late as 1903. Those issued in the classic period are noted elsewhere.

417-421 The issues of the United States of Colombia in the classic period were lithographed by Ayala and Medrano as before and every design continued to feature the national coat of arms. A great variety of frames and shapes (octagonal and triangular as well as more orthodox formats) was utilized, but the oddest shape of all was the scalene triangle used for the 2½ c stamp of 1869. This is a triangle in which all three sides are of different lengths. This stamp, produced on various types of paper, is the only one of this format ever issued.

CORFU

Although British stamps are known to have been used in Corfu, on mail from the British garrison in the Ionian Islands in the mid-nineteenth century, these are extremely rare and point to the fact that this facility was denied to the civilian population. Distinctive stamps were introduced in May 1859. They were undenominated but those in orange were sold for 5 obols or a ½ d, those in blue for 10 obols or 1 d, and those 422 in carmine for 20 obols or 2 d. The denominations were omitted to avoid offending either the Greek community or the British authorities. The stamps bore a profile of Queen Victoria, but were inscribed in Greek 'IONIKON KRATOS' (Ionian Government)—the only stamps from the nineteenth-century British Empire which were not inscribed in English. The Greek language had been used frequently on postmarks in the pre-adhesive period and it was

adopted on stamps to appease Greek nationalist sentiment in the islands. The stamps were recess-printed by Perkins Bacon and are rare in used condition, particularly on cover. They were discontinued in May 1864 when the islands were handed over to the kingdom of Greece.

BAHAMAS

An important development in the postal history of the British West Indies was the decision, taken in March 1858 by the Treasury in London, to permit the use of British adhesive stamps in the Caribbean colonies. This privilege was also extended to the Bahamas, often, though erroneously, classed with the West Indies. British stamps used in that colony may be recognized by the A 05 obliterator used at Nassau.

The introduction of British stamps encouraged the islanders to demand their own distinctive stamps and in 1858–9 there was correspondence between the Governor of the colony, the Colonial Office, the Post Office in London and Perkins Bacon. In 1860 the British Post Office relinquished control over the Bahamas and this coincided with the production of a distinctive 1 d stamp, intended for internal postage between the islands of the colony, hence the inscription 'INTERINSULAR POSTAGE'. 440 This stamp, bearing a portrait of Queen Victoria, was issued on June 10th 1859. British adhesives were discontinued in May 1860, however, and for more than a year the islanders were forced to use multiples of the 1 d stamp, or revert to the use of hand-struck postal markings, on external letters. Other denominations were not produced by Perkins Bacon until December 1861.

In 1862 responsibility for printing the stamps passed to De La Rue who continued to use the Perkins Bacon plates. Their first penny stamps were issued without a watermark and can be distinguished from the Perkins Bacon printings only by means of the perforation gauge. From 1863 to 1882, however, the Crown CC watermark was used. The interinsular stamp, in all its variations of shade, watermark and perforation, remained in use for twenty-five years—a remarkably long lifespan. It bore the Chalon portrait of the queen, flanked by a pineapple and a conch shell. Perkins Bacon used the Chalon portrait against an engine-turned background for the 4 d and 6 d stamps issued in 1861. Although De La Rue retained the Perkins Bacon plates for 1, 4 and 6 d stamps, they reverted to their more traditional method of production in 1869 when they typographed a 1 shilling stamp with a profile of the queen engraved by Joubert. The pineapple and conch motifs were retained.

FRENCH COLONIES

A decade after stamps were introduced in the mother country France made provision for her overseas territories. Hitherto it had been left to the individual initiative of colonial administrators to make arrangements for the handling of mail, and in one case only, Réunion (1852), was the use of adhesive stamps adopted. By 1859 adhesive stamps had been adopted individually by many British colonies while the West Indian group were using British stamps. In that year the French authorities introduced a series of stamps featuring the Imperial eagle and inscribed 'COLONIES DE L'EMPIRE FRANÇAIS'. The stamps were engraved by Albert Barre and typographed in Paris on tinted paper. At first 10 and 40 centimes stamps were issued, but between 1862

and 1865, 1, 5, 20 and 80 c values in the same design were issued. A curious variety of the 10 c consists of pairs in which one stamp is turned sideways in relation to the other. The stamps were issued imperforate but examples are recorded pin-perforated unofficially. This series remained in use until the end of 1871, more than a year after the Empire which they proclaimed had ceased to exist. Ironically they were then superseded by a series portraying the Emperor Napoleon III whose surrender at Sedan in September 1870 had brought down the Second Empire.

ROMAGNA (ITALY)

The most ephemeral series of stamps issued by the erstwhile states of Italy was that issued by Romagna in September 1859, for it was suppressed barely five months later, when the state was taken over by the House of Savoy. The stamps of Romagna consisted of ½, 1, 2, 3, 4, 5, 6, 8 and 20 bajocchi in a utilitarian design with the value in the centre and the inscription 'FRANCO BOLLO POSTALE ROMAGNE' on the four sides of the frame. The electrotypes were made by Amoretti Brothers and the stamps typographed in black on various coloured papers by Volpe and del Sassi of Bologna. On account of their short life, these stamps are generally more valuable in used condition, and collectors should beware of stamps with forged cancellations.

SIERRA LEONE

Prior to 1852 the British West African colony of Sierra Leone had a postmaster but no post office; he was solely responsible for making up and delivering the mail but had nothing to do with the collection of postage. A post office was opened in Freetown in 1853 and two years later the rate on letters to England was fixed at 6 d per half ounce. In 1859 adhesive stamps were introduced and a fine of 6 d, in addition to the postage, was levied on unpaid letters. The following year prepayment of mail was made compulsory. No attempt was made to institute inland postage until 1872, and this explains the fact that a solitary 6 d value was all that was required until that year.

Sierra Leone's 6 d stamp, introduced on **423** September 21st 1859, was typographed by De La Rue on unwatermarked paper and remained in use until 1885. Inexplicably the obsolete Crown CC, instead of Crown CA, watermark was then adopted. The very long life of the unwatermarked sixpenny testifies to the minimal amount of mail handled in that period. The first printings were perforated 14 and may be found in various shades on bluish or white paper. The gauge of perforation was changed to 12 ½ in 1872.

CHAPTER VI
THE 1860s: THE POSTAGE STAMP COMES OF AGE

Over seventy countries adopted adhesive postage stamps in the 1850s. A new-fangled device, confined to a few isolated countries in the first decade, had by the end of 1859 extended to all parts of the world and was beginning to be accepted as a necessity rather than a luxury. The negotiation of postal treaties and the simplification of international accountancy also stimulated the spread of postage stamps. In 1850 postage stamps were still sufficiently novel to be regarded with suspicion by governments and the general public alike. The use of postage stamps for the prepayment of postage did not become compulsory in many countries till long after their introduction.

By the end of the decade, however, the convenience of the postage stamp was universally accepted. It is a wonder that so many countries still contrived to get by without this convenience. Of the then existing countries of Europe, all had adopted adhesive stamps by the end of the decade except the Balkan countries—Greece, Turkey, Serbia and Montenegro, the German state of Mecklenburg-Strelitz and the tiny states of San Marino and Monaco (both of the latter used the stamps of other countries —Sardinia and France respectively). Elsewhere in the world the emergent nations of that period embraced adhesive stamps less readily, though by the end of the classic period (1870) only the empires of the Far

East and one or two backward countries in Latin America had not adopted stamps.

Seven countries adopted adhesive stamps in 1860, four British colonies and three others scattered as far afield as Europe, West Africa and the South Pacific.

NEW CALEDONIA

The year began with the issue of a 10 centimes stamp in the French Pacific colony of New Caledonia. It is probable the colonial authorities at Noumea were unaware of the decision to issue a general series for use throughout the French colonies, at the time their stamp was in preparation. Surprisingly it was allowed to continue in circulation until September 17th 1862, when it was withdrawn in favour of the general series.

New Caledonia's stamp was lithographed at Noumea and bore a passable portrait of the Emperor Napoleon III. The design was engraved on a stone with a pin by Sergeant Triquerat and compares favourably with the primitives of Mauritius and the Philippines produced under similar conditions. Used examples of this stamp are comparatively scarce but unused copies are reasonably plentiful. It was not until 1881 that New Caledonia re-emerged as a stamp-issuing entity.

444

POLAND

Also on New Year's Day 1860 the solitary stamp of the kingdom of Poland made its debut. A separate postal administration for Poland had been established in 1858 during a period of liberalization. Russian stamps were used at first, distinguished only by the type of cancellation used by the Polish post offices, but steps were taken in 1859 to produce a distinctive stamp for use in Poland. The resulting 10 kopek stamp was very similar in design to the contemporary Russian stamps featuring the Imperial double-headed eagle. The inscription, however, was in Russian and Polish, and a minute Polish white eagle was superimposed on the breast of the Tsarist emblem. The stamps were typographed in varying shades of blue, with a centre and background in red shades, ranging from rose to carmine. The stamps were produced at the Government Printing Office in Warsaw and appeared both imperforate and perforated with gauges from 11½ to 12½. After the Insurrection of 1863 the Russians confiscated the printing press and the use of Polish stamps was gradually phased out. Examples on cover are known as late as 1865, but Russian stamps and Russian-style postmarks were then substituted. Poland Number One, as this forerunner of the issues of independent Poland is known, has been the subject of intensive study over the past century, its several printings, plate flaws and numeral cancellations having been the subject of considerable research.

QUEENSLAND

The stamps of New South Wales were used in Queensland from 1850 to the end of 1860.

444 *New Caledonia, 10 c, 1860*

445 *Poland, 10 k, 1860*

446 *Queensland, 6 d, 1860*

444

445

446

In 1859, however, Queensland was separated from New South Wales and philatelic, as well as political, independence became inevitable.

446 Perkins Bacon won the contract to print the first stamps, in denominations of 1, 2 and 6 pence. The stamps reproduced the Chalon portrait of Queen Victoria in a small upright format and were recess-printed on paper watermarked with a large star. The stamps were put on sale on November 1st 1860. The first supply was imperforate, but various experimental perforating machines were used and stamps of this issue may be found perforated 14 × 15½. Of these the 2 d is recorded vertically imperforate between pairs. A small star watermark was substituted in later printings and a shilling stamp added to the set later in November 1860. A 3 d denomination was introduced in April of the following year. In January 1861 an undenominated stamp inscribed 'REGISTRATION' was released for use on registered letters.

Later issues were produced at Brisbane by Ham. They are easily distinguishable from the London printings because they were rougher and coarser in their general appearance, the colours were less clear and the perforations differed. In addition various types of paper were used. The colonial printers were supplied with a thick toned unwatermarked paper, a paper watermarked QUEENSLAND POSTAGE POSTAGE STAMPS STAMPS in three lines, paper watermarked with a small truncated star, and a paper watermarked with a crown and letter Q. When additional values were required Ham produced 4 d, 2 s, 2 s 6 d, 5 s, 10 s and 20 s stamps by using lithographic transfers from the dies of other values. Many flaws and varieties in the lettering occurred. The Chalon Heads of Queensland were in use for some twenty years and the many printings, papers,

watermarks and perforations have made this series a very popular one for philatelic study.

JAMAICA

Jamaica, in common with the other British colonies in the West Indies, took over responsibility for its postal affairs in 1860. Since 1858 British adhesive stamps had been in use, identified by the numeral obliterators from A 01 to A 78. British stamps 455, 456 were officially withdrawn from use in August 1860 and the Jamaicans were forced to revert to the former practice of indicating prepayment of postage by means of handstruck markings. Examples of British stamps used after that date have been recorded exceptionally. Meanwhile a contract was placed with De La Rue to print stamps in denominations of 1, 2, 4, 6 d and 1 s. These stamps were not available in Jamaica until November 23rd 1860. The stamps bore a laureated profile of Queen Victoria and were typographed on paper with a distinctive pineapple watermark. A 3 d denomination was added to the series in September 1863. The stamps varied considerably in shade, but the most outstanding variety was the so-called 'Dollar Error' which appeared as a vertical stroke through the S of SHILLING. This occurred once on every sheet of the 1 s stamp.

The Crown Agents took over the supply of stamps to Jamaica in 1867, from the agents of the Jamaican government, Messrs Thomson Hankey & Co. The transfer was not immediately reflected in the stamps because a stock of pineapple watermarked paper was still on hand at the printers, but from October 1869 onwards, Jamaican stamps were produced on the standard Crown CC paper then in use in the colonies.

MALTA

Throughout most of the nineteenth century the Maltese post office functioned as a branch of the General Post Office in London. British adhesive stamps were introduced in 1857 and became compulsory in March 1858. These stamps, identified by the A 25 numeral obliterator, remained in use till 1885 when the island's post office was separated from London. In 1859 it was decided to reduce the Maltese internal letter rate from 1 d to ½ d per half ounce. As there was no British stamp of that value at the time a distinctive halfpenny stamp became necessary. The Crown Agents placed the contract with De La Rue and the ½ d stamp came into use on December 1st 1860. For twenty-five years this was Malta's only stamp, but in that long period it underwent numerous changes of shade, paper, perforation and watermark. Officially the colour of the stamp was described as yellow, but in practice this varied from buff to brown-orange and every shade of yellow in between. The stamp was typographed with a profile of Queen Victoria on a relatively simple background.

ST LUCIA

St Lucia was the next of the West Indian colonies to substitute its own stamps for the British adhesives. At that time St Lucia came under the control of Barbados and thus it was the governor of that island who was responsible for making the necessary arrangements for a supply of stamps to be printed for St Lucia. In July 1860 an order for stamps was placed by the Crown Agents with Perkins Bacon. Thriftily Perkins Bacon used one plate for the production of all three denominations required. The design, featuring the queen's profile and the inscription 'ST LUCIA POSTAGE', was undenominated, the values being indicated by the different colours used—red (1 d), blue (4 d) and green (6 d). The stamps were shipped to St Lucia in November and were placed on sale on December 18th 1860. The stamps were normally perforated in gauges ranging from 14 to 16 but all three values are known imperforate between horizontal pairs.

De La Rue took over the contract in 1863. Apart from the distinctive shades, the De La Rue stamps may be recognized by the Crown CC watermark, the Perkins Bacon stamps being on their star watermarked paper. The colours of the stamps were changed in 1864 and subsequently the gauges of perforation altered. These attractive recess-printed stamps remained in use until 1882 when they were superseded by a series typographed by De La Rue.

LIBERIA

The last of the countries to commence the issue of stamps in 1860 was the West African republic of Liberia, at that time, with Ethiopia, the only country on the African continent which was independent of other foreign powers. For over twenty years Liberia made use of one stamp design, in a large upright format featuring Liberty and a sailing ship. If this design seems suspiciously like the Britannia reverse on contemporary British coinage it is hardly surprising, since the stamps were produced by a London firm, Dando, Todhunter & Smith. Although Liberia had a decimal currency (the dollar of 100 cents), the denominations of the stamps were 6, 12 and 24 c, conforming to the postal rates of neighbouring Sierra Leone, through which the external mail of Liberia was routed.

The first printing was on thick paper with rich colours. A subsequent printing, made in 1864, was on medium to thin paper in lighter colours. The frame-line between stamps was omitted in 1866 and very thin paper and pale colours were used in 1867. These stamps remained in use till 1880 when the colours were changed and lower values of 1 and 2 c were added to the series.

BRITISH COLUMBIA

The discovery of gold in British Columbia in 1858 led to the rapid development of the westernmost colony in British North America. A rudimentary postal service was established that year and the postal rate on letters fixed at 5 cents. The following year adhesive stamps were ordered from De La Rue and these were put on sale about April 1860. The stamps were inscribed 'BRITISH COLUMBIA & VANCOUVER'S ISLAND', although these were administered as separate colonies at that time. The value was given as 2½ d, the sterling equivalent of 5 cents. The stamps bore a profile of Queen Victoria. The first printing was imperforate but was never put into circulation though unused copies are known. Stamps perforated 14 are known in various shades of reddish rose. Between June 1864 and November 1865 this stamp was sold at 3 d, following an increase in the letter rate, though no surcharge was made on the stamps to indicate the increase.

Separate issues for Vancouver Island and British Columbia were introduced in September and November 1865 respectively. Vancouver's 5 and 10 c stamps depicted the queen as before, but British Columbia's 3 d stamp featured the crown and royal monogram with the heraldic flowers of the United Kingdom in the background. The release of separate issues for the two colonies became necessary when Vancouver adopted Canadian decimal currency while British Columbia retained sterling. In November 1866 the two colonies were combined and their respective stamps were henceforward used in both parts. British Columbia adopted decimal currency in 1868. The 3 d stamp was printed in various colours (like the St Helena 6 d) and surcharged in values from 2 c to $ 1. In 1871 British Columbia joined the Canadian Confederation and withdrew distinctive stamps on July 20th of that year.

Five of the seven countries which entered the stamp album in 1861 were in the Western hemisphere. Three of these were British colonies in the West Indies, Nevis, Grenada, and St Vincent, following the lead of Jamaica and the Bahamas.

GRENADA

Grenada's 1 d and 6 d stamps, issued in June 1861, were recess-printed by Perkins Bacon in a small upright format reproducing the Chalon portrait of Queen Victoria on laid unwatermarked paper. The 6 d was also produced on wove paper but no used copies have been found. A fresh consignment was sent to Grenada at the beginning of 1863. These were printed on paper watermarked with a small six-pointed star. There were numerous shades of this issue, especially the 6 d which varied from rose to vermilion. In addition the vermilion variety has been recorded doubly printed and stamps in the dull rose-red shade are known with the watermark sideways. These stamps remained in use till 1883, undergoing a number of variations in paper and watermark. Unlike the majority of the Perkins Bacon contracts of this period, those relating to Grenada were never surrendered to De La Rue, though the latter company typographed the stamps of Grenada from 1883 onwards.

NEVIS

459 The stamps of Nevis, printed in London by Nissen & Parker, at first from line-engraved plates and subsequently by lithog-
453 raphy, consisted of 1, 4, 6 d and 1 s values reproducing the vignette from the Great Seal of the colony. An allegorical group of two ladies giving succour to a third is an allusion to the medicinal springs with which the island abounds. The frames of these stamps derived their inspiration from contemporary British stamps of the corresponding value. Between 1861 and 1876 the stamps were recess-printed, first on blued paper, then on greyish paper and finally, in 1866, on white paper. A lithographed version of the series appeared in 1876, to be superseded three years later by the inevitable De La Rue typographed set portraying Queen Victoria.

ST VINCENT

British stamps were used in the West Indian island of St Vincent from 1855 to 1861, distinguished by the A 10 numeral canceller. On June 14th 1860 an Act was passed by the colonial legislature authorizing the appointment of a colonial postmaster and transferring to the government of St Vincent control of the post office. The Act also envisaged the introduction of distinctive postage stamps and a contract to this end was placed with Perkins Bacon. Ini-

447 *Liberia, 12 c, 1860*

448 *St Lucia, 1 d, 1860*

449 *British Columbia and Vancouver's Island, 2 1/2 d, 1860*

450 *Vancouver Island, 5 c, 1865*

451 *British Columbia, 3 d, 1865*

452 *Grenada, 1 d, 1861*

453 *Nevis, 1 s, 1861*

454 *St Vincent, 1 d, 1861*

447

448

449

450

451

452

453

454

tially two denominations, 1 d for local mail and 6 d for letters to the United Kingdom, were provided, the stamps being brought into use in May 1861. Further consignments were sent out to St Vincent up to 1866 but considerable variety exists in the perforation of the different printings. Stamps in a similar design, in denominations of 4 d and 1 s, were added in August 1866. The colour of the 1 s stamp was changed from grey to indigo in April 1869 and again, this time to brown, in September of the same year. At the same time the colour of the 4 d value was changed from blue to bright yellow. The earliest issues were printed on unwatermarked paper but in 1871 a small star watermark was adopted.

The St Vincent stamps bore a profile of Queen Victoria against an upright oval background of engine-turning in characteristic Perkins Bacon style. These attractive stamps remained in use till 1899, undergoing numerous changes in the thirty-eight years of their currency. It was not until 1882 that De La Rue succeeded in wresting the St Vincent contract from Perkins Bacon and the original plates were destined for employment for a further seventeen years.

The 1860s were the heyday of the small independent printers in London who vied with the major companies, Perkins Bacon and De La Rue, for crumbs of colonial and foreign stamp contracts. In many cases these printers were able to secure contracts for one territory only, but often they retained the contract for a number of years. A typical example was Charles Whiting, of Beaufort House in the Strand, London. An unsuccessful contender in the Treasury Competition of 1839 for Britain's first stamps, Whiting is now remembered philatelically for printing all but one of the stamps issued by the Canadian province of Prince Edward Island. Whereas the other smaller printers clung to traditional methods of recess-printing or lithography Whiting emulated De La Rue and made use of typography.

PRINCE EDWARD ISLAND

The Canadian Post Office Act of 1851 gave Prince Edward Island an independent postal service but a decade elapsed before adhesive stamps were introduced, the island being the last of the Canadian colonies to adopt this facility. The first stamps, released on New Year's Day 1861, consisted of 2 d, 3 d and 6 d denominations bearing profiles of Queen Victoria in different frames. At first an unusually large gauge 460 of perforation was used but this made it virtually impossible to separate the stamps. Both 2 d and 3 d stamps were officially au- 461 thorized to be bisected and used at half their face value. The 2 d stamp is also known to have been rouletted, but in 1862 a finer perforation, gauging 11 instead of 9, was adopted. Between 1863 and 1868 stamps in denominations of 1, 2, 3, 4, 6 and 9 d were typographed by Whiting on yellowish toned paper. The perforations of these stamps varied from 11 to 12 and included compounds of these gauges. Coarse wove bluish paper was substituted in 1867–8 for 2, 3 and 4 d values.

The sole exception to the Whiting monopoly was the 4½ d stamp issued in June 463 1870. Recess-printed by the British American Bank Note Co. of Montreal and Ottawa, it depicted the Chalon portrait of the queen. A feature of this stamp, copying Canadian precedents, was the value rendered as 4½ d currency or 3 d sterling. Whiting produced a new series for Prince Edward Island in 1872 following the introduction of Canadian currency. The

462 stamps, in values from 1 to 12 cents, are comparatively plentiful unused since the island's stamps were withdrawn from circulation in July 1873 when Prince Edward Island entered the Confederation of Canada.

CONFEDERATE STATES OF AMERICA

Politically the most important event of 1861 was the secession of eleven of the southern slave-owning states of the United States to form the Confederate States of America. In December 1860 a state convention in South Carolina formally repealed the 1788 Act ratifying the constitution of the United States. This was tantamount to secession from the Union, and within eight weeks six other states—Mississippi, Florida, Alabama, Georgia, Louisiana and Texas—had followed suit. Delegates from the seven breakaway states met in Montgomery, Alabama, in February 1861 and formed the government of the Confederate States, with Jefferson Davis of Mississippi as president and Alexander Stephens of Georgia as vice-president.

The southern states feared that the postal system would be used by the Federal government as a means of spreading anti-southern propaganda and immediately took steps to establish their own postal administration. John H. Reagan of Texas was appointed Postmaster General and at the beginning of April tenders were invited for distinctive postage stamps. Surprisingly enough, the advertisement even appeared in several northern newspapers. Three of the firms which submitted contracts were 'Yankee', including the American Bank Note Co. which printed the US government stamps!

Before any definitive arrangements could be made, however, the simmering conflict

455 *Jamaica, 1 d, 1860*

456 *Jamaica, 4 d, 1860*

457 *Malta, ¹/₂ d, 1860*

458 *British Columbia, 2 c, 1868*

459 *Nevis, 1 d, 1861*

460 *Prince Edward Island, 3 d, 1861*

461 *Prince Edward Island, 9 d, 1862*

462 *Prince Edward Island, 2 c, 1872*

463 *Prince Edward Island, 4 ¹/₂ d, 1870*

455

456

457

458

459

460

461

462

463

464

465

466

467

468

469

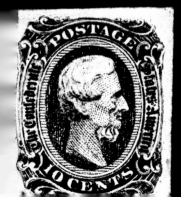

473

474

475

476

exploded when Confederate artillery attacked the Federal garrison at Fort Sumter in Charleston Harbour on April 12th. President Lincoln immediately mobilized his forces, and although hostilities did not break out on a grand scale for several months, the war had begun. By the end of May 1861, Virginia, Arkansas, Tennessee and North Carolina had joined the Confederate States.

The Confederacy declared US postage stamps and postal stationery invalid, but pending proper Confederate issues it had to make do with various makeshifts. The first consisted of hand-stamps inscribed 'PAID' with the figure of value. Many different types of hand-stamp were used. In some cases the figure of value was incorporated in the paid hand-stamp, in others it was struck separately, and in some cases the value was added in manuscript.

The hand-struck paid marks were used intermittently throughout the Civil War, particularly west of the Mississippi where post offices could not get hold of the Confederate general series. Some postmasters issued their own provisional stamps. Some were either struck or printed on the envelopes, so that strictly they rank as postal stationery. Others were actually struck or printed on sheets of paper which were then cut up and used as adhesive stamps in the normal way. The standard catalogues list approximately forty towns which produced their own stamps, although more than 160 different places are believed to have produced their own distinctive issues. Many of them were crude woodcuts or type-set labels. Others, such as the stamps of Athens, Charleston, Knoxville and Mobile, were typographed or lithographed in a highly professional manner. Many of the Confederate local issues are extremely rare, while several are believed to be unique.

464, 465
466, 467

468 Hoyer & Ludwig of Richmond, Virginia—the only firm in the Confederacy to apply for the contract—were commissioned to produce the first definitive stamps. These were issued in September 1861 and consisted of 5 c green and 10 c blue values competently lithographed with portraits of Jefferson Davis and Thomas Jefferson respectively. The colours of these stamps were changed the following year to blue for the 5 c and rose for the 10 c. A 2 c green portraying Andrew Jackson was introduced at the same time.

469 Another 5 c blue portraying Jefferson Davis was issued in April 1862. It was typographed by De La Rue—the first stamp produced by this ubiquitous company for any foreign country and, incidentally, the only stamp used in the Continental United States not actually produced in that country. De La Rue also produced a 1 c yellow

471 stamp portraying John Calhoun but it was never issued, since postal rates were increased before it reached the Confederacy. Subsequent printings of the De La Rue 5 c were made in Richmond by Archer & Daly. Wartime exigencies meant using several different kinds of paper and ink.

Archer & Daly recess-printed a new series which appeared in 1863. It consisted of 2, 10 and 20 c stamps showing respec-

470 tively Andrew Jackson, Jefferson Davis and

472 George Washington. Apart from numerous shades and different papers used in the printing there were three distinct types of the 10 c stamp. In 1864 the contract to print 10 c stamps passed to Keatinge & Ball of Columbia, South Carolina, and this resulted in yet another version of this stamp, distinguished by the very rough impression, brown patchy gum and deep blue colour. The defeat of the Confederacy in 1865 was followed by the the suppression of these stamps and the re-introduction of US issues in the southern states.

479 *Greece, 2 lepta, Hermes, 1861*
480 *Bergedorf, 1 1/2 s, tête-bêche pair, 1861*

479

480

GREECE

Reference has already been made to the so-called 'Tessarakonta lepta' stamp of 1831 (see page 17) and the controversy which surrounds its status. Fully thirty years went by after its appearance, however, before Greece introduced adhesive stamps in the accepted sense. It was a sad commentary on the decline of the arts and crafts in Greece at the time of independence from the Turks that no printer or engraver could be found capable of producing the stamps locally and the contract was therefore given to the French. Albert Barre engraved the dies and E. Meyer typographed the stamps in denominations of 1, 2, 5, 20, 40 and 80 lepta. The common design featured the profile of Hermes, messenger of the gods. The 10 lep stamp was inscribed with the numerals of value on the gummed side as a security measure, but the other denominations were unmarked. The Hermes Heads remained in use for twenty-five years and during that long period there were numerous changes in paper, ink, gum and security numerals on the back.

The printing plates were shipped to Athens where printings were produced from November 1861 onwards. In the Paris prints the shading on the neck of Hermes consisted of fine lines and dots, whereas in the Athens printings the lines were thicker and unbroken. The Athens prints show numerals of value on the backs of all but the 1 and 2 lep. Over the years the various printings differed radically as the plates were subject to wear or were cleaned and refurbished.

BERGEDORF

From 1420 to 1867 the North German city of Bergedorf was jointly owned by Hamburg and Lubeck. This fact was referred to in the stamps of Bergedorf, introduced on November 1st 1861, which bore the letters LHPA (Lubeck Hamburg Post Anstalt) in the corners. The stamps, in denominations of ½, 1, 1 ½, 3 and 4 schillings were in similar designs but progressively larger sizes. The design featured the combined arms of Hamburg (a castle) and Lubeck (an eagle). The series was lithographed in black on coloured paper by Charles Fuchs of Hamburg. Prior to the general release of stamps in November a trial printing was made in June 1861. The trial stamps were imperforate, whereas those actually put on sale were rouletted, and the colours of paper were rather different.

In August 1867 Hamburg bought out the rights of Lubeck in Bergedorf. Having acquired complete jurisdiction, Hamburg replaced the stamps of Bergedorf with its own issues, though the latter were in use for barely four months pending the introduction of the stamps of the North German Confederation.

ITALY

Considering that the *Risorgimento* had been completed by 1860 it seems surprising that stamps for the newly established kingdom of Italy did not appear till two years later. Presumably the architects of the Italian state had more important matters commanding their attention. An interesting parallel a decade later was the German Empire, proclaimed at Versailles in January 1871, but without its own distinctive stamps till 1872.

In the interim the stamps of the erstwhile regimes were tolerated and then superseded by the contemporary issues of Sardinia, the last printing of which appeared as late as

1863. Significantly the first stamps of the kingdom of Italy consisted of the Sardinian series, but with the added refinement of perforations. These stamps were typographed by Francisco Matraire of Turin. A new printing of the 15 c, lithographed instead of typographed, appeared in January 1863 and then an entirely new lithographed design was adopted for this denomination in the following month. Newspaper stamps of 2 c value, typographed in yellow with 474 the numeral of value embossed in colourless relief in the centre appeared in May 1862. These stamps were regarded merely as stopgaps, pending the release of a new series which was being typographed by De La Rue in London.

477 The De La Rue series, in denominations from 1 centesimo to 2 lire, was released on December 1st 1863 in three basic designs, 475 a numeral motif for the 1 c and profiles of 476 King Victor Emmanuel II in two different frames for the higher values. De La Rue printed these stamps until the end of 1865 and during this period two further denominations were produced in London, a 2 c 478 in a numeral design, and a provisional 20 c, made by surcharging the 15 c value.

The State Printing Works in Turin took over the production of Italian stamps in January 1866. To all intents and purposes the Italian printings are indistinguishable from the London version. De La Rue produced a 20 c stamp in a new portrait design in May 1867. Subsequent printings of this value were made in Turin. Although De La Rue had earlier hoped to secure a lengthy contract to produce Italian stamps they had to be content with manufacturing the plates and other equipment, and, like Perkins Bacon before them, consigning the initial printing of the stamps together with the necessary equipment to the country concerned. Subsequently De La Rue were

to print stamps for Belgium on the same basis and provide Portugal with equipment and materials for stamp production.

ANTIGUA

The West Indian island of Antigua used British stamps from 1858 to 1860 and these may be recognized by the A 02 numeral obliterator of St John's. A hiatus of two years followed, before the introduction of a 6 d stamp in August 1862. This was 481 followed by a 1 d stamp for local postage in January 1863. Both stamps were recessprinted by Perkins Bacon with a profile of the queen against an engine-turned background. This simple design fell below the usual Perkins Bacon standard, the background being coarse and the portrait severe. Perkins Bacon continued to print these stamps for Antigua for a decade before the plates had to be surrendered to De La Rue. Though De La Rue eventually typographed other denominations, the Perkins Bacon 1 d and 6 d stamps lasted till 1903, undergoing numerous variations in perforation, shade and watermark in those forty years.

NICARAGUA

On December 2nd 1862 the Central American republic of Nicaragua issued its first stamps. The American Bank Note Co. recess-printed 2 and 5 centavos stamps de- 482 picting the five mountains emblem formerly used by the Central American Federation to which Nicaragua had belonged. The emblem was, however, given a naturalistic treatment, resembling a landscape. The earliest printings of these stamps were on yellowish paper, but thin white paper was introduced in 1869, when other denominations of 10 and 25 c were issued. Different frames were used for each value of the series.

HONG KONG

Prior to 1860 control of the Hong Kong postal administration had been vested in the General Post Office in London. Following the transfer of responsibility to the colony, adhesive stamps were planned, but not actually put into circulation until December 8th 1862. De La Rue typographed the stamps in a simple design bearing a profile of the queen, with inscriptions in English **488** and Chinese in the horizontal and vertical panels respectively. This simple but effective design remained in use till 1903, undergoing variations in watermark and colour, and was revived in 1938 with a profile of King George VI substituted.

OTTOMAN EMPIRE

The year 1863 was the quietest in the philatelic development of the world since the 1840s. Four names entered the stamp album for the first time that year and of these only one was a country of major im- **489** portance. The Ottoman Empire introduced adhesive stamps on January 1st, a series from 20 paras to 5 piastres being printed in black on various coloured paper with a band in a second colour across the foot of the design. The stamps were oriental in appearance, the *toughra*, or sign manual of the sultan, forming the principal motif, and the inscriptions entirely in Arabic script, signifying 'Ministry of Finance of the Sublime Government'. After making use of stamps lithographed at Constantinople, the Turkish authorities placed an order for stamps with the firm of Poitevin in Paris who were responsible for the typographed series released in January 1865. This series, ranging from 10 paras to 25 piastres, showed **490** the crescent and star emblem surrounded by an oval band containing the inscription in Arabic lettering. Despite their oriental appearance these stamps were designed, engraved and printed in Paris and remained in use till 1876. During that period they were overprinted with Turkish inscriptions to signify 'Post of the Government of Turkey'. Many different settings and types of these overprints were employed, adding greatly to the complexity of these stamps. In 1868 the plates were sent to Constantinople and subsequent printings were made there.

RUSSIAN POST OFFICES IN THE LEVANT

Though many European powers had maintained post offices in the Turkish Empire since the early eighteenth century, the first of these to provide special stamps for use there was Russia which, in January 1863, issued a large square 6 kopek stamp **484** emblazoned with the Imperial eagle and bearing an inscription in Russian which signified 'Despatch under wrapper to the East'. This stamp was typographed at St Petersburg on various types of paper between 1863 and 1866.

In 1865 a series of stamps was introduced for use on mail handled by the Russian Company for Navigation and Trade, better known by its initials as ROPIT. The stamps, lithographed at Odessa, featured a sailing ship and bore the initials of the company in Cyrillic. The stamps were undenominated but different colours and designs were used for the 2 and 20 k values **491** at which they were sold. Stamps in a numeral design inscribed 'Vostochnaya Korrespondentsia' (eastern correspondence) were typographed at St Petersburg, issued in 1868, and remained in use till the 1890s.

493

COSTA RICA

In April 1863, Costa Rica issued ½ and 2 reales stamps. Other values of 4 r and 1 peso appeared the following year. The stamps were recess-printed by the American Bank Note Co. and showed a sailing ship off the coast of Costa Rica. These stamps remained in use till 1881.

492

BOLIVAR

The other stamp-issuing entities of 1863 consisted of a Colombian state and a Russian district. Bolivar issued 10 centavos and 1 peso stamps between 1863 and 1866 featuring the coat of arms of Colombia, which in size ranked as the tiniest ever issued. They remained in use till 1872.

483

WENDEN

The town of Wenden in the Russian province of Livonia was governed by the Teutonic Knights and, as such, enjoyed special privileges under the Tsarist Empire, including a separate postal administration which lasted till the early years of the twentieth century. The earliest stamps consisted of undenominated labels inscribed in German either 'Briefmarke' (letter stamp) or 'Packenmarke' (parcel stamp) 'Wendenschen Kreises' (of the district of Wenden). These stamps were sold at 2 and 4 kopeks respectively. An undenominated stamp

494

486

481 *Antigua, 6 d, 1862*

482 *Nicaragua, 2 c, 1862*

483 *Bolivar, 1 p, 1863*

484 *Russian Levant, 6 k, 1863*

485 *Mecklenburg-Strelitz, ¼ sgr, 1864*

486 *Wenden, 2 k, 1863*

487 *Holstein, 1 ¼ s, 1864*

481

482

483

484

485

486

487

sold for 2 k also appeared in 1863 with a blank central oval. The following year this stamp was re-issued with the arms of the province of Livonia (a winged horse) engraved in the oval. The status and origin of the Wenden stamps puzzled early philatelists, and the use of German inscriptions on stamps emanating from part of the Russian Empire only served to confuse the matter further. A circular blue device inscribed 'WENDENsche KREIS BRIEF POST' is sometimes met with; this is believed to have been an essay for postage stamps but never used for this purpose.

MECKLENBURG-STRELITZ

Four countries joined the ranks of the stamp-issuing territories in 1864. The grand duchy of Mecklenburg-Strelitz, taking a leaf out of the book of neighbouring Mecklenburg-Schwerin, introduced a series that year, ranging from ¼ to 2 silbergroschen. Stamps in denominations of ¼, ⅓ sgr and 1 schilling were in a rectangular design, while the 1 and 2 sgr stamps had octagonal frames. Both were engraved by Otto of Güstrow in Mecklenburg-Schwerin, and typographed at the Prussian State Printing Works in Berlin. The coat of arms of the grand duchy was embossed in the centre. These stamps were relatively short-lived, being withdrawn at the end of 1867 when Mecklenburg-Strelitz joined the North German Confederation.

SCHLESWIG-HOLSTEIN

The Schleswig-Holstein question, which had been raised briefly in 1850 when the inhabitants tried to assert their independence, remained unanswered until 1864 when there was a confrontation between Denmark and the German Confederation over the future of the two duchies. First troops of the Confederation, and latterly the forces of Austria and Prussia, were involved in war with Denmark. Finally Austria and Prussia quarrelled over the administration of the occupied districts and this precipitated the Seven Weeks' War of 1866 which saw Prussia emerge as the dominant state in Germany. Philatelically the situation in Schleswig-Holstein was almost as confusing as the political wrangle. In Schleswig the Austrian and Prussian powers made a joint issue of stamps in August 1864. In Holstein, which was technically a member of the Confederation, the German Federal Commissioners issued distinctive stamps modelled on the contemporary Danish designs but inscribed cryptically H.R.Z.G.L. F.R.M. (Herzogliche Freimarke = ducal postage stamp). These stamps remained in use till August 1865.

Austria and Prussia made a joint issue of stamps for use in both duchies in February 1865, pending the settlement of their claims in the area. The Convention of Gastein, signed later that year, gave Austria control over Holstein while Prussia gained Schleswig and the duchy of Lauenburg in the extreme south of Holstein. Stamps inscribed for Schleswig-Holstein were superseded in November 1865 by separate issues released independently by Austria and Prussia for use in the districts under their control. Both sets were similar in design, consisting of the value in an upright oval surrounded by the inscription HERZOGTH (duchy) and the name of the duchy concerned.

Prussia violated the Convention of Gastein on June 7th 1866 by invading Holstein. On June 21st the joint issue of Schleswig-Holstein was re-introduced and remained in use till January 1868 when it was superseded by the stamps of the North German Confederation.

NETHERLANDS INDIES

Reference has already been made to the Batavian land-mail labels of the 1840s, but the Netherlands Indies did not adopt postage stamps in the normally accepted sense until April 1864. Like the contemporary Dutch series, the 10 cents stamp of the Netherlands Indies was engraved by J. W. Kaiser and recess-printed at the Utrecht Mint. Unlike the Dutch issues, however, this stamp bore a full-face portrait of King William III and was inscribed 'NEDERL.
512 INDIE POSTZEGEL' with the value across the top. Originally it was released imperforate, but those issued from 1868 to 1870 were perforated. The solitary 10 c
500 stamp was superseded in 1870 by a series typographed by Enschede bearing a profile of the king. This series, with many variations in paper, perforation and shade, remained in use for some twenty years.

SORUTH

Although adhesive stamps had been in use in British India since 1852, more than a decade passed before they were adopted by any of the princely states. The first to do so was the territory known as Soruth; 1 anna stamps were hand-stamped in black watercolour on paper of various shades and
513 types. The stamps were extremely primitive in appearance, consisting of three lines of Sanskrit lettering in a horizontal format. The exact date of issue is not known but is believed to have been some time in 1864. Four years later a series ranging from 1 to 4 a was crudely type-set. The stamps are of interest on account of the numerals expressed in either Nagri or Gujarati script. Thus two distinct versions exist of the 1 and 4 a denominations. As before, a wide va-

488 *Hong Kong, 48 c, 1862*

489 *Turkey, 20 paras, 1863*

490 *Turkey, 20 paras, 1868*

491 *Russian Levant, ROPIT, 1865*

492 *Costa Rica, ¹/₂ r, 1863*

493 *Russian Levant, 1 k, 1868*

494 *Wenden, 2 k, 1863*

495 *Wenden, Essay, 1863*

496 *Mecklenburg-Strelitz, 1 sgr, 1864*

497 *Schleswig, 1 ¼ s, 1864*

498 *Holstein, 1 ¼ s, 1864*

499 *Schleswig-Holstein, 1 ¼ s, 1865*

488

489

490

491

493

Briefmarke des WENDEN= schen Kreises.

494

495

496

497

498

499

500

501

502

503

504

505

506

507

508

509

510

511

riety of different papers was employed in the production of these stamps.

There was a slight increase in the number of new countries issuing stamps in 1865. Apart from the introduction of separate issues for British Columbia and Vancouver Island, already noted, these were stamps for the first time from two Latin American republics, Ecuador and the Dominican Republic, and the international community in Shanghai, while Bermuda, which had had local 'Postmasters' issues since 1848, finally got around to making a government issue of stamps.

ROMANIA

The Danubian principalities of Moldavia and Wallachia adopted the name of Romania in 1864. This change became evident in stamps released on January 1st 1865 bearing the profile of Prince Alexander Cuza. The 517 stamps were lithographed in Bucharest in denominations of 2, 5 and 20 parales. For the first time the Roman alphabet was used exclusively and the Cyrillic of the previous issues was omitted. Alexander was deposed in 1866 and succeeded by Prince Charles of Hohenzollern-Sigmaringen. Stamps in the same values as the preceding series but bearing the profile of the new ruler ap- 515 peared on August 1st 1866. The first printings were on thick paper but the following year much thinner paper was introduced. The currency of Romania was changed to the leu of 100 bani, and similar stamps, in 501 denominations of 2, 4 and 18 b, were released on New Year's Day 1868. A new design with the same portrait of Prince Charles came out at the end of 1868 in the same three values and remained in use till 1871.

500 *Netherlands Indies, 10 c, 1870*

501 *Romania, 18 b, Prince Charles, 1868*

502 *Bermuda, 6 d, 1865*

503 *Shanghai, 1 c, 1867*

504 *Egypt, 5 paras, 1866*

505 *British Honduras, 1 d, 1866*

506 *Honduras, 2 r, 1866*

507 *Bolivia, 5 c, 1868*

508 *Serbia, 1 p, Prince Michael, 1868*

509 *Serbia, 10 p, Prince Milan, 1869*

510 *British Virgin Islands, 4 d, 1867*

511 *British Virgin Islands, 1 s, 1867*

ECUADOR

Ecuador, racked by civil war continuously since independence, entered a period of comparative tranquility and prosperity under President Moreno. A British postal agency was established on the coast at Guayaquil in 1865, to handle external mail, and Ecuador introduced stamps for use on internal mail at the same time. The first stamps of Ecuador were engraved by Emilio Rivadeneira and typographed by M. Rivadeneira in Quito. The design of the ½ and 516 1 real stamps was faintly reminiscent of contemporary French stamps, with Grecian borders and a circular vignette. The principal motif was the national coat of arms, which appeared on the majority of Ecuadorean stamps from then until the end of the century. The stamps of this series ranged enormously in shade and in the quality of the paper.

A 4 r stamp with a more ornate frame design appeared in 1866. These stamps remained in use till 1872.

DOMINICAN REPUBLIC

The history of the Dominican Republic in the first half of the nineteenth century was a chequered one, with brief turbulent periods of independence interspersed by domination by the neighbouring republic of Haiti. The Spaniards, who had been driven out in 1821, reconquered their portion of the island in 1861 and for four years the erstwhile republic reverted to the original name of Santo Domingo. In this period adhesive stamps of the Spanish colonial series intended for use in Cuba and Puerto Rico were employed and can only be identified by means of the postmarks.

The Spanish government was overthrown by a revolution in 1865. The republic was

512 *Netherlands Indies, 10 c, 1864*

513 *Soruth, 1 a, 1868*

514 *Dominican Republic, ¹/₂ r, 1865*

515 *Romania, 2 p, Prince Charles, 1868*

516 *Ecuador, ¹/₂ r, 1865*

517 *Romania, 5 p, Prince Alexander Cuza, 1865*

518 *Shanghai, 16 c, 1865*

519 *Egypt, 20 paras, Sphinx and Pyramid, 1867*

520 *Egypt, 5 piastres, 1866*

512

513

514

515

516

517

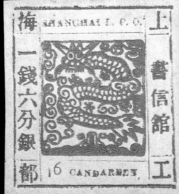

518

519

520

restored and distinctive stamps were introduced on October 19th of that year. The first stamps consisted of a ½ real value typographed in black on rose paper and a 1 real value in black on green paper. The stamps are known on wove or, more rarely, on laid paper. They depicted the coat of arms with CORREOS and the value in words, at the sides. A larger design, in vertical format, was introduced between 1866 and 1874. These stamps were typographed in black on paper of various colours and quality. All of the typographed stamps of 1865–74 were printed by Garcia Brothers in Santo Domingo.

BERMUDA

The last of the Postmasters issues is believed to have been made in Bermuda in 1861. There was then a four-year hiatus before the introduction of a series typographed in denominations of 1 d, 6 d and 1 s by De La Rue. A 2 d value was added the following year and a 3 d stamp in 1873. This series, bearing a profile of Queen Victoria, lasted in some cases as late as 1904, with various changes in watermark, perforation and shade in that long period.

SHANGHAI (CHINA)

Although China was the last of the major world powers to adopt stamps (1878), these convenient pieces of paper had been introduced by foreign merchants in the various Treaty Ports and the British colony of Hong Kong in the previous decade. In 1865 the international community in Shanghai organized a local Post Office and introduced a series of adhesive stamps featuring a dragon motif. The first stamps were type-set locally in values from 2 to 16 candareens. Two versions exist, showing the name of the currency in plural and singular forms. The dragon continued to grace all the stamps of Shanghai down to the closing years of the century, but smaller and neater designs, lithographed by Nissen and Parker of London, were adopted in 1866 with the value rendered in cents. A similar set, in candareens, appeared a year later.

During the remaining years of the classic period the number of new stamp-issuing administrations rose steadily. This may be attributed to the gradual process of consolidation, in which the remaining countries of the world emulated their neighbours. Nevertheless there were still large areas of the world in which the adhesive postage stamp had still not made its presence felt. The continent of Africa, for example, was represented in the stamp album by the British territories in the south and west, the only independent administration being that of Liberia.

EGYPT

The international importance of Egypt as a commercial centre was reflected in the fact that postal services were operated from the consulates and embassies of Austria, Britain, France, Greece, Italy and Russia. A domestic postal service was organized as early as 1821 by Carlo Meratti and took on the curiously misleading title of Posta Europea in 1842. In 1864 Meratti's former partner, Giacomo Muzzi, was granted a ten-year monopoly to run the Egyptian postal service, provided that he carried all government mail free of charge. Large circular seals, known to collectors as 'interpostals' were used on official mail, and although they are not postage stamps in the strict sense, they are regarded as the fore-runners of Egyptian philately.

Muzzi's service proved to be so success-ful that Ismail Pasha decided to nationalize it. He bought back the concession, offered Muzzi a title of nobility and appointed him first Postmaster General. Muzzi invited a number of foreign printers to tender for the production of Egyptian stamps and even-tually Pellas Brothers of Genoa won the contract. The series, released in January 1866, was not entirely satisfactory. The Turkish inscriptions fulfilled domestic re-quirements but complaints soon arose from European postal administrations that their clerks could not recognize either the coun-try of origin or the value of the stamps. As a result, a new series was ordered. A Ger-man engraver named Hoff prepared dies depicting the Sphinx and Pyramid in the centre, with Cleopatra's Needle and Ha-drian's Column in Alexandria in the side panels. The inscriptions were still rendered in Turkish but the numerals of value were given in European style. These stamps were issued in August 1867 and remained in use till 1872. The colours of the 10 and 20 paras denominations were changed in July 1869.

BRITISH HONDURAS

Both Honduras and British Honduras in-troduced stamps in January 1866. British stamps had been used in the latter territory from 1858 to 1860, identifiable by the nu-meral obliterator A 06, but these were with-drawn in May 1860 and the archaic system of hand-stamping mail was re-introduced. Adhesive stamps for the colony were or-dered from De La Rue in 1865 and put on sale early in January 1866. The series consisted of 1 d, 6 d and 1 s, typographed

in a design with an unusual crowned profile of Queen Victoria. As an economy measure all three denominations were printed in the same sheet separated by horizontal and ver-tical gutter margins. The sheet comprised two panes of sixty 1 d stamps at the top, with panes of sixty 6 d and 1 s stamps at bottom right and left, so that interpanneau pairs of stamps of different denominations are possible, though extremely rare. Later printings of the 1 d stamp were made in sheets without the other denominations.

HONDURAS

Attempts to organize a postal service in the republic of Honduras were made in 1865, and stamps prepared for this purpose appeared the following January, but it is unlikely that they were put into use. It was not, in fact, until 1877 that Honduras was able to place its postal services on an effi-cient footing. The 2 reales stamp of 1866 was typographed in black on green or rose coloured paper showing the national coat of arms. These stamps were revalidated in 1877 by means of surcharges in various de-nominations from ½ to 2 reales. Examples of the unsurcharged series of 1866 rank among the cheapest and most plentiful of all classic issues.

BOLIVIA

Elsewhere in Latin America Bolivia adopted stamps in 1866, after a false start some three years earlier. A decree of February 1863 invited tenders from printers for a series of postage stamps and a decree of the fol-lowing month awarded the contract to Justiniano Garcia who prepared a series of stamps in denominations from ½ to 4 reales. These stamps were to have been released on June 1st 1863, but the contract was abruptly suspended by a further decree dated April 29th. By that time, however, the stamps had been printed. Though never officially issued, examples have been recorded on cover. They featured the coat of arms in a central medallion and are known in either black or blue.

521 In 1866 a 5 centavos stamp featuring the national bird, the condor, was introduced for use on domestic correspondence. Originally printed in various shades of green, this stamp changed colour to mauve in 1868. In the same year other denominations in the same design were released, ranging from 10 to 100 c. The Condor stamps of Bolivia rank among the most complex issues of the classic era. The 5 c plate was completely re-engraved four times and broadly retouched six times, making possible eleven clearly defined states of the plate.

507 The American Bank Note Co. recess-printed a series showing different versions of the coat of arms and these stamps, from 5 to 100 c, were issued in April 1868. In the original version nine stars appeared at the foot of the medallion, but the design was redrawn in 1871 to show eleven stars.

JAMMU AND KASHMIR (INDIA)

Postage stamps were adopted by the Indian state of Jammu and Kashmir in March 1866, with values of ½, 1 and 2 annas. The de-
522 signs were circular and featured the sun as the central motif, with the denominations in the centre and the inscription, in Nagri and Arabic lettering, round the perimeter. The stamps were hand-struck from brass dies in watercolours, on a wide variety of locally made paper. A disconcerting feature

of the stamps of Jammu and Kashmir was the tendency to print all denominations in the same colour, and to change that colour at frequent intervals. Separate issues for both Jammu and Kashmir were issued later the same year. The Jammu series was printed in blocks of four consisting of three ½ a stamps and one 1 a value. Kashmir's first separate issue consisted of a ½ a printed in black from a single die. This was followed by rectangular ½ and 1 a stamps printed in sheets of twenty-five, the four upper rows being ½ a stamps and the fifth row being 1 a stamps. Yet another rectangular series for Kashmir was issued in 1867, again with different denominations printed side by side in the same sheet. Combined issues for Jammu and Kashmir were re-introduced in 1878.

SERBIA

Under Prince Michael Obrenovich (1860–8) the Balkan principality of Serbia was rapidly modernized. Among the important reforms which he instituted was a postal service complete with adhesive stamps, introduced on May 1st 1866. Stamps in denominations of 1 and 2 paras were typographed
523 at the State Printing Works in Belgrade and featured the national coat of arms with the Cyrillic inscription K. S. Pochta (Royal Serbian Post) at the top. Various shades and types of paper were used in the production of these stamps. Higher denominations of 10, 20 and 40 p appeared in July 1866
508 and portrayed Prince Michael. This series was initially typographed at the Imperial Printing Works in Vienna but later printings were made in Belgrade. The Vienna and Belgrade printings may be distinguished by differences in perforation, shade and quality of paper. The Austrian printers

were also responsible for the manufacture of plates for a series portraying the young
509 Prince Milan who succeeded his father in 1868. Early printings of these stamps, from 1869 to 1872, were made in Vienna and subsequent printings in Belgrade; again the various gauges of perforation, type of paper and shade are useful guides to the classification of these stamps, but the plates were also reset with margins of varying widths.

BRITISH VIRGIN ISLANDS

The last of the stamp-issuing territories of 1866 consisted of the British Virgin Islands which introduced 1 d and 6 d stamps during
524 that year. The stamps, lithographed by Waterlow & Sons from plates manufactured by Nissen & Parker, featured St Ursula, patron saint of the colony. The stamps are known on both white and toned paper of various sorts. They remained in use till 1899 and inevitably underwent numerous variations in perforation and watermark in that period, being produced by De La Rue from 1879 onwards.

In 1867–8 larger designs were produced
510 for 4 d and 1 s stamps, both portraying a
511 female figure. The 1 s stamp, originally printed in one colour, was superseded shortly afterwards by a similar design in which the virgin was depicted in black. A few examples have been recorded with the black printing omitted, thus giving rise to the famous 'Missing Virgin' error.

TURKS ISLANDS

The extension of adhesive stamps to the West Indian colonies continued in 1867,
525 with the Turks Islands releasing 1 d, 6 d and 1 s stamps on April 4th of that year. These stamps were among the last to be recess-printed in the classic period by Per-

521 *Bolivia, 5 c, Condor, 1866*

522 *Jammu and Kashmir, 4 a, 1866*

523 *Serbia, 1 p, 1866*

524 *British Virgin Islands, 1 d, St Ursula, 1866*

525 *Turks Islands, 1 s, 1867*

526 *North German Confederation, ¼ g, 1868*

527 *Austrian Levant, 15 s, 1867*

521

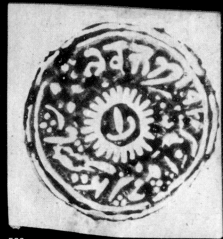

522

523

524

525

527

kins Bacon and, with their fine profile of the queen on an engine-turned background, conformed to the standards which characterized the work of this company. They remained in use, with variations in shade, perforation and watermark, till De La Rue typographed a new set in 1881. The chief interest of the Perkins Bacon issues, however, lies in the numerous provisional surcharges made to create ½, 2½ and 4 d denominations, on the same principles as St Helena.

HELIGOLAND

Two other British colonies began issuing their own stamps in 1867. The North Sea island of Heligoland, occupied by Britain since the Napoleonic Wars, had previously belonged to Denmark, but had a predominantly German population and close economic ties with Germany. Prior to 1867 the stamps of Hamburg were used on the island. Distinctive stamps, portraying Queen Victoria and with values in Ham-
528 burg currency from ½ to 6 schillings, were typographed at the Prussian State Printing Works in Berlin with the queen's profile embossed. A singular feature of all Heligoland's stamps was their production in combinations of green and red, the island's colours. The German Imperial currency of 100 pfennigs to the mark was adopted in 1875 and stamps were released that year in values from 1 to 50 pf. In addition the stamps bore the corresponding value in British currency, from ¼ d to 6 d.

STRAITS SETTLEMENTS

The Straits Settlements (Singapore, Malacca and Penang) had formed part of the Indian postal administration until September 1867 and accordingly used Indian stamps. When the administration was separated, Indian stamps surcharged in Straits cents were used pending the supply of distinctive stamps by De La Rue in December of the same year. 529, 530 The series, depicting a profile of the queen, consisted of 2, 4, 6, 8, 12, 24, 32 and 96 c stamps. A 30 c value was added in December 1872. This series, with variations, remained in use till 1892.

AUSTRIAN POST OFFICES IN THE TURKISH EMPIRE

The Austrians operated the largest network of post offices in the Turkish empire of any foreign power in the nineteenth century. At first ordinary Austrian stamps were used and then, between 1863 and 1867, the stamps of Austrian Italy (Lombardo-Venetia) were used. After the loss of Lombardo-Venetia in the Seven Weeks' War of 1866 these stamps were withdrawn from use. A new series, in the same design as the Austrian set of 1867, but inscribed in values of soldi, was produced and put on sale in the Austrian post offices in the Turkish Empire in June of that year. The stamps ranged from 2 to 50 s and varied considerably in shade 527 during the nine years of their currency.

In Central America, Salvador issued a set of four stamps in 1867 featuring the national emblem, a mountain and eleven stars. The stamps, recess-pinted by the American 531 Bank Note Co., remained in use till 1874.

NORTH GERMAN CONFEDERATION

New Year's Day 1868 was a red letter day in the philatelic calendar. On that day

279

separate issues of all the German states (except Bavaria, Baden and Wurttemberg) were withdrawn and replaced by the series of the North German Confederation. Two sets were typographed at the Prussian State Printing Works, inscribed in groschen and kreuzer values for use in northern and
26 southern districts respectively. The first printings of the stamps were rouletted but in February 1869 perforation was adopted.
533 In March 1869 10 and 30 g stamps for use on parcels were released. These stamps were not normally available to the public in unused condition, but were affixed in the post office to parcels requiring them and cancelled with pen and ink. Because of the different currency used in Hamburg, an undenominated stamp sold for ½ schilling was used on local mail between the city boundaries. A series of stamps for official use was released in 1870. The stamps of the
534 North German Confederation were superseded in January 1872 by the issues of the German Empire.

ORANGE FREE STATE

For almost half a century (1852–1902) the Orange Free State was, as its name implied, an independent sovereign state. Nevertheless its close proximity to Cape Colony meant that it came under a considerable amount of British influence, to a greater
543 degree than its sister Boer republic in the Transvaal. Thus it was not surprising that the burghers of the OFS should turn to London, rather than the continent, for their stamps, once the decision was taken to adopt this convenience.

From 1856 onward a series of hand-struck stamps inscribed 'BETAALD' (paid) were used at the main post offices of the country but the idea of introducing adhesive stamps

528 *Heligoland, 6 s, 1867*

529 *Straits Settlements, 3 c, 1867*

530 *Straits Settlements, 2 c, 1868*

531 *Salvador, ¹/₂ r, 1867*

532 *Tolima, 5 c, 1870*

533 *North German Confederation, 1 k, 1868*

534 *North German Confederation, ¼ g, official stamp, 1870*

535 *Cundinamarca, 5 c, 1870*

536 *Hungary, 1 k, journal tax stamp, 1868*

537 *Gambia, 6 d, 1869*

538 *St Christopher, 1 d, 1870*

539 *Fiji, Times Express, strip of four (6 d, 1 s, 1 d, 9 d), 1870*

528

529

530

531

532

536

537

538

FIJI TIMES EXPRESS
6 PENCE.

FIJI TIMES EXPRESS
1 SHILLING.

FIJI TIMES EXPRESS
1 PENNY.

FIJI TIMES EXPRESS
9 PENCE.

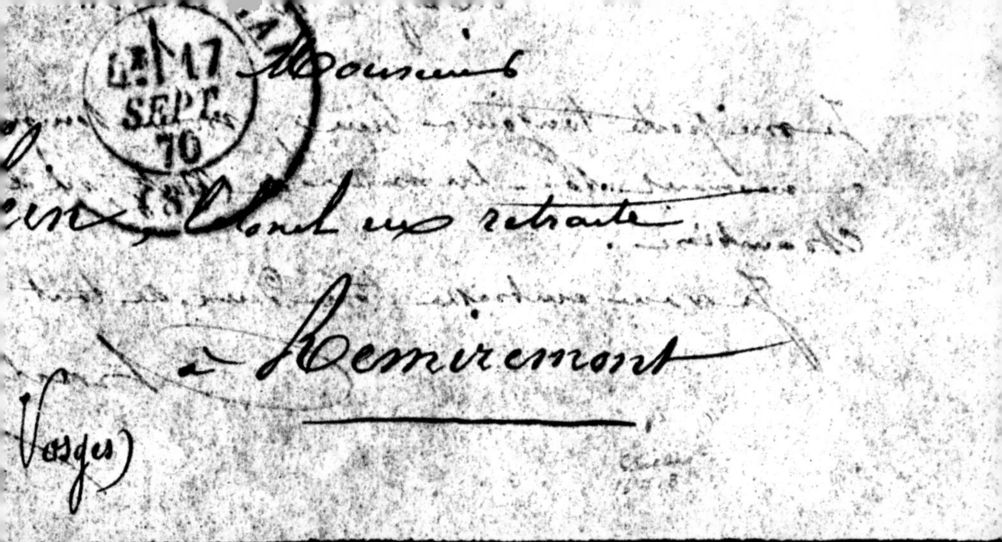

Monsieur

... Colonel en retraite

à Remiremont

(Vosges)

ON MONTÉ.

PD

PARIS

N... & C

Londres

EMP. RE FRANCAIS 20C POSTES 20C

EMPIRE FRANCAIS 10 C POSTES 10 C

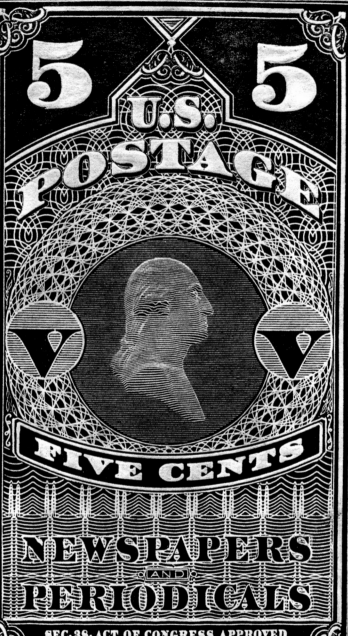

was not mooted until 1865, when the Consul General of the Free State in London contacted De La Rue for a quotation. This preliminary discussion was fruitless, but two years later this company was again approached, and this led to the production of 1 and 6 penny and 1 shilling stamps, typographed in a simple design featuring the orange-tree emblem of the state. The OFS authorities were obviously satisfied with this design since it remained in use till 1903, when the country had ceased to exist and had been redesignated, after the Anglo-Boer War, as the Orange River Colony.

The original trio was put on sale on New Year's Day, 1868. Between that date and 1903 few changes other than shade were made to the basic set; 4 d and 5 s stamps were added to the series in 1878 and ½ d, 2 d and 3 d in 1883–4, while the ½ d, 1 d and 1 s changed colour between 1894 and 1900. But the principal interest of these stamps during their long period of use was the numerous provisional surcharges produced over the years by Borkenhagen of Bloemfontein. It is interesting to note that the plates of these stamps, held by De La Rue in London, were surrendered to the Foreign Office in 1900 as enemy property and are now preserved in the British Museum.

AZORES AND MADEIRA

Also on New Year's Day 1868 the first of the Portuguese overseas territories began issuing stamps. The contemporary Portuguese series portraying King Luiz was overprinted ACORES or MADEIRA for use in the respective islands. In both cases imperforate stamps were used at first. Madeira also used ordinary Portuguese stamps with the experimental *perce en croix*

540 *Papillon de Metz, 1870*

541 *Letter 'par ballon monté', from the Siege of Paris, 1870*

542 *United States, 5 c, newspaper stamp, 1865 (the largest stamp of the classic period)*

544

roulette and overprinted stamps are also known with this unusual form of separation. Perforated stamps were released later in 1868. Overprinted Portuguese stamps continued to be used in these islands for many years, until ordinary Portuguese stamps were re-introduced.

ANTIOQUIA, TOLIMA AND CUNDINAMARCA

Following the lead of Bolivar, the Colombian state of Antioquia began issuing stamps in 1868. Four stamps, in denominations of 2½, 5, and 10 centavos and 1 peso, were lithographed by Ayala of Bogotá and featured the national coat of arms. A new series in the same values and including a 20 c stamp appeared between 1869 and 1871. With the encouragement of the federal authorities other states of Colombia soon introduced their own stamps. Both Tolima and Cundinamarca released stamps from 1870 onwards. Tolima's first issue was a type-set 5 c, with the value and inscription surrounded by printer's ornament. Successive issues, from 1871 onwards, clung to the Colombian tradition of showing the coat of arms in various frames, a practice emulated by Cundinamarca also.

HUNGARY

Had the revolution of 1848 been successful it is likely that Hungary would have had the honour of producing some of the incunabula of philately, those stamps of the first decade. The suppression of the Kossuth uprising, however, set back the movement for Hungarian independence by almost twenty years. Not until the *Ausgleich* of 1867, which led to the Dual Monarchy,

543 *Orange Free State, 6 d, Orange Tree, 1868*
544 *Madeira, 100 r, 1868*
545 *Antioquia, 5 c, 1868*
546 *Persia, 8 sh, 1868*

543

544

545

546

could the Magyars of Hungary re-assert their individuality. In that year a new series of postage stamps was issued throughout the Hapsburg dominions, portraying Kaiser Franz Josef (Kiralyi Ferenc Joszef) and the inscription confined to the abbreviation kr which could stand for kreuzer or krajczar, depending which side of the frontier the stamps were used. These 'neutral' stamps preceded the separation of the Austrian and Hungarian postal administrations, and the release of separate stamps in both countries, but this was not effected till 1871.

A forerunner of Hungary's own stamps, however, was provided in June 1868 when 536 a separate issue of journal tax stamps was made. Like their Austrian counterparts these stamps did not prepay postage but represented a tax, collected by the Post Office, on newspapers. Nevertheless it could be argued that these stamps possessed a certain franking validity since newspapers thus taxed were exempt from normal postal charges. These journal tax stamps are therefore listed by postage stamp catalogues. The stamps consisted of 1 and 2 kr denominations with the value in the centre and the Hungarian coat of arms in the frame. They were in use till the end of the century.

PERSIA

546 Under Shah Nasir-ud-Din (1848–96) Persia was transformed into a modern state, and among the many reforms instituted by this enlightened ruler was a reasonably efficient postal service. Turkey adopted adhesive postage stamps in 1863 and the idea was soon taken up by Nasir-ud-Din. In 1865 he despatched a deputation to Paris to make enquiries on the subject of stamps for postal purposes. A Monsieur A. M. Riester got to hear of this and, on his own initiative,

prepared a series of essays for Persian stamps, printed in various colours, and these were actually shown at a fine arts exhibition in Paris that year. In the meantime, however, the deputation contacted Albert Barre at the French Mint and he subsequently prepared the lion and sunburst design which was ultimately adopted by the Persian authorities. Despite the fact that this design was produced in Europe it has a singularly un-European appearance, heightened by the omission of any inscription other than the numerals in Arabic script. Copper clichés were made from Barre's original dies and the stamps typographed in Teheran. A wide variety of papers was used for this series and the shades of the stamps also varied considerably. The stamps were issued in Persia some time in 1868. The exact date of their release is not known.

There was no method of cancellation—far less a dated postmark—in use at that time and consequently most of the first issue are to be found without defacement. A few have been recorded with cancellation by pen strokes. The public was not permitted to purchase unused stamps, the stamps being affixed to correspondence by the post office clerks. The relatively few examples in genuinely unused condition, complete with original gum, could only have been obtained by influence. The stamps were in values of 1, 2, 4 and 8 shahi and remained in use until 1875, when the design was modified by the substitution of European numerals in the lower corners.

FERNANDO PO

The Spanish West African island of Fernando Po issued a 20 centimos de escudo stamp in September 1868. The stamp was typographed and bore a profile of Queen Isabella. For some inexplicable reason 547 (perhaps economy) it was decided to dispense with separate issues for the island, and in December 1868 the stamp was withdrawn. From then until 1879 the stamps of Cuba and Puerto Rico were employed in Fernando Po. Examples of these, identifiable by their postmark, are of considerable interest and rarity.

All four countries which began issuing stamps in 1869 were in the British sphere of influence. In March the West African colony of the Gambia, and the state of Sarawak in south-east Asia, introduced distinctive stamps. Later in the year the South African Republic (Transvaal), which owed the nominal suzerainty of Britain, and the Indian state of Hyderabad, also adopted adhesives.

GAMBIA

For the Gambia, De La Rue typographed 537 4 and 6 penny stamps with an unusual (for them) embossed profile of Queen Victoria. The Gambia 'Cameos' remained in use for some thirty years—first unwatermarked and subsequently with the contemporary colonial watermarks. All the stamps up to 1880 were released imperforate, something of an anachronism after perforation had been well established for over a decade.

SARAWAK

548 Sarawak's first stamp, a 3 cents issued on March 1st 1869, was lithographed by Maclure, Macdonald & Co. of Glasgow and portrayed the first of the white rajahs, Sir James Brooke. The corners of the stamp

547 *Fernando Po, 20 c, 1868*

548 *Sarawak, 3 c, Rajah Brooke, 1869*

549 *Transvaal, 6 d, 1869*

550 *Angola, 50 r, 1870*

551 *Hyderabad, 1 anna, 1869*

552 *St Thomas and Prince Islands, 50 r, 1870*

553 *Paraguay, 1 r, 1870*

554 *Afghanistan, official stamp, 1870*

555 *Alsace-Lorraine, 10 c, 1870*

547

548

549

550

551

552

553

554

555

bore the letters JBRS—James Brooke, Rajah of Sarawak. Sir James, however, had died on June 11th 1868, after the contract for the stamps had been placed. This stamp therefore ranks as the first to portray a ruler posthumously.

TRANSVAAL

549 The Transvaal's first series consisted of 1 and 6 pence and 1 shilling and were typographed by Otto of Güstrow. The stamps featured the arms of the republic and were inscribed in Dutch 'POSTZEGEL' (postage stamp) at the top and 'Z. AFR. REPUBLIEK' (South African Republic) at the foot. The first printings are known imperforate or rouletted. The same basic design was retained for all stamps of the Transvaal down to 1878 when the republic was taken over by the British, but during that brief period the combinations of paper, shade, roulette and printing plates rendered the classic issues of the Transvaal exceedingly complex.

HYDERABAD

Despite its oriental appearance, with Arabic lettering set in arabesque ornament, the 1 anna stamp issued by Hyderabad in 1869 551 was designed and engraved by a Mr Rapkin of London and recess-printed by Nissen & Parker. This stamp, perforated 11 ½, is also known imperforate or partially perforated.

ST CHRISTOPHER (ST KITTS)

By contrast with the preceding year, only one of the eight new countries of 1870 was a British colony. On April 1st the West Indian island of St Christopher (St Kitts) 538 released 1 d and 6 d stamps, for inland letters and letters to Britain respectively. Like the other British Caribbean colonies St Christopher had enjoyed the use of British stamps at one time (1858–60) and these may be recognized by the A 12 obliterator then used in Basseterre, the island's capital. It seems astonishing in retrospect that fully ten years should have been allowed to pass without the benefit of adhesive stamps, having once appreciated their convenience, particularly in view of the fact that the neighbouring island of Nevis had had its own stamps since 1861. The stamps of St Christopher were typographed by De La Rue, rapidly approaching that point of virtual monopoly in British and colonial stamp production which they were to enjoy unassailed for more than forty years.

Significantly the design of the St Christopher stamps was a foretaste of things to come. Not only was there no attempt to provide different frames for the different denominations (as De La Rue had previously done for other colonies) but the design itself was suspiciously like those used for Lagos (1874) and Tobago (1879). In a sense this simple but adaptable design was the forerunner of the long range of colonial keyplates which were the dreary hallmark of British colonial stamps in the middle period (1880–1920). Uniformity and economy were achieved at the expense of interest and variety. But that era of monotony was still far off in 1870 when the classic period drew to its close.

ANGOLA AND THE ST THOMAS AND PRINCE ISLANDS

A further two Portuguese colonies adopted stamps in 1870. One cannot blame the

Crown Agents and De La Rue for the concept of keytype designs, since Portugal had thought of it so much earlier. The series provided for Angola in July 1870 was simple and pleasing, with the Portuguese crown set in a circular Grecian border. The name of the colony appeared at the top and the value across the foot. The same design, in a modified form, was used for the stamps issued by St Thomas and Prince Islands later the same year. Instead of the name across the top there appeared the word CORREIO, and the upper arc of the Grecian border was erased to make way for the name of the colony. This design remained in use for many years and, as other colonies adopted stamps, it was adapted to suit their requirements. Thus Mozambique (1876), Cape Verde Islands (1877), Guinea (1881), Macao (1884) and Timor (1886) were all later to use the crown keytype.

PARAGUAY

The stamps of the Colombian state of Cundinamarca have already been mentioned. Elsewhere in South America, Paraguay introduced stamps on August 1st 1870. The stamps, consisting of 1, 2 and 3 reales depicting the lion emblem of the republic in various frames, were lithographed by R. Lange of Buenos Aires. Subsequently Paraguay made use several other Argentinian printers, and even went as far as Giesecke & Devrient of Leipzig in the 1880s, but did not produce stamps locally till 1901.

AFGHANISTAN

Afghanistan's neighbours—India, Russia and Persia—had all adopted adhesive stamps, and at the very end of the classic period the practice was extended to this remote kingdom. The first stamps were circular in shape and their design, showing a lion's head surrounded by the inscription in Arabic lettering, was reminiscent of the stamps of Jammu and Kashmir. The stamps bore the date 1288 in the Moslem calendar; since this corresponds with 1870-1 in the Christian calendar it is just possible that the stamps did not appear till 1871, but one must give them the benefit of the doubt and include them with the classics.

The stamps, in various denominations from 1 shahi to 1 abasi, were lithographed together on the same plates (although there was also one plate entirely composed of the shahi stamp). Circular stamps remained in use in Afghanistan until 1890, though the rectangular format had demonstrated its convenience and had been adopted practically everywhere else. As regards the cancellation of stamps Afghanistan was also a law unto itself. Instead of using a postmark or pen-cancellation, it was customary for postal clerks to lift a corner of the stamp from the letter and tear out a piece. Thus Afghan stamps in damaged condition are quite collectable, since it indicates that they have been postally used.

FIJI

Before 1870 mail destined for the Pacific island kingdom of Fiji was addressed to the care of the British consul who acted as an unofficial postmaster and arranged for the collection and delivery of mail. This system was more or less adequate until 1869 when the European population was increased by new settlers. The local newspaper, the *Fiji Times*, which was founded in 1869, was vociferous in condemning the inadequacies of the postal service and eventually took the matter into its own hands by establishing its own postal service on November 1st 1870.

The paper organized an efficient postal service and parcel delivery through its agents in the various islands. The news-539 paper produced 1 d, 3 d, 6 d and 1 s stamps, type-set in a utilitarian design. They were printed in black on rose-tinted paper, arranged in four rows of 6 d, 1 s, 1 d and 3 d stamps respectively. Though a private venture the Fiji Times Express paved the way for the reorganization of the government service which began issuing its own stamps in November 1871.

OCCUPIED FRANCE

The last of the new issues in the classic period may be described as the first of that modern phenomenon, the war stamp. The Franco-Prussian War broke out on July 19th 1870 but actual hostilities did not develop till the beginning of August. A series of lightning victories by the German armies, however, led to the downfall of the Second Empire. Large areas of France were occupied by August 10th, and four days later the Germans established a postal administration in the occupied territory. Special

stamps were introduced in September. In their design they reflected the efforts of the German authorities to avoid upsetting local French sentiments, being inscribed in French and printed in the colours of the corresponding denominations used in unoccupied France. The design showed the values, from 1 to 25 centimes, with the 555 word POSTES at the top. The stamps were typographed at the State Printing Works in Berlin.

These stamps were used in all parts of occupied France during the latter part of 1870, but remained current in the districts of Alsace and Lorraine until the end of December 1871 when ordinary stamps of the German Empire were introduced.

The Franco-Prussian War had other important repercussions on philately. Letters were flown out of the beleaguered cities of Metz and Paris by pigeons and balloons. 540 The pigeon *pellicules* of the Siege of Paris foreshadowed the airgraphs of the Second World War, while the specially printed letter sheets inscribed 'Par Ballon Monté' were 541 the ancestors of the aerogrammes of the present day. In this way aerophilately—now one of the most important branches of philately—had its tentative beginnings, though more than forty years elapsed before the aerial transmission of mail was seriously considered in times of peace.

CHAPTER VII
THE GROWTH OF PHILATELY

In the short space of thirty years the adhesive postage stamp had spread across the globe and evolved in the manner and shape in which it is familiar to this day. Indeed, from the very outset, the small upright rectangular format of the Penny Black was that favoured by the stamps of most countries, and which is regarded to this day as the most convenient in everyday use. Yet in that formative period many weird and wonderful shapes of stamps appeared—the circular stamps of Scinde and the triangles of the Cape of Good Hope and Colombia—but for all practical purposes the upright rectangle was the most popular shape.

Printing techniques made enormous strides in the classic period. Yet it is significant that the press used by Perkins Bacon for the Penny Black in 1840 was still in use a century later, printing the 5 cents Caribou stamp of Newfoundland when an emergency short-run printing was required. Recess-printing was the process favoured by printers and postal administrations alike since it was the technique least likely to be well imitated by the forger. The secret of Perkins Bacon's success over their early competitors lay not in their use of this process, but in the incorporation of intricate geometric engraving in the background to the stamps, achieved on the improved rose engine which was patented by the company. Nevertheless, lithography was also a popular printing process, mainly on account of its cheapness. Several examples are known in which stamps were produced lithographically from recess-printed originals or master dies—Trinidad, Chile, Western Australia and the Virgin Islands being notable in this context. A compromise between cheapness and security against the forger was effected by De La Rue in the mid-1850s combining typography with the use of special fugitive inks (which, if not proof against the forger, at least prevented dishonest individuals from washing off the postmark and re-using the stamp). De La Rue scored heavily over their rivals, Perkins Bacon, not so much by virtue of their cheaper process, but because they were more security-conscious. The easy-going business approach of Perkins Bacon irritated the Crown Agents, who took away the lucrative colonial contracts from the firm in 1862 and forced them to hand over the plates and equipment to De La Rue. Significantly, although De La Rue's fortune was made on the strength of the much-vaunted typographic process, this firm continued to recess-print stamps for many colonies, using Perkins Bacon plates, for many years after 1862.

One of the attractions of the classic period is the multiplicity of printers who competed as pioneers in this field. In Britain alone, for example, there were upwards of a dozen different printers producing stamps for foreign or colonial postal administrations. Nissen & Parker, Barclay & Fry, Dando, Todhunter & Smith, Maclure & Macdonald—hopefully they competed with the giants, but inevitably they were elbowed out of what was to become a fiercely competitive market. Only Waterlow & Sons, of the lesser printers of this period, survived eventually to enter the big league (though taken over by De La Rue in 1962). Oddly enough, there has been a mushroom growth of security printers in Britain in recent years, as a result of the growing demand by postal administrations for more and more stamps and even Perkins Bacon (eclipsed before the Second World War) has made a partial comeback in this field.

By contrast, however, many of the major printers of the past century had not emerged in the classic period. Bradbury Wilkinson did not begin to print stamps till 1878 and the great maestros of photogravure—Vaugirard, Courvoisier and Harrison—did not enter the field till the present century. Of the other great commercial companies only Enschede of Haarlem had begun to print stamps by the end of the classic period, entering on their monopoly of Dutch stamps in 1866. Elsewhere stamp production was in the hands of government printers, in Austria, France, Prussia, Belgium, Italy and Sweden. In the United States, home of free enterprise, a number of commercial printers fought for the stamp contracts in the classic period, but since 1895 the majority of American stamps have been produced by the United States Bureau of Engraving and Printing.

Stamp design in the classic period was relatively unimaginative, despite the scope offered by the four printing processes then in use. In practice the most popular subjects for stamp designs were the features of the ruler or the national coat of arms. The majority of portrait stamps followed the lead of Great Britain and adopted a formal profile of the ruler. The youthful effigy of Queen Victoria, which remained unaltered till the day of her death in 1901, at the age of 84, gave to British and British colonial stamps a quality of sameness, mitigated only in the classic period by the ingenious use of different frames and backgrounds. Nevertheless a fair proportion of portrait stamps used a 'proper' portrait (in the heraldic sense), either full or three quarter face. The most successful stamps of Queen Victoria in this genre were those which reproduced the painting by Edward Chalon (Canada, New Zealand, Tasmania, Bahamas, Natal and Grenada). Several of the Australian states attempted originality in royal portraiture, but with varying degrees of success. Among the best stamp portraits of the period were those of Washington, Franklin and other American statesmen on the stamps of the United States, but after experimenting with proper portraiture the Americans also settled for profiles based on statues and medals.

Much of the charm of the classic period lies in the fine quality of the work produced by Perkins Bacon and the American Bank Note Co. who well deserve the title of the Old Masters of philately. The handsome engraving and carefully balanced designs of their stamps rendered them as works of art in miniature. Yet part of the charm of the classics also lies in the Primitives, produced in remote parts of the world by semi-skilled craftsmen labouring under difficult conditions. The Napoleon etched by Sergeant Triquerat in New Caledonia may not be the faithful likeness which Barre engraved for France, not poor, half-blind Barnard's 'Post Office' stamps of Mauritius be more than a parody of the British Penny Red, but both of these Primitives have exercised a powerful charm on collectors over the years. In their ugliness and simple naiveté, the Primitives possess a fascination which outweighs their aesthetic shortcomings.

Apart from portraiture and heraldry the most popular device on the classic stamps was the figure of value. There was a higher proportion of purely numeral designs in this period than in any other, mainly on grounds of expediency and utilitarianism. In this category come the primitive type-set stamps of Hawaii, Réunion and Tolima, but it also includes ornamental designs such as those of Uruguay and the sensitive designs of Thurn and Taxis. From heraldry it is but a short step to the use of an emblem in an allegorical setting. Thus the seated figure of Hope, on the stamps of the Cape of Good Hope, or the orange-tree of the neighbouring Orange Free State were derived from heraldry, though placed in a pictorial context. Taking this a stage farther we find the beaver on Canada's 3 d stamp of 1851—and the way is open to fully pictorial designs. Significantly it was in Canada and the other colonies of British North America that pictorialism in stamp design first began, though it was many years before the idea became popular elsewhere.

The development of postal services in the nineteenth century was still in a transitional state between the old haphazard methods and fully efficient, nationalized institutions. Thus the private companies and semi-official carriers of the United States performed useful and much-needed services alongside the government postal organization. In Russia, though the *zemstvo* (district) posts were not officially authorized till 1870, local posts were in existence at least five years earlier. In Germany and Scandinavia private companies handled large quantities of local mail as well as parcels. In each case distinctive stamps were produced by these companies and boosted the number of collectable items which preoccupied the early philatelist. In Britain alone was there positive discouragement to private enterprise. The Postmaster General, jealously guarding his monopoly, suppressed the college postal services at Oxford and Cambridge as well as the cut-price circular delivery companies that operated briefly in the major cities.

Philately, the study of postage stamps, grew up with the postage stamp itself. Dr John Gray of the British Museum claimed to be the world's first philatelist since he purchased blocks of Penny Blacks and Twopence Blues in May 1840 to preserve as examples of an important social innovation. For the most part, however, stamp collecting did not become a popular pursuit until the mid-1850s when there was a sizeable number of stamps to pursue. Dealers in stamps were in existence in Paris and London by 1860. In 1861 the first tentative catalogues of stamps were published by Oscar Berger-Levrault of Strasbourg and Alfred Potiquet of Paris, while the first English catalogues, those of Frederick Booty and William Mount Brown, appeared the following year. Magazines devoted to stamp-collecting were first published in 1862, when the ephemeral *Monthly Advertiser* appeared in England, followed by *The Stamp Collector's Magazine* and *Le Timbre Poste* in 1863. Zschiesche & Koder of Leipzig produced the first priced catalogue of stamps, followed by the better known works of Moens (Brussels), Maury (Paris), Gibbons (Plymouth and later London) and Scott (New York). A philatelic society, formed in Paris in 1865, was short-lived. The oldest club now in existence, the Royal Philatelic Society of London, was founded in April 1869.

Most collectors were content to collect on a global scale and on a simplified basis. Watermarks were of little interest to them and perforation, introduced on British stamps in the 1850s, was still too newfangled for its finer points to be appreciated. Such collectors were deemed to belong to the English School. On the Continent, however, such stalwarts as Georges Herpin and Dr J. A. Legrand had founded the French School which took heed of the technical minutiae of stamp production and design. It was Herpin who coined the term *philatélie*, in place of the earlier words *timbromanie* or *timbrologie*, which has been used ever since. In 1866 Legrand invented the *odontomètre* (perforation gauge) and first classified the different gauges of perforation found on stamps of that period. The first stamp albums were published in France, Belgium and England in the early 1860s and about the same time the first philatelic handbooks appeared. Significantly they dealt with fakes and forgeries, indicating how serious a menace to the hobby these 'album weeds' had become at that early date. Competent engravers were ten a penny in the mid-nineteenth century, when all book and magazine illustration was hand-engraved. Conversely the early philatelists did not have the advantage of well illustrated catalogues and periodicals to assist them in determining whether a stamp was genuine or not. The market in the rarer stamps was sufficiently brisk by 1860 to encourage the forger, though it should also be noted that many of the forgeries of that period were produced in order to defraud the postal administration rather than to deceive collectors.

The rapid growth of philately in the 1860s had undesirable side effects in that it encouraged unscrupulous dealers, such as Samuel Allan Taylor of Boston, Massa-

556 *Local stamp, Helsingfors (Finland), 1860*

557 *Local stamp, Tammerfors (Finland), 12 p, 1866*

558 *Local stamp, Constantinople (Turkey), 20 paras*

559 *Zemstvo stamp, Kotelnich, 1869*

560 *Zemstvo stamp, Novgorod, 1870*

561 *Local stamp, T. B. Morton and Co., 2 piastres, 1866*

562 *Zemstvo stamp, Novaya Ladoga, 1867*

563-4 *Zemstvo stamps, Rzhev (2), 1867–8*

556

557

558

559

560

561

562

565

566

567

568

569

570

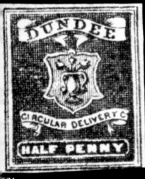

571

572

573

565 *Zemstvo stamp, Schlusselburg, 1865*

566 *Zemstvo stamp, Riazan, 1867*

567 *Zemstvo stamp, Soumy, 1868*

568 *Local stamp, British Circular Delivery stamp, Clark and Co., 1867*

569 *British Circular Delivery stamp, London and District, 1867*

570 *British Circular Delivery Stamp, London Circular Delivery Co., 1867*

571 *British Circular Delivery Stamp, Dundee Circular Delivery Co., 1867*

572 *British Circular Delivery Stamp, Glasgow Circular Delivery Co., 1867*

573 *British Circular Delivery Stamp, Aberdeen Circular Delivery Co., 1867*

574 *British Circular Delivery Stamp, Liverpool Circular Delivery Co., 1867*

575 *British Circular Delivery Stamp, Edinburgh and Leith Circular Delivery Co., 1867*

chusetts, to produce entirely bogus stamps. These stamps were for places and postal administrations which belonged in the realms of phantasy or anticipated by some years the genuine issues of real places. Thus bogus stamps of Guatemala were circulating in the stamp trade years before that country began producing them. It was not long either before certain countries realized that considerable revenue was to be gained from selling unused stamps to collectors, without the necessity of performing any postal service. It is highly probable that the potential philatelic market inspired the totally unnecessary issue of a provisional surcharged series in Uruguay in January 1866—barely a week before an entirely new series was due to be released anyway. Such practices brought loud condemnation in the pages of the embryonic philatelic press all over the world, but did not deter certain countries from abusing their position.

Mercifully the philatelist of the classic period did not have to contend with commemorative stamps, charity or semi-postal stamps, miniature or souvenir sheets or First Day covers and postmarks. The first of these unnecessary abuses did not manifest itself until 1876, when the United States produced commemorative envelopes for the Centennial Exposition of Philadelphia, and adhesive stamps for commemorative purposes did not appear till 1888. This, of course, is one more reason why the stamps of the classic period are so popular today—they are so innocent of the abuses and excesses by which every postal administration in recent years has sought to divert more and more of the collector's money into its coffers. The law of diminishing returns applies to philately as to everything else, and the tendency of the countries of today to over-issue stamps is forcing philatelists to turn increasingly to the classic stamps.

APPENDICES

CHRONOLOGICAL ORDER OF ADOPTION OF THE POSTAGE STAMPS

1840

6 May 1840	Great Britain

1842

1 February 1842	United States (private City Despatch Post of New York)

1843

March 1843	Swiss canton of Zurich
1 August 1843	Brazil
1 October 1843	Swiss canton of Geneva

1845

1 July 1845	Swiss canton of Basle
12 July 1845	First Postmasters' stamps issued in New York

1847

16 April 1847	Trinidad (Lady McLeod Steamship stamp)
1 July 1847	United States government issues
21 September 1847	Mauritius

1848

1848	Bermuda Postmasters' stamps

1849

1 January 1849	France
1 July 1849	Belgium
1 November 1849	Bavaria

1850

1 January 1850	New South Wales
	Spain
3 January 1850	Victoria
May 1850	Switzerland (Federal issues)
1 June 1850	Austria
	Austrian Italy (Lombardo-Venetia)
29 June 1850	Saxony
1 July 1850	British Guiana
15 November 1850	Prussia
	Schleswig-Holstein
1 December 1850	Hanover

1851

1 January 1851	Sardinia

1 April 1851	Tuscany	18 July 1855	New Zealand
	Denmark	November 1855	Danish West Indies
23 April 1851	Canada		
1 May 1851	Baden	**1856**	
1 September 1851	New Brunswick		
	Nova Scotia	1 January 1856	St Helena
4 October 1851	Hawaii	1 March 1856	Finland
15 October 1851	Wurttemberg	1 July 1856	Mecklenburg-Schwerin
		1 August 1856	Mexico
1852		2 August 1856	Corrientes
		1 October 1856	Uruguay
1 January 1852	Réunion		
	Brunswick	**1857**	
	Netherlands		
	Papal States	1 January 1857	Newfoundland
5 January 1852	Oldenburg	1 April 1857	Ceylon
29 January 1852	Thurn and Taxis	May 1857	Natal
15 April 1852	Barbados	1 December 1857	Peru
1 June 1852	Modena		
	Parma	**1858**	
1 July 1852	Scinde		
15 September 1852	Luxembourg	1 January 1858	Russia
			Naples
1853		29 April 1858	Buenos Aires
		1 May 1858	Argentine Confederation
1 July 1853	Portugal		
	Chile	15 July 1858	Moldavia
1 September 1853	Cape of Good Hope	28 October 1858	Cordoba
1 November 1853	Tasmania (Van Diemen's Land)		
		1859	
1854		1 January 1859	Hamburg
			Lubeck
1 February 1854	Philippine Islands		Sicily
1 August 1854	Western Australia		Venezuela
1 October 1854	India	15 May 1859	Ionian Islands
		10 June 1859	Bahamas
1855		August 1859	Granadine Confederation (Colombia)
1 January 1855	Norway	1 September 1859	Romagna
	Cuba and Puerto Rico	21 September 1859	Sierra Leone
	South Australia	1859	French Colonies (general series)
10 April 1855	Bremen		
1 July 1855	Sweden		

1860

1 January 1860	New Caledonia
	Poland
April 1860	British Columbia and
	Vancouver's Island
1 November 1860	Queensland
23 November 1860	Jamaica
1 December 1860	Malta
18 December 1860	St Lucia
1860	Liberia

1861

1 January 1861	Prince Edward Island
May 1861	St Vincent
June 1861	Grenada
September 1861	Confederate States of
	America
1 October 1861	Greece
1 November 1861	Bergedorf

1862

February 1862	Italy
August 1862	Antigua
2 December 1862	Nicaragua
8 December 1862	Hong Kong

1863

1 January 1863	Turkey
January 1863	Russian post offices in
	the Levant
April 1863	Costa Rica
1863	Bolivar
	Wenden

1864

1864	Mecklenburg-Strelitz
1 March 1864	Holstein
10 March 1864	Schleswig
1 April 1864	Netherlands Indies
1864	Soruth

1865

1 January 1865	Romania (formerly
	Moldo-Wallachia)
15 February 1865	Ecuador
19 September 1865	Vancouver Island
25 September 1865	Bermuda (government
	issues)
19 October 1865	Dominican Republic
1 November 1865	British Columbia
1865	Shanghai

1866

1 January 1866	Egypt
	Honduras
January 1866	British Honduras
1866	Bolivia
March 1866	Jammu and Kashmir
1 May 1866	Serbia
1866	Virgin Islands

1867

4 April 1867	Turks Islands
1867	Heligoland
June 1867	Austrian post offices in
	the Turkish Empire
1 September 1867	Straits Settlements
1867	Salvador

1868

1 January 1868	North German Confed-
	eration
	Orange Free State
	Azores
	Madeira
1868	Antioquia
	Persia
20 June 1868	Hungary (journal tax
	stamps)
September 1868	Fernando Po

1869

March 1869	Gambia
1 March 1869	Sarawak
1869	Transvaal (South African Republic)
	Hyderabad

1870

1 April 1870	St Christopher
July 1870	Angola
1 August 1870	Paraguay
September 1870	German occupation of France (Alsace-Lorraine)
1870	St Thomas and Prince Islands
	Cundinamarca
	Tolima
	Afghanistan
1 November 1870	Fiji (Times Express)

TABLE OF VALUES OF CLASSIC STAMPS (UNUSED)

according to the four principal world catalogues (GB : Stanley Gibbons; US : Scott; France : Yvert; Germany : Michel)

The stamps in the table have the same numbering as in the captions. No prices are given for the local stamps—American, Russian *zemstvo* and the steamship companies—since these are usually omitted from the standard catalogues. Apparent anomalies in the pricing merely reflect regional or national variations in the stamp market.

		Gibbons (in £)	Scott (in $)	Yvert (in FF)	Michel (in DM)
1	Great Britain, Penny Black, 1840	80-125	120	900	800
2	Great Britain, Penny Red, 1841	5-9	13	75	35
3	Great Britain, Twopence Blue, 'white lines', 1841	60-150	125	750	450
4	Great Britain, Penny Red with perforations, 1858	0.40	0.65	5	4
5	Great Britain, 1/2 d, 1870	1.25	2.25	17.50	12.50
6	Great Britain, 1 1/2 d, 1870	5	10	75	40
7	Great Britain, 6 d, embossed, 1854	10-200	135	1000	600
8	Great Britain, 4 d, surface-printed by De La Rue, 1855	200	800	1750	1350
9	Great Britain, 6 d, 1856	25-40	55	375	220
10	Great Britain, 3 d, wing-margin, 1862	30-70	60	400	300
11	Great Britain, 4 d, 1862	25-30	50	375	250
12	Great Britain, 9 d, 1862	45	70	550	450
13	Great Britain, 3 d, 1865	30	57.50	400	300
14	Great Britain, 6 d, 1865	20	40	275	200
15	Great Britain, 10 d, 1867	35	85	550	450
16	Great Britain, 1 s, 1865	25-35	45	325	250
17	Great Britain, 2 s, 1867	70	85	600	700
20	United States, 3 c, City Despatch Post, 1842	32	95	550	420
87	United States Carriers' stamp, U.S.P.O. Despatch, 1849	2	5.50	35	40
88	United States Carriers' stamp, One Cent Despatch, 1852	16	55	125	120
89	United States Carriers' stamp, Honour's City Post Paid, 1851	25	70	350	500
90	United States Carrriers' stamp, Government City Dispatch., 1860	5	13.50	100	80
92	United States Government issue, 5 c, Franklin, 1847	110	350	1350	950
93	United States Postmaster's stamp, 5 c, New York, 1845	70-550	200-3500	1350-7000	1150
94	United States Government issue, 10 c, Washington, 1847	550	1600	5000	3500
95	United States Government issue, 15 c, inverted centre, 1869	1800	5500	25000	19000
96	United States Government issue, 24 c, inverted centre, 1869	1300	4500	20000	15000
97	United States Government issue, 30 c, inverted centre, 1869	4500	17000	60000	37000
98	United States Postmaster's stamp, 10 c, 'St Louis Bear', 1845	475	1100	9000	4500
99	United States Postmaster's stamp, Providence, Rhode Island, 1846	25	60	400	300
100	United States Postmaster's stamp, Brattleboro P.O., Vermont, 1846	2500	7500	16000	9000

		Gibbons (in £)	Scott (in $)	Yvert (in FF)	Michel (in DM)
101	United States Postmaster's stamp, Baltimore 5 c on cover, December 1845	750–2000	5000	11000	8000
102	United States Government issue, 1 c, Franklin, 1851	22	70	400	310
103	United States Government issue, 3 c, Washington, 1851	4	18.50	75	60
104	United States Government issue, 5 c, Jefferson, 1856	375	1250	5500	4000
105	United States Government issue, 10 c, Washington, 1855	75	235	1200	900
106	United States Government issue, 12 c, Washington, 1856	70	225	1200	900
107	United States Government issue, 24 c, Washington, 1860	30	100	450	360
108	United States Government issue, 30 c, Franklin, 1860	28	100	475	360
109	United States Government issue, 90 c, Washington, 1860	130	350	1600	1250
110	United States Government issue, 1 c, Franklin, 1861	5	26.50	110	85
111	United States Government issue, 3 c, Washington, 1861	2	8.50	40	26
112	United States Government issue, 5 c, Washington, 1861	25	42.50	150	125
113	United States Government issue, 10 c, Washington, 1861	10	32.50	150	95
114	United States Government issue, 12 c, Washington, 1861	16	57.50	250	175
115	United States Government issue, 24 c, Washington, 1862	12	42.50	225	150
116	United States Government issue, 30 c, Franklin, 1861	25	80	350	280
117	United States Government issue, 90 c, Washington, 1861	65	225	900	770
118	United States Government issue, 2 c, Jackson, 'Black Jack', 1863	8	30	135	90
119	United States Government issue, 15 c, Lincoln (the world's first mourning stamp), 1866	28	110	450	330
120	United States Government issue, 1 c, Franklin, 1896	16	67.50	300	200
121	United States Government issue, 2 c, Pony Express Rider, 1869	9	37.50	175	120
122	United States Government issue, 3 c, Locomotive, 1869	5	20	85	75
123	United States Government issue, 6 c, Washington, 1869	30	110	450	350
124	United States Government issue, 10 c, Shield and Eagle, 1869	30	115	475	400
125	United States Government issue, 12 c, Steamship Adriatic, 1869	30	110	450	350
126	United States Government issue, 15 c, Landing of Columbus, 1869	38	375	550	400
127	United States Government issue, 24 c, Declaration of Independence, 1869	80	300	1250	950
128	United States Government issue, 30 c, Shield, Eagle and Flags, 1869	100	365	1500	1000
129	United States Government issue, 90 c, Lincoln, 1869	250	825	3500	2800
130	United States Government issue, 1 c, Franklin, 1870	1.75	12.50	90	85
131	United States Government issue, 2c Jackson, 1870	3	12.50	60	38
132	United States Government issue, 3 c, Washington, 1870	1.25	9	40	25
133	United States Government issue, 6 c, Lincoln, 1870	10	60	250	160
134	United States Government issue, 7 c, Stanton, 1871	19	70	300	230
135	United States Government issue, 10 c, Jefferson, 1870	3	60	250	200

		Gibbons (in £)	Scott (in $)	Yvert (in FF)	Michel (in DM)
136	United States Government issue, 12 c, Clay, 1870	25	100	425	290
137	United States Government issue, 15 c, Webster, 1870	6.50	75	350	270
138	United States Government issue, 24 c, Winfield Scott, 1870	30	85	400	370
139	United States Government issue, 30 c, Hamilton, 1870	24	190	850	630
140	United States Government issue, 90 c, Commodore Perry, 1870	65	270	1200	900
141	Brazil, 60 r, 'Inclinado', 1844	2.25	7	55	55
142	Brazil, 10 r, 'Bull's Eye', 1843	140	425	2500	2700
143	Brazil, 30 r, 1850	0.30	0.75	5	7.50
144	Brazil, 10 r, Dom Pedro II, 1866-8	1.00	2.75	13.50	17.50
145	Brazil, 20 r, Dom Pedro II, 1866-8	1.00	2.75	13.50	17.50
146	Brazil, 50 r, Dom Pedro II, 1866-8	0.85	2.75	13.50	17.50
147	Brazil, 80 r, Dom Pedro II, 1866-8	1.75	5.50	30	40
148	Brazil, 100 r, Dom Pedro II, 1866-8	0.90	2.75	15	18
149	Brazil, 200 r, Dom Pedro II, 1866-8	2.00	6.50	35	50
150	Brazil, 500 r, Dom Pedro II, 1866-8	7	22.50	120	145
151	Zurich, 4 rappen (the unique strip of five varieties), 1843	5-10000	25000	162500	52500
152	Geneva, 5 + 5 c, 'Double Geneva', 1843	3500	15000	75000	32000
153	Geneva, 5 c, 'Small Eagle', 1845	250	900	4500	1750
154	Geneva, 5 c, cut-out envelope stamp, 1849	35	80	500	350
155	Zurich, 2½ r, 1850	450	1650	8500	4500
156	Geneva, 4 c, 1849	2250	11000	15000	5500
157	Basle, 2½ r, 'Little Basle Dove', 1845	900	3000	17500	7000
158	Geneva, 5 c, 1850	650	2500	15000	5500
159	France, 10 c, tête-bêche pair, 1850	650	2000	12000	4500
160	France, 25 c, Napoleon III, 1853	130	375	2500	900
161	France, 20 c, Napoleon III, laureated profile, 1867	7	25	160	110
162	Bavaria, 1 kreuzer, 'Schwarzer Einser', 1849	90	300	1350	1500
163	Belgium, 10 c, 'Epaulettes', 1849	225	700	3500	1800
164	France, 20 c, Ceres, 1849	15	60	350	150
165	France, 1 c, Napoleon III, perforated, 1862	2.75	8.50	55	25
166	France, 2 c, Napoleon III, laureated profile, 1862	2.25	7.50	50	10
167	France 1 c, Ceres, Third Republic, 1870	5	15	100	40
168	France, 10 c, Ceres, Third Republic, 1870-3	12	55	1000	150
169	France, 10 c, postage due, 1859	1.25	2	17.50	9
170	Bavaria, 12 k, 1850	16	50	250	280
171	Bavaria, 12 k, Coat of Arms, 1867	60	165	750	1000
172	Bavaria 1 k, perforated, 1870	0.05	0.25	65	3-80
173	Belgium, 20 c, 'Medallion', 1863	30	90	100	1000
174	Belgium, 40 c, 1866	14	50	300	100
175	Belgium, 5 c, 1866	7	25	150	60
176	Belgium, 1 c, 1869	0.35	1.25	8	3
177	Trinidad, 5 c, Lady Macleod, 1847	850	2500	15000	18000

		Gibbons (in £)	Scott (in $)	Yvert (in FF)	Michel (in DM)
179	Steamship Company Stamp, Danube Steam Navigation Company, 17 k	—	—	1250	—
180	Steamship Company Stamp, St Thomas and La Guaira, ½ centavo, 1864	—	—	50	—
181	Steamship Company Stamp, Asia Minor Steamship Co, 2 piastres, 1868	—	—	10000	—
182	Steamship Company Stamp, Turkish Admiralty Stamp, 1859	—	—	8500	—
184	Bermuda, 1d, 'Perot', 1848	6000	27500	200000	75000
186	Mauritius, 4 d, Britannia, 1854	95	300	1600	1800
187	Mauritius, 1d, 'Post Office', stamp on cover, 1847	15000	35000	275000	220000
188	Mauritius, 2 d, 'Post Office', 1847	22000	45000	350000	300000
189	Mauritius, 1 d, 'Post Paid', 1848	4000	7000	50000	50000
190	Mauritius, 1 d, 1859	4.75	15	75	85
191	Mauritius, 4 d, 1860	45	80	500	480
192	Mauritius, 6 d, 1861	45	100	625	700
193	Mauritius, 2 d, 'Tête de Singe', 1859	150	750	7500	7800
194	New South Wales, 1 d, 'Sydney View', 1850	150	550	4000	5000
195	Spain, 6 reales, 1850	160	700	4000	2400
196	New South Wales, 2 d, 'Laureated Queen,' 1851	45	200	500	530
197	New South Wales, 5 d, 1855	55	175	1350	950
198	New South Wales, 1 d, 1856	5	20	125	145
199	New South Wales, 2 d, 1862	5	12	90	110
200	Victoria, 1 d, 'Half Length', 1850	300	75	6000	1250
201	Victoria, 1 s, 1854	8	20	450	170
202	Victoria, 2 d, 'Queen Enthroned', 1852	10	35	275	160
203	Victoria, 1 d, 1856	8	25	75	150
204	Victoria, 6 d, 1854	5.50	22.50	250	150
205	Victoria, 1 d, 1857	8	11	75	60
206	Victoria, 3 d, 1860	3.50	13	75	70
207	Victoria, 6 d, 1860	9	30	175	190
208	Victoria, 2 d, 1863	1.90	4.75	30	30
209	Victoria, 2 d, 1870	0.90	3	17.50	18
210	Victoria, 5 s, 1867	22	40	175	190
211	Spain, 6 cuartos, 1850	16	80	400	220
212	Spain, 6 cuartos, 1851	10	40	200	120
213	Spain, 12 cuartos, 1852	100	300	1350	1000
214	Spain, 3 cuartos, Madrid local stamp, 1853	950	3500	17500	11000
215	Spain, 2 cuartos, 1854	160	450	2500	1500
216	Spain, 4 cuartos, 1855	20	60	300	170
217	Spain, 4 cuartos, 1860	1.50	6	35	20
218	Spain, 4 cuartos, 1862	0.25	0.90	5	3
219	Spain, 4 cuartos, 1864	0.30	1.00	6	3.50

	Gibbons (in £)	Scott (in $)	Yvert (in FF)	Michel (in DM)
220 Spain, 2 cuartos, 1865	10	37.50	225	150
221 Spain, 4 cuartos, 1867	1.50	5.50	32.50	20
222 Spain, 5 milesima, 1867	2.75	10	60	35
223 Spain, 1 milesima, 1870	0.25	1.25	7	4
224 Spain, 1 onza, official stamp, 1854	0.07	1.15	4.50	4
225 Spain, 4 onza, official stamp, 1855	0.12	1.25	4	4
226 Spain, 2 reales, error of colour (blue instead of red), 1851	10000	45000	200000	—
227 Spain, 12 cuartos, with frame inverted, 1865	95	375	2000	3500
228 Switzerland, 15 rappen, 'Strubbeli', 1854	45	150	225	500
229 Switzerland, 5 rappen, 'Rayon I', 1850	35-90	600	3000	2200
230 Switzerland, 30 c, 'Helvetia', 1862	35	135	450	450
231 Austria, 2 k, 1858	80	300	4000	2500
232 Austria, 15 k, 1861	26	90	450	250
233 Austria, 25 k, 1867	9	12.50	60	30
234 Austria, 6 k, 'Red Mercury', newspaper stamp, 1856	4000	16000	75000	45000
235 Austria, 3 k, 1863	14	50	750	400
236 Saxony, 3 pf, newspaper stamp, 1850	400	2500	12500	11500
237 Austrian Italy, 10 c, 1850	150	500	2750	1350
238 Austria, 1 k, newspaper stamp, 1867	2	12	50	20
239 Austria, 9 k, with Andreaskreuz, 1850	110	550	25000	1000+
240 Saxony, 3 ngr, Frederick Augustus II, 1851	18	60	350	350
241 Saxony, 5 ngr, John I, 1855	6	20	150	150
242 Saxony, 3 pf, newspaper stamp, 1851	10	30	200	480
243 Saxony, 1/2 ngr, 1863	0.05	0.30	1.50	1.25
244 Saxony, 2 ngr, 1863	0.12	0.80	5	5
245 Prussia, 4 pf, 1858	9	35	45	50
246 Prussia, 3 pf, 1865	1.50	15	20	18
247 Hanover, 2 gr, George V, 1859	3	10	50	50
248 Hanover, 1/2 gr, 1860	12	60	300	250
249 Prussia, 1 sgr, 1850	11	35	150	180
250 Schleswig-Holstein, 1 sch, 1850	30	100	500	500
251 British Guiana, 4 c, 'Cottonreel', 1850	7000	22500	225000	75000
252 Hanover, 1/10 th, 1851	25	75	400	360
253 Hanover, 3 pf, newspaper stamp, 1853	45	120	650	650
254 Tuscany, 1 crazia, Lion, 1851	120	500	2000	1850
255 Tuscany, 3 lire, Arms of Savoy, 1860	5000	18000	85000	42500
256 Sardinia, 40 c, Victor Emmanuel II, 1851	130	700	3500	1650
257 British Guiana, 4 c, 1856	850	2500	40000	35000
258 Baden, 3 k, 1851	40	90	850	500
259 Wurttemberg, 3 k, 1851	10	27.50	275	200
260 Wurttemberg, 6 k, 1857	32	80	650	650
261 British Guiana, 4 c, 1853	90	300	2250	1700

		Gibbons (in £)	Scott (in $)	Yvert (in FF)	Michel (in DM)
262	British Guiana, 4 c, 1860	3.75	12	50	90
263	Sardinia, 40 c, 1855	0.12	0.80	6	3
264	Sardinia, 1 c, newspaper stamp, 1861	0.05	0.30	3	1.50
265	Denmark, 4 s, 1864	9	12.50	70	40
266	Denmark, 2 rbs, 1851	225	900	4500	2500
267	Baden, 3 k, 1860	12	37.50	200	220
268	Baden, 18 k, 1862	70	200	1000	1000
269	Baden, 1 k, 1868	0.35	1.50	8	8
270	Wurttemberg, 9 k, 1869-73	3	11	65	65
271	Hawaii, 1 c, Princess Victoria Kamamalu, 1871	0.50	2.85	15	6
272	Hawaii, 2 c, Kamehameha IV, 1864	0.50	3	15	7
273	Hawaii, 5 c, Kamehameha V, 1866	1.00	12	50	30
274	Hawaii, 6 c, Kamehameha V, 1871	0.90	4	20	12.50
275	Hawaii, 18 c, Mataio Kekuanaoa, 1871	3	12	50	35
276	Canada, 10 c, Prince Albert, 1859	32	100	650	400
277	Canada, 3 c, Small Cents, 1870	0.75	5	15	5
278	Hawaii, 2 c, 'Missionary', 1851	12000	35000	22500	100000
279	Hawaii, 5 c, 'Missionary', 1852	2500	7500	40000	15000
280	Hawaii, 13 c, 'Missionary', 1852	2500	8000	45000	40000
281	Hawaii, 2 c, Inter-island Post, 1859	150	575	2250	2000
282	Hawaii, 5 c, Kamehameha III, 1853	18	385	50	200
283	Canada, 3 d, Beaver, 1851	60	2000	17500	9000
284	Canada, 12 d, mint pair from bottom of sheet, 1851	15000	25000	160000	120000
285	Canada, 12½ c, Large Cents, 1868	25	35	250	100
286	New Brunswick, 1 s, 1851	2000	1900	25000	29000
287	Nova Scotia, 1 d, 1853	120	200	2000	2000
288	Nova Scotia, 10 c, 1860	0.65	1.60	30	35
289	Trinidad, 1 d, Britannia, 1851	1.75	5	25	35
290	Brunswick, 3 sgr, 1852	350	900	10000	4500
291	Oldenburg, 1/10 th, 1852	120	165	2250	2800
292	Oldenburg, 1/3 1859	350	550	6000	5500
293	Thurn and Taxis, 3 sgr, 1852	30	75	550	350
294	Thurn and Taxis, 6 k, 1852	50	110	650	475
295	Parma, 5 c, 1852	7	22.50	110	62
296	Modena, 10 c, 1852	20	125	600	150
297	Papal States. ½ b, 1852	20	50	135	400
298	Papal States, 2 b, 1852	15	60	135	200
299	New Brunswick, 1 c, Locomotive, 1860	1.25	2.00	20	35
300	New Brunswick, 12½ c, Steamship, 1860	1.50	6	30	35
301	New Brunswick, 2 c, Queen Victoria, 1863	1.25	1.00	20	27
302	New Brunswick, 5 c, Connell, 1860	500	850	7500	8000
303	New Bunswick, 5 c, Queen Victoria, 1860	1.25	0.75	20	30

		Gibbons (in £)	Scott (in $)	Yvert (in FF)	Michel (in DM)
304	New Brunswick, 17 c, Prince of Wales, 1860	1.40	3	30	33
305	Nova Scotia, 1 c, 1860	0.25	0.70	4	5
306	Trinidad, 4 d, Britannia, 1859	4	35	175	360
307	Trinidad, 5 s, 1869	1.75	15	75	110
308	Brunswick, 4/4 ggr, 1857	4	15	75	80
309	Brunswick, 1 gr, 1865	0.10	0.70	4	4
310	Thurn and Taxis, 30 k, 1859	0.20	1.00	4	4.50
311	Oldenburg, 1 gr, 1862	0.75	3.50	20	18
312	Papal States, 4 b, 1852	15	50	275	500
313	Parma, 15 c, 1859	10	45	225	150
314	Modena, 20 c, Cross of Savoy, 1859	5	15	85	50
315	Parma, 20 c, 1859	25	125	600	300
316	Modena, 10 c, newspaper stamp, 1859	4	12.50	650	300
317	Réunion, 15 c, 1852	1700	5500	27500	19000
318	Réunion, 30 c, 1852	1700	5500	27500	19000
319	Netherlands, 5 c, William III, 1852	90	275	1250	900
320	Luxembourg, 10 c, 1852	250	800	3500	2500
321	Barbados, 1/2 d, block of four 1852	60	130	900	640
322	Portugal, 25 r, Pedro V, 1855	30	110	600	500
323	Portugal, 5 r, Maria II, 1853	160	550	3000	1650
324	Scinde, 1/2 anna, 1852	275	600	4000	3000
325	Chile, 20 c, Columbus, 1861	11	25	200	100
326	Cape of Good Hope, 4 d, triangular, 1853	25	250	1750	1700
327	Cape of Good Hope, woodblock pair showing 4 d error of colour, 1861	—	5500	70000	46000
328	Tasmania, 1 d, 1853	150	375	3500	2750
329	Tasmania, 4 d, 1853	50	110	1100	1000
330	Tasmania, 2 d, 1855	4.50	275	2750	2300
331	Philippine Islands, 5 c, Isabella II, 1854	95	350	1750	1250
332	Netherlands, 10 c, 1854	30	80	500	300
333	Netherlands, 10 c, 1867	11	35	150	150
334	Netherlands, 1 1/2 c, 1869	3.50	15	65	45
335	Luxembourg, 1 c, rouletted, 1870	1.10	6	25	12.50
336	Luxembourg, 12 1/2 c, 1859	15	60	425	300
337	Barbados, 1 s, 1866	3.50	12	70	70
338	Portugal, 5 r, Luiz, 1862	4	15	100	50
339	Portugal, 5 r, 1867	9	25	175	60
340	Cape of Good Hope, 1 d, rectangular, 1864	3	9	50	55
341	Tasmania, 1 s, 1858	17	42.50	325	300
342	Tasmania, 1 d, 1864	0.65	2	15	20
343	Philippine Islands, 5 c, 1861	1.40	6	35	30
344	Philippine Islands, 5 c, 1859	2	5.50	40	35
345	Philippine Islands, 3 1/8 c, 1864	0.35	1.25	7.50	8

	Gibbons (in £)	Scott (in $)	Yvert (in FF)	Michel (in DM)
346 India, ½ a, 1856	1.00	2.75	25	20
347 India, 8 p, 1860	15	47.50	300	360
348 Norway, 2 s, 1867	1.25	4	20	12.50
349 Cuba and Puerto Rico, 10 c, 1868	0.15	0.70	5	5
350 New Zealand, 2 d, local printing, 1855	225	450	3250	2300
351 New Zealand, 2 d, worn plate, 1862	14	40	225	210
352 New Zealand, 6 d, perforated, 1864	6	18	110	85
353 St Helena, 6 d, 1856	38	100	350	600
354 St Helena, 2 d, 1868	0.25	11	50	30
355 Finland, 5 p, 1866	20	35	450	200
356 Mecklenburg-Schwerin, 4/4 s, 1856-64	6	17.50	75	100
357 Mexico, 1 p, Hidalgo, 1864	0.12	1.25	2	3
358 Uruguay, 180 c, Montevideo Sun, *tête-bêche* pair, 1858	2750	6250	40000	35000
359 Uruguay, 12 c, 1864	1.50	4.50	25	30
360 Uruguay, 1 c, 1866	0.35	1.10	7	8
361 Uruguay, 5 c, 1866	0.45	2.00	12.50	16
362 Western Australia, 1 d, 'Black Swan', 1854	50	60	500	800
363 Western Australia, 1 s, 1854	18	45	225	350
364 Western Australia, 4 d, 'Inverted Swan' error, 1854	2000	6500	37500	50000
365 India, ½ a, 1854	80	225	1100	1000
366 India, 2 a, 1854	3.75	12.50	65	85
367 India, 4 a, 1854	50	145	2000	2000
368 Norway, 4 s, Oscar II, 1856	14	35	200	125
369 Cuba and Puerto Rico, 1 r, 1855	0.05	2.75	20	20
370 South Australia, 1 d, 1855	190	375	2750	2000
371 South Australia, 4 d, 1867	1.40	11	50	60
372 Sweden, Stockholm local stamp, 1856	35	90	550	200
373 Sweden, 24 s, 1855	700	2000	10000	4000
374 New Zealand, 1 d, London printing, 1855	1000	2000	20000	14500
375 Bremen, 5 g, 1856	12	50	300	300
376 Finland, 5 k, 1856	1000	2200	12000	3500
377 Danish West Indies, 3 c, 1855	4	30	175	240
378 Mecklenburg-Schwerin, 5 s, 1856	20	90	300	500
379 Corrientes, 2 c, 1864	5	8.50	70	55
380 Mexico, ½ r, Hidalgo, 1856	2	7.50	45	50
381 Mexico, 2 r, Eagle 1864	0.45	1.50	20	20
382 Mexico, 13 c, Maximilian, 1866	0.75	6	50	45
384 Mexico, Guadalajara local issue, 1867	10	30	225	240
385 Newfoundland, 3 d, 1857	3.75	70	600	850
386 Newfoundland, 1 d, 1857	3	12.50	75	70
387 Ceylon, 1 d, 1857	18	40	250	250
388 Natal, 3 d, 1859	3.75	17	85	95

	Gibbons (in £)	Scott (in $)	Yvert (in FF)	Michel (in DM)
389 Ceylon, 4 d, strip of four, 1859	2600+	6000	44000	30000
390 Newfoundland, 2 d, Codfish, 1866 (with imprint of American Bank Note Co.)	6	11	125	120
391 Newfoundland, 5 c, Seal, 1866	50	85	750	750
392 Newfoundland, 13 c, Schooner, 1866	7	12.50	110	90
393 Newfoundland, 4 d, 1862	1.40	4	30	30
394 Newfoundland, 6 d, 1862	1.40	3.75	30	30
395 Newfoundland, 10 c, Prince Albert, 1866	5	25	125	145
396 Newfoundland, 12 c, Queen Victoria, 1866	1.40	5	30	27
397 Newfoundland, 24 c, Queen Victoria, 1866	2	5	30	40
398 Newfoundland, 1 c, Prince of Wales, 1868	2.25	7.50	45	55
399 Newfoundland, 6 c, Queen Victoria, 1870	0.50	1.50	10	12
400 Ceylon, ½ d, 1857	20	50	325	250
401 Natal, 1 d, POSTAGE overprint, 1869	2.50	6.50	65	45
402 Peru, 2 r, Pacific Steam Navigation Co, 1857	130	250	550	1600
403 Peru, 1 p, 1863	9	28.50	225	190
404 Peru, 5 c, 1866	0.50	1.50	20	10
405 Peru, 10 c, 1866	0.50	1.50	20	15
406 Russia, 5 k, 1863	1.50	5	20	20
407 Naples, ½ t, Victor Emmanuel II, 1861	0.50	2.50	18	11
408 Argentina, 5 c, Rivadavia, 1864	25	70	500	300
409 Argentina, 5 c, 1862	6	11	100	60
410 Hamburg, 1¼ s, 1864	12	25	60	135
411 Lubeck, 1 s, 1863	10	40	175	250
412 Venezuela, ½ r, Eagle, 1863	0.15	1.50	11	15
413 Venezuela, ½ r, 1864	0.45	1.65	10	15
414 Venezuela, 1 r, 1859	2.50	8.50	50	75
415 Columbia, 10 c, United States of Colombia, 1862	15	50	250	370
416 Colombia, 1 c, 1865	0.65	2	10	15
417 Colombia, 2½ c, triangular, 1865	1.00	3.50	25	30
418 Colombia, 10 c, 1865	1.25	4	20	15
419 Colombia 2 c, 1870	0.20	0.75	5	6
420 Colombia, 5 c, 1870	0.20	1.10	7	9
421 Colombia, 25 c, 1870	2.50	8.50	50	67
422 Ionian Islands, ½ d, Queen Victoria, 1859	12	25	160	75
423 Sierra Leone, 6 d, 1859	8	20	180	120
424 Peru, 1 d, 1858	8	32.50	600	600
425 Russia, 10 k, 1858	500	500	2500	1750
426 Naples, 1 g, 1858	50	80	350	225
427 Naples, ½ t, Trinacria, 1860	5000	16000	90000	60000
428 Naples, ½ t, Cross of Savoy, 1860	1300	5000	25000	15000
429 Buenos Aires, 5 p, 'Barquito', 1858	300	750	8000	3000

	Gibbons (in £)	Scott (in $)	Yvert (in FF)	Michel (in DM)
430 Argentina, 15 c, 1858	1.00	2.50	25	20
431 Moldo-Wallachia, 30 p, 1862	4	15	75	70
432 Moldavia, 80 p, 'Bull', 1858	45	140	15000	12000
433 Moldavia, 81 p, 'Bull', 1858	2250	6500	32500	20000
434 Sicily, 1 g, 'Bomba Head', 1859	10	35	175	90
435 Cordoba, 10 c, 1858	170	400	5000	2500
436 Hamburg, 3s, 1859	18	30	300	350
437 Lubeck, 4 s, 1859	2	8	40	45
438 Venezuela, 1/4 c, 1861	3.50	9	50	50
439 Colombia, 2 1/2 c, Granadine Confederation, 1859	4.50	16	85	120
440 Bahamas, 1 d, Interinsular, 1859	4.50	13.50	70	85
441 Bahamas, 6 d, 1861	140	300	1600	1280
442 French Colonies, 20 c, 1859	2.50	8.50	50	30
443 Romagna, 1/2 b, 1859	2	7.50	40	30
444 New Caledonia, 10 c, 1860	10	30	150	135
445 Poland, 10 k, 1860	75	250	1600	1200
446 Queensland, 6 d, 1860	30	60	500	480
447 Liberia, 12 c, 1860	3.75	17.50	225	250
448 St Lucia, 1 d, 1860	12	27.50	200	170
449 British Columbia, and Vancover's Island, 2 1/2 d, 1860	250	500	600	450
450 Vancover Island, 5 c, 1865	20	55	375	300
451 British Columbia, 3 d, 1865	5	17.50	100	80
452 Grenada, 1 d, 1861	4	22.50	125	140
453 Nevis, 1 s, 1861	80	200	1350	1450
454 St Vincent, 1 d, 1861	2.50	15	75	90
455 Jamaica, 1 d, 1860	5	15	75	85
456 Jamaica, 4 d, 1860	22	50	325	300
457 Malta, 1/2 d, 1860	200	400	1250	800
458 British Columbia, 2 c, 1868	6	17.50	125	90
459 Nevis, 1 d, 1861	3	42.50	250	290
460 Prince Edward, Island, 3 d, 1861	2	5	30	35
461 Prince Edward Island, 9 d, 1862	3	10	40	40
462 Prince Edward Island, 2 c, 1872	0.40	2.50	7.50	5
463 Prince Edward Island, 4 1/2 d, 1870	2	10	30	33
464 Confederate States of America, Memphis, 5 c, 1861	8	20	800	160
465 Confederate States of America, Mobile, 5 c, 1861	11	25	150	200
466 Confederate States of America, Rheatown, 5 c, 1861	300	600	3500	4800
467 Confederate States of America, Petersburg, 5 c, 1861	40	150	450	680
468 Confederate States of America, 5 c, Jefferson Davis, 1861	6	25	75	130
469 Confederate States of America, 5 c, Jefferson Davis, 1861	0.85	2	10	14
470 Confederate States of America, 10 c, Jefferson Davis, 1863	0.60	2.25	11	14
471 Confederate States of America, 1 c, John Calhoun, 1862	8	23.50	110	130

		Gibbons (in £)	Scott (in $)	Yvert (in FF)	Michel (in DM)
472	Confederate States of America, 20 c, George Washington, 1863	2.50	7	35	40
473	Bergedorf, 4 s, 1861	2.50	9	45	50
474	Italy, 15 c, Victor Emmanuel II, 1862	10	50	240	175
475	Italy, 60 c, Victor Emmanuel II, 1863	0.30	2.50	20	18
476	Italy, 2 lire, 1863	1.75	10	40	10
477	Italy, 1 c, Numeral, 1863	0.08	0.50	4	2
478	Italy, 2 c, Numeral, 1865	0.45	4	16	8
479	Greece, 2 lepta, Hermes, 1861	3.00	15	75	30
480	Bergedorf, 1¹/₂ s, *tête-bêche* pair, 1861	8	20	150	250
481	Antigua, 6 d, 1862	80	125	1000	500
482	Nicaragua, 2 c, 1862	0.10	1.25	7.50	5
483	Bolivar, 1 p, 1863	2.25	4.50	25	20
484	Russian Levant, 6 k, 1863	20	65	450	300
485	Mecklenburg-Strelitz, ¹/₄ sgr, 1864	20	65	275	330
486	Wenden, 2 k, 1863	8	20	100	80
487	Holstein, 1¹/₄ s, 1864	3.75	25	110	120
488	Hong Kong, 48 c, 1862	45	115	650	670
489	Turkey, 20 paras, 1863	5	15	75	100
490	Turkey, 20 paras, 1868	0.05	0.40	6	1.50
491	Russian Levant, ROPIT, 1865	2.50	10	40	30
492	Costa Rica, ¹/₂ r, 1863	0.10	0.25	2	1.50
493	Russian Levant, 1 k, 1868	1.75	8	40	30
494	Wenden, 2 k, 1863	28	50	400	175
495	Wenden, Essay, 1863	0.50	1.25	5	5
496	Mecklenburg-Strelitz, 1 sgr, 1864	18	60	600	720
497	Schleswig, 1¹/₄ s, 1864	3.50	15	70	60
498	Holstein, 1¹/₄ s, 1864	8	12.50	60	50
499	Schleswig-Holstein, 1¹/₄ s, 1865	1.25	6	150	33
500	Netherlands Indies, 10 c, 1870	1.25	5.50	20	27
501	Romania, 18 b, Prince Charles, 1868	12	50	275	300
502	Bermuda, 6 d, 1865	1.25	4	22.50	30
503	Shanghai, 1 c, 1867	0.40	1.35	6	7.50
504	Egypt, 5 paras, 1866	2.75	7	60	60
505	British Honduras, 1 d, 1866	2.75	8	40	35
506	Honduras, 2 r, 1866	0.05	0.10	0.50	0.70
507	Bolivia, 5 c, 1868	1.10	3	17.50	14
508	Serbia, 1 p, Prince Michael, 1868	4.50	10	50	35
509	Serbia, 10 p, Prince Milan, 1869	0.50	3	12	10
510	British Virgin Islands, 4 d, 1867	5	10	75	60
511	British Virgin Islands, 1 s, 1867	20	75	500	500
512	Netherlands Indies, 10 c, 1864	25	80	500	400

	Gibbons (in £)	Scott (in $)	Yvert (in FF)	Michel (in DM)
513 Soruth, 1 a, 1868	3	9	60	60
514 Dominican Republic, 1/2 r, 1865	30	90	500	550
515 Romania, 2 p, Prince Charles, 1868	0.25	1.00	8	7
516 Ecuador, 1/2 r, 1865	0.75	2.75	18	15
517 Romania, 5 p, Prince Alexander Cuza, 1865	0.75	3	16	15
518 Shanghai, 16 c, 1865	6	18.50	150	180
519 Egypt, 20 paras, Sphinx and Pyramid, 1867	5	14	70	75
520 Egypt, 5 piastres, 1866	38	100	650	500
521 Bolivia, 5 c, Condor, 1866	0.25	2	15	10
522 Jammu and Kashmir, 4 a, 1866	5	20	90	120
523 Serbia, 1 p, 1866	7	25	250	175
524 British Virgin Islands, 1 d, St Ursula, 1866	4	10	50	60
525 Turks Islands, 1 s, 1867	3	20	100	110
526 North German Confederation, 1/4 g, 1868	1.00	7	40	40
527 Austrian Levant, 15 s, 1867	1.50	6	7	18
528 Heligoland, 6 s, 1867	2.50	5	30	18
529 Straits Settlements, 3 c, 1867	4	13	75	75
530 Straits Settlements, 2 c, 1868	0.35	1.10	5	6
531 Salvador, 1/2 r, 1867	0.15	0.40	2.50	2.70
532 Tolima, 5 c, 1870	12	32.50	200	250
533 North German Confederation 1 k, 1868	1.00	6	30	35
534 North German Confederation 1/4 g, official stamp, 1870	2.50	10	50	60
535 Cundinamarca, 5 c, 1870	0.65	1.50	15	13
536 Hungary, 1 k, journal tax stamp, 1868	0.20	0.50	3	1.50
537 Gambia, 6 d, 1869	40	135	750	900
538 St Christopher, 1 d, 1870	2.50	8	50	50
539 Fiji, Times Express, strip of four, (6 d, 1 s, 1 d, 9 d), 1870	150	500	2000	2260
542 United States, 5 c, newspaper stamp, 1865 (the largest stamp of the Classic period)	10	30	160	175
543 Orange Free State, 6 d, Orange Tree, 1868	0.50	0.75	6.50	4.20
544 Madeira, 100 r, 1868	25	90	525	500
545 Antioquia, 5 c, 1868	120	275	1500	1800
546 Persia, 8 sh, 1868	12	25	125	140
547 Fernando Po, 20 c 1868	30	120	850	330
548 Sarawak, 3 c, Rajah Brooke, 1869	3.50	7.50	50	50
549 Transvaal, 6 d, 1869	12	32.50	175	190
550 Angola, 50 r, 1870	1.50	6.50	50	35
551 Hyderabad, 1 anna, 1869	3.25	6	35	60
552 St Thomas and Prince Islands, 50 r, 1870	1.00	4.25	35	28
553 Paraguay, 1 r, 1870	0.50	1.50	10	15
555 Alsace-Lorraine, 10 c, 1870	3.75	35	200	160

BIBLIOGRAPHY

Graveson, Samuel (ed) *Penny Postage Centenary*, Postal History Society, London, 1940.
Hurt, E. F. and Williams, L. N. and M. *Handbook of the Private Local Posts*, Fritz Billig, New York, 1950.
Lowe, Robson *The British Postage Stamp of the Nineteenth Century*, National Postal Museum, London, 1968.
Mackay, James A. *The Tapling Collection*, British Museum, London, 1964.
The International Encyclopedia of Stamps, International Publishing Corporation, London, 1970–1.
Melville, Fred J. *Postage Stamps Worth Fortunes*, Melville, London, 1908.
Nicklin, John W. *Fabulous Stamps*, Hastings House, 1939.
Stocken, Nevile L. *Stamps of Great Price*, Hopkins, Bath, 1932.
Williams, L. N. and M. *Famous Stamps*, Chambers, London, 1940.
Stamps of Fame, Blandford Press, London, 1949.
The Postage Stamp, Penguin Books, London, 1956.
Rare Stamps, Weidenfeld and Nicholson, London, 1967.
Wilson, Sir John *The Royal Philatelic Collection*, Dropmore Press, 1953.
Wolff, J. W. *Philatélique 1965: Les Classiques*, Grapheion, Augusta, Vienna, New York, 1965.

Many of the above-mentioned works include bibliographies listing the monographs and handbooks dealing with the stamps of individual countries.

INDEX

Franco-Prussian War   161, 295
Frankfurt-am-Main   136, 157, 171
Franklin, Benjamin   48, 51, 151, 298
Franz Josef, Emperor of Austria   117, 286
Fraser, G.G.   211
Frederick Augustus II, King of Saxony
   118
Frederick William IV, King of Prussia
   118
Freetown   235
Freire, Francisco Borjade   173
Fremantle   188
French colonial general series   167-8, 234,
   237
Frenckell, J.C.   96
Frere, Sir Bartle   172-3, 191
Fuchs, Charles   257

Galicia   117
Gambia   290
Garcia Brothers   273
Garcia, Justiniano   274
Garibaldi, Giuseppe   220
Gastein, Convention of   263
Gauthier Frères   82
General Post Office, London   129, 147,
   151, 233, 242, 259
Geneva   66-72, 75, 113, 203
Genoa   274
George V, King of Great Britain   84
George VI, King of Great Britain   259
George V, King of Hanover   129
Georgetown, British Guiana   129
Georgia   248
German-Austrian Postal Union   117, 126,
   135, 143, 157, 158, 171
German Confederation   117, 263
German Empire   136, 226, 257, 280, 295
Germany   11, 117, 279, 299
Gibbons, Stanley   62, 132, 299
Giesecke & Devrient   118, 294
Gillett, H.C.   177
Girardin, Emile de   76
Glasgow   208, 290

Gomm, Sir William   83
Gonvea, Clementino G. de   61
Gotha   157
Government Printing Works, Madrid   104
Government Printing Works, Warsaw   238
Granadine Confederation   230
Grand Ducal Printing Office, Florence
   131
Gray, Dr John E.   15
Great Britain   10, 19-30, 51, 52, 76, 126,
   143, 152, 171, 177, 191, 197, 201, 211,
   233, 235, 247, 273, 279, 293, 298, 299,
   300
Greece   17, 233, 237, 257, 273
Greig, Alexander D.   31, 46
Grenada   243-4, 298
Grey, Earl   83
Guadalajara   207
Guatemala   303
Guayaquil   270
Guildhall Medal   25
Guinea   294
Güstrow   203, 263, 293

Haiti   270, 280
Ham of Brisbane   241
Ham, Thomas   100, 103
Hamburg   11, 225-6, 257, 279
Hanover   11, 125-9, 135, 197
Hapsburg Empire   117, 289
Harris, Lord   155
Harris, R.   182
Harrison & Sons   298
Hasper of Karlsruhe   136
Havana   195
Hawaii   7, 9, 144-7, 299
Heath, Charles and Frederick   19, 23
Heligoland   279
Hermes Heads   257
Herpin, Georges   300
Hessen-Darmstadt   157
Hessen-Kassel   157
Heyl, J.B.   93
Hidalgo, Manuel   204

The text of this book, the color illustrations and the jacket were printed by the Imprimerie Paul Attinger S. A., Neuchâtel. – The black and white illustrations were printed by Roto-Sadag S. A., Geneva. – Photolithos by Schwitter A. G., Basle. – Binding by Eugène Clerc & Cie, Lausanne. – Editorial : Giles Allen.
– Layout and design by Franz Stadelmann.

Printed in Switzerland